Job Evaluation:
The Myth of Equitable Assessment

- public service.

Job Evaluation:
The Myth of Equitable Assessment

MAEVE QUAID

UNIVERSITY OF TORONTO PRESS
Toronto Buffalo London

© University of Toronto Press Incorporated 1993
Toronto Buffalo London
Printed in Canada

ISBN 0-8020-2904-3

Printed on acid-free paper

Canadian Cataloguing in Publication Data

Quaid, Maeve
    Job evaluation : the myth of equitable assessment

    Includes index.
    ISBN 0-8020-2904-3

    1. Job evaluation.   I. Title.

    HF5549.5.J62Q3 1993   658.3'125   C93-093041-X

This book has been published with the help of a grant from the Social
Science Federation of Canada, using funds provided by the Social Sciences
and Humanities Research Council of Canada.

This book is dedicated to my parents,
Niall and Georgina Quaid

Contents

Acknowledgments ix

1 Introduction 3

Part I *Job Evaluation: The Debate to Date* 17
2 The History of Formal Job Evaluation: The Bureaucratization of Job Worth 19
3 What Is Job Evaluation Supposed to Do? Some Unexamined Assumptions 48

Part II *Job Evaluation in 'Atlantis': A Case-Study* 81
4 Why Job Evaluation? The Case for a 'Rational' System 83
5 Preparing for a 'Rational' System: Job-Description Writing and Employee Socialization 117
6 Evaluating the Jobs: The Objective of Internal Equity 133
7 Pricing the Jobs: The Objective of External Competitiveness 154
8 Organizational Reaction to a 'Rational' System 175

Part III *Job Evaluation Reconsidered* 199
9 The Failure of Job Evaluation: A Triumph of Political Action over Bureaucratic Logic 201
10 The Success of Job Evaluation: The Creation of an 'Institutional Myth' 223

Appendices 255
A Guide Chart for Measuring Working Conditions 256
B Correlation 258

C Employee Questionnaire 260

References 267

Index 279

Acknowledgments

I thank the Mackenzie King Travelling Scholarship Trust for providing me with the financial support required to undertake the research for this book. I also thank the people of 'Atlantis' for permission to use their organization as the site of my case-study. I appreciate the time that they devoted to answering my questions and sharing their recollections with me.

This book draws upon research that I conducted for a doctoral thesis at the University of Oxford. To the late Eric Batstone, Nuffield College, I owe a great debt for supervising my research with enthusiasm, patience, and insight.

I thank the late Dan Gowler, Templeton College, University of Oxford, who also supervised my research. He led me into a world which I sensed was there, but could never have reached without him. I will be forever grateful for all that Eric and Dan taught me. Their memory will always be with me.

Job Evaluation:
The Myth of Equitable Assessment

1 Introduction

Job evaluation technique has undergone a surprising rebirth. The basis of this second coming has, of course, been the pay equity movement. Formal job evaluation technique has become the measurement instrument endorsed by the pay equity movement as the technical device for eliminating gender-based pay discrimination. It has become enshrined as the exclusive tool used to operationalize the concept of pay equity.

Since its first recorded application in the nineteenth century, job evaluation has been portrayed as sophisticated, complex, and rational. Many view the technique as a 'knight in shining armour' or 'gladiator' with the ability to defeat pay inequities wherever they exist. Even leading feminist researchers (Acker 1989) have embraced the technique (accepting the rational-technical premises, while seeking to make modifications to the process through the purging of 'sex bias'). Professional job evaluators have, themselves, been accorded high-priest status (as rational technocrats) and, in turn, have elevated the personnel function, according it further (longed for) enhanced status. Consultants have experienced a major boom in business, claiming specialized expertise in the application of the technique. Myriad high-paying jobs have been created in state-organized pay equity bureaus, redressing the gender balance in the pay equity problematic, at least for the élite group charged with the responsibility of increasing pay levels for their marginalized 'sisters' in the workforce.

At its simplest, job evaluation is a job-worth measurement technique that seeks to 'establish' a hierarchy of jobs. A variety of job evaluation methods exists – from simple whole ranking to highly analytical point schemes – but I focus my attention here on the latter

– schemes requiring assessment of jobs under a number of different factors, such as skill, responsibility, effort, and working conditions – which are advocated by pay equity bureaus and legislators.

Despite the recent widespread interest in and application of job evaluation technique, this book claims that we know very little about the more fundamental properties of the technique and that we have become satisfied with a number of unexamined assumptions. In fact, this book demonstrates that the function of job evaluation does not itself lie in 'evaluation,' but rather in the more diffuse area of 'meaning management.' Using examples from a real-life organizational context, I hope to demonstrate that many qualities that have been attributed to job evaluation are unfounded and that, in fact, despite its many claims, at the 'rational' level job evaluation accomplishes little, if anything at all.

I do not suggest here that job evaluation provides organizations with nothing of value. On the contrary, I make the case that job evaluation serves other, more useful functions through the cultural processes of myth, ritual, and ceremony. For example, it is shown how the technique is important to organizations because it cloaks the puzzling and uncertain task of establishing the income hierarchy in a myth of 'rationality' and 'scientificity' and in so doing fosters the perception that the technique is objective and fair. In short, the answer to the question 'What does job evaluation do?' is that it resolves the irresolvable. Job evaluation functions as a 'myth' – presented in the form of bureaucratic order and logic – to perform the indeterminable task of mediating between internal organizational equity and external market competitiveness. Seeing job evaluation in this way will be difficult for many readers, as it requires a departure from the dominant and comfortable 'rational' view of the world into the realm of the 'symbolic' (a realm, for the most part, outside the purview of the compensation literature). Arguably, it will be all the more difficult to accept my 'symbolic' interpretation because I present the mythical character of job evaluation within the logic of the 'bureaucratic' (a logic not normally associated with the 'mythical').

Job evaluation is a 'myth' because it is not possible to scientifically, or objectively, determine the relative value or worth of jobs. Job evaluation provides organizations with a language and a set of rituals and rhetoric that transport an otherwise impossible process into the realm of the possible and the determinable. In this way, what job evaluation serves to do is to code existing biases and value systems in order to re-present them as 'objectifiable' data.

If women are now finding that their jobs are being upgraded as a result of formal job evaluation reviews, it is not because job evaluation has objective powers to determine 'appropriate' value, but because women have become empowered to the extent that they can 'recode' the technique to inform value in one direction and not another. While women's groups have not yet appreciated the symbolic aspects of job evaluation technique, it could be said that they sense the power of its rational-technical aura to provide needed legitimacy in making claims on finite compensation resources. In one sense, it could be said that job evaluation disguises the 'political' aspects of pay determination, turning the 'subjective' into the 'objective.'

The positing of job evaluation as myth should not appear unusual; organizations and societies have often been found to invent myths when confronted with ambiguity and intangible outputs. When there is no apparent logic or rationale for an activity, organizations and societies need to invent one, if only to cope with the management of this uncertainty. Job evaluation can be seen as expressing and enhancing beliefs and, thus, as a vital ingredient in the production of organizational reality. Job evaluation 'codifies' issues and feelings which otherwise could not be handled, or might be handled in a much more 'primitive' and possibly detrimental way.

Job evaluation fits the definitional requirements of myth to the extent that it is a process in which people 'believe.' The idea that the relative value of jobs can be 'evaluated' or measured is 'believed' by workers, practitioners, consultants, feminists, and academics alike. it is believed to the extent that it has become 'taken for granted,' part of reality. It is true because it is believed.

It is possible to argue that job evaluation gains its power as a myth because of its rational aura. The elaborate rational basis of job evaluation, with its detailed statistical charts, complex scoring devices, 'systematic' descriptions, and 'definitive' job evaluation criteria (skill, effort, responsibility, working conditions, and so on) lends credence to the idea that it is possible to place a 'correct' value on jobs. The rational framework helps to ensure that job evaluation (or the myth that the worth of jobs can be measured) is seen as a valid process, able to do the things that it purports to do.

The rationalized rules and procedures associated with modern job evaluation techniques provide the concrete substance of the myth. These rules and procedures can be viewed as an elaborate story or narrative which serves to help managers explain to workers why jobs are valued as they are and, more recently, to aid women lodge claims directed at rectifying perceived pay inequities. As is the case for any system of beliefs, the job evaluation process provides a framework for 'interpreting' events. Without such a narrative or story, managers (and women's groups) would be at a loss as to how to make sense of an existing hierarchy. These narratives or stories are not unique but vary from culture to culture and from nation-state to nation-state. The kind of narrative or story told by job evaluation will likely be based in the wider cultural belief about what constitutes 'fairness' in the evaluation of jobs.

In the former Soviet Union, for instance, job evaluation systems invest considerably more importance in working conditions. Their narrative or story is, therefore, different from that used in North America and Europe. Universally, however, the instrument is viewed as producing 'objective' results. Just as Western societies need myth to sort out the vexing problems associated with the valuation of jobs, so, too, do other cultures. Job evaluation provides a firm logic with which to buttress existing societal views about job worth. Viewed in this way, job evaluation is not a universal scientific device, but simply a reflection of a society's beliefs at a specific time.

The idea that job evaluation simply reflects the beliefs of society at a given time is evidenced by the tendency in the recent pay equity movement to use the technique as the tool or device with which to pursue pay claims on behalf of women. It is interesting to note that organizations which used systematic job evaluation technique prior to the advent of the pay equity movement seemingly did not recognize (within the narrative of that time) the importance of certain female-based jobs. It was only through a shift in values (and the empowerment of women) that job evaluation could be used to reinterpret its own 'narrative' and allow for pay adjustments for these 'ghettoed' positions.

The findings in this book challenge the rational-logical basis of job evaluation and many of the basic premisses of feminist commentators on the role of job evaluation within the pay equity problematic. Central to my argument is that commentators on job evaluation (including the feminist strand) have been held captive by the rational model of organization. I propose to take this debate in another direction, into the terrain of the symbolic and, ultimately, into the realm of 'socially constructed reality' (Berger and Luckmann 1966).

It is possible to suggest that the bulk of what has been written on job evaluation has emerged from and within a *rational* level of analysis. This suggestion should not be surprising, as job evaluation is (at least, at its surface level) an eminently rational device. It has been assigned the power of providing a higher 'rationality' to the process of salary administration. It has, apparently, the power to subdue the dreaded chaos associated with the wage-determination process. The economic jungle of the labour market and employer/employee 'smash and grab' tactics are seen to be replaced by a scientific and formal process for determining wage rates.

Job evaluation technique, which is basically a systematic way of comparing jobs within an organization, has, for the most part, been seen by researchers as a 'rational' tool. Indeed, the increase in the use of formal job evaluation technique appears to have grown hand in hand with complex bureaucratic structures. Job evaluation can, in fact, be seen as a derivative of the classical school of management. While job evaluation is often associated with 'state of the art' organizational principles, it is deeply rooted within a 'classical-bureaucratic' logic. Traditional bureaucratic management depends, for instance, on a steep, well-reinforced hierarchy. Since job evaluation technique measures differences in terms of hierarchical' relationships, it can be said to fit and reinforce the bureaucratic logic.

This book attempts to shift the focus of job evaluation research to a deeper social context, taking the research out of its predominantly rational context. It argues that this rational paradigm leads us to see and interpret job evaluation in a distinctive, yet partial, way.

The answer to the question 'What does job evaluation do?' has been, in other words, directly conditioned by the model of organization employed. The rational metaphor of organizational analysis has tended to highlight certain interpretations of job evaluation while backgrounding or disguising others and producing a unidimensional view of this technique. Little has changed since Gellerman (1960: 28) made the following plea for new ways of looking at wage and salary research in general: 'Few other areas of industrial practice have the layers upon layers of traditional thinking that characterize wage and salary administration. We are in danger of being trapped in a kind of institutional way of dealing with the problem simply because we have done for so long. We have made the same assumptions and not tested nor questioned them. Practices have developed and become fixed simply by past practice. If only for these reasons, we badly need fresh air and light into the field by new lines of empirical research and by other facets of theory.'

As the model of organization is altered, so, too, is the answer to the question of what job evaluation does. An attempt is made to consider the question not only from the rational perspective but also from a competing sociological perspective, and specifically from within social constructionism or institutional theory (Berger and Luckmann 1966; Meyer and Rowan 1977). The social-constructionist or institutional perspective places attention on the way in which social reality is enacted and re-enacted. Reality, from within this perspective, consists of a set of socially constructed images, myths, and rationales (a set of images, myths, and rationales that gives meaning to an otherwise chaotic array of actions). The meaning and utility of job evaluation will be seen to shift dramatically as the model of organization is varied.

The 'social construction of reality' theory shifts the level of analysis from a surface level (based on an analysis of rules and procedures) to a deeper level (codes). It requires us to take the conventional language normally associated with job evaluation procedure ('classification,''job description,' 'standardization,' and so on) and reinterpret it in terms of 'rhetoric,' 'ritual,' and 'symbols' of equity, utility, performance, and legitimacy. This method of analysis is not always easy, and often lends itself to a story or a 'narrative.' This book, in the end, is a 'story' of job evaluation and, in this sense, provides one possible interpretation of what job evaluation does. Because I view job evaluation through a different set of paradigmatic lenses from those of the rational tradition, the story that I tell departs, sometimes dramatically, from traditional analysis.

This change of analytical focus is important because the treatment of job evaluation technique from within a sociological perspective has been negligible. The important exceptions (see, for instance, Acker 1989; Burton 1987; Collins 1969; Hyman and Brough 1975; Offe 1976) have importantly turned the debate into the realm of the 'political' but nevertheless retain an underlying rational model of organization. For this group, 'rationality' is imputed to be coalition rather than organizationally based. The lack of rigorous research on job evaluation from within sociology is particularly glaring when one compares the amount of research conducted on 'work study' or 'scientific management' (for example, Lupton 1957; Brown 1973; Braverman 1974). While work study and scientific management have been accorded 'celebrity' status within the 'labour process' school, job evaluation has basically remained untouched from within sociology.

This book is based on an extended case-study of a single organization. The case-study relates to the introduction of a formal job evaluation plan to the government of one of Canada's ten provinces. This province is referred to here by the pseudonym 'Atlantis.' The introduction of formal job evaluation to Atlantis was a major project, involving 1,200 (non-unionized) supervisory, managerial, and professional government employees (the 10,800 unionized employees refused to have the formal job evaluation plan applied to their group – as the union president told the researcher: 'We don't need it!').

The particular type of job evaluation technique introduced in Atlantis is known as the 'Hay' plan and is by far the most widely used single job evaluation plan in the world. Although this type of job evaluation scheme is applied mostly to white-collar jobs ∠ (Torrington and Hall 1987), it is also being increasingly used for blue-collar jobs (Incomes Data Services 1979).

I was directly involved (as an internal job evaluator) with the introduction and maintenance of this job evaluation system for a period of two and a half years, from April 1980 to September 1982. I returned to Atlantis for three months in 1985, some two and a half years after the plan's implementation, wearing not the hat of the practitioner, but rather the hat of the 'inquisitive' field-worker. This opportunity to 'change hats' and return to a managerial-change project for subsequent academic analysis is rare but by no means unique (see, for instance, Klein 1976).

The research method I used is based on a *case-survey* approach, which can be referred to as qualitative and 'interpretive' in design. As White (1981a: 50) describes it :

The [case-survey] method applies survey techniques within a particular organization to investigate the situation there. A standard set of measures applicable to any organization is neither used nor considered something potentially desirable. Rather, independent investigation of each situation leads to the development of a survey questionnaire which brings out the features of special interest. And although the questionnaire survey enables the theories to be operationalized and tested, the full interpretation depends equally upon a qualitative account of the situation: 'a case analysis.'

The social phenomenon to be studied here – an open-ended organizational change, rich in symbolic modes of discourse – suggested a need for both interpretive and systematic (e.g., survey) design techniques. Morgan and Smircish (1980) have suggested that the particular method or approach brought to bear on a piece of research needs to be matched to the nature of the social phenomenon explored. The analysis of situations of 'social change,' for instance, is considered to be more amenable to qualitative than to structured approaches. This type of 'matching' is precisely what I have attempted in my own research.

The main emphasis of this book, however, is on the 'case-study,' a qualitative ethnographic approach that has a number of features to which I was attracted. The focus of this interpretive approach is not only on the 'concrete' activities that take place but also on the 'meanings' that can be attributed to these activities and the nature of shared definitions. Much of the rational tradition has researched job evaluation solely in terms of a 'concrete' activity. The basic epistemological stance within this tradition has been either to study systems or processes or to map out contexts.

The ontological assumption embraced in this research is that reality is neither a 'concrete structure' nor a 'concrete process' but, rather, is defined variously in terms of 'symbolic discourse' and 'social discourse.' In this sense, the basic epistemological stance of this research is to understand patterns of symbolic discourse and how social reality is created. What I have done with this research is to take a phenomenon that has been traditionally treated as a 'concrete process' and attempt to apply different ontological assumptions so as to leave open the possibility that job evaluation is something more than a concrete process – possibly an aspect of symbolic discourse, possibly a social construction.

From my experience as a job evaluator, I began to have my own 'doubts' about the ability of job evaluation to do what the rational tradition claims it can do. These concerns about the powers of job evaluation in fulfilling a wide-ranging set of rational objectives have been used to form the basis for the following inquiry. What I have attempted to do in this book is to take my unsystematic 'hunches' about the job evaluation process and to analyse them in a more systematic, rigorous, and sociological manner.

These practitioner's 'hunches' have directly, therefore, informed the direction of this book. The main 'hunch' to which I refer is that job evaluation does not do what it purports to do. This, then, is the first objective of the book – to determine whether or not job evaluation fulfils or meets its rational objectives, as laid out by the rational tradition. If job evaluation does not fulfil these specific objectives, it is suggested, it is only logical – because we need some explanation for the popularity and proliferation or the technique – for us to ask ourselves what other objectives or functions job evaluation may perform or fulfil. This second line of inquiry can be put in a more compelling manner: 'What does job evaluation really do?'

The Organization of This Book

This book is divided into three main parts. Part I (chapters 2 and 3) consists of a discussion of the definition and history of job evaluation as well as a summary of the stated objectives of the process from within the managerial/rational perspective. Part II (chapters 4–8) is devoted to the case-study. Part III (chapters 9 and 10) reconsiders job evaluation in the light of case-study findings.

Chapter 2, 'The History of Job Evaluation: The Bureaucratization of Job Worth,' provides a definition of job evaluation and traces the evolution of job evaluation as a formal measurement technique. While the basic act of deciding that one job is worth more, less, or the same as another might be considered to be as old as industry itself, this discussion pieces together, from a wide variety of primary and secondary sources, the relatively obscure origins of job evaluation.

In this chapter, I explore the way in which job evaluation developed and changed over time. The history of formal job evaluation was difficult to research simply because all organizations, regardless of the epoch considered, have relied on some form of job evaluation. There is agreement in the literature, however, that job evaluation technique was officially developed in the United States and then spread to other countries. The transfer of job evaluation to Canada and pay equity's impact on the proliferation of the technique in Canada are also outlined. In the final analysis, the history of job evaluation is defined in terms of the ever-increasing 'formalization' of the technique. Chapter 2 suggests that we have witnessed the increasing bureaucratization of job evaluation processes over time. In discussing the early pioneering work, this chapter points to a number of factors that are likely to have influenced the rapid spread of the technique. Moreover, the past two decades have seen evidence of

increasing state intervention (through equal pay and pay equity legislation) in the matter of what does and does not constitute job
evaluation. Organizations that, at one time, may have relied on 'informal' evaluation processes are replacing these with formal procedures and rules. The formalization of job evaluation can, in this way,
be seen as an important aspect of the bureaucratization of organizational life.

Chapter 3, 'What Is Job Evaluation Supposed to Do? Some
Unexamined Assumptions,' outlines the various claims made in the
literature about what job evaluation can do (e.g., establishing the
order of jobs within an organizational hierarchy, determining job
differentials, and setting pay levels). In this chapter, I examine the
claims of three diverse literatures: the personnel-management school,
the industrial-relations school, and the feminist school. I begin by
suggesting that the personnel-management perspective has, perhaps,
too much faith in the job evaluation process in terms of its ability to
construct the wage structure, determine fair and equitable pay rates,
and establish appropriate pay differentials. Job evaluation is seen to
be able to determine job worth rationally and scientifically.

Writers from within the industrial-relations school have expended
much effort on delineating the control aspects of the technique and
have launched an assault on the device for diminishing the role of
collective bargaining. Finally, I suggest that the feminist school has,
for the most part, taken for granted many of the unexamined personnel-management claims about job evaluation (principally job
evaluation's role in 'evaluation' itself). It is maintained that each of the
three schools has perhaps oversold or misunderstood job evaluation.

Chapters 4–8 are devoted to the case-study. The material and ideas
presented here derive from the analysis of the implementation and
day-to-day operation of formal job evaluation in the province of
Atlantis. This case-study analysis spans a five-year period, from 1980
to 1985.

The actual case is divided into six sections. The first provides a
background to the case. Each of the subsequent sections represents a
key stage of the job evaluation project: why job evaluation arose
when it did (chapter 4), the writing of job descriptions (chapter 5), the
evaluations of jobs (chapter 6), the pricing of jobs (chapter 7), and the
organization's reaction to the 'results' (chapter 8). Although organizations may vary somewhat in the procedure used to introduce job
evaluation, these main phases are basically those that would occur in

any organization undertaking a similar project.

Chapter 4, 'Why Job Evaluation? The Case for a "Rational" System,' describes how the notion of job evaluation arose in the province of Atlantis when it did. This chapter demonstrates that the technique was presented to certain key individuals and groups in such a way that each, no matter what the frame of reference, stood to 'gain' as a result of its introduction. Chapter 4 is important because it addresses an issue that is usually skirted in the job evaluation literature: why job evaluation is introduced. In the case of Atlantis, it is suggested that job evaluation formed part of a highly visible 'efficiency' strategy on the part of the government as well as a response to the consultants' identification of 'problems' with the old salary-administration system. The 'problems' the consultants pointed to were precisely those which managerialist literature suggests job evaluation can resolve.

Chapter 5, 'Preparing for a "Rational" System: Job-Description Writing and Employee Socialization,' demonstrates the 'critical' activity of job-description writing in the job evaluation process. It will be seen that, in Atlantis, great emphasis was placed upon the need for each of the individual employees to prepare his or her own job description in a strict and exacting format. The importance of this process becomes more apparent as the case-study progresses, when we reinterpret it from rational 'process' to 'symbolic' activity. Only after the results of the evaluations are announced do we begin to see that the 'critical' role played by job descriptions was not to be found in its function as a basis for evaluating jobs, but, rather, in the actual *requirement* that a job description be written. The writing of job descriptions drew employees into the system and into their own evaluations. Here the process of writing job descriptions is seen as an important 'ritual' activity for the dissemination of the rhetoric of job evaluation.

Chapter 6, 'Evaluating the Jobs: The Objective of Internal Equity,' reviews the process in which key jobs, or benchmarks, were 'evaluated' by the most senior personnel in the government, deputy ministers. This chapter reveals the highly subjective and political nature of the job evaluation process. The process was not seen to provide an objective or scientific basis for the evaluation of jobs. Rather, it provided the deputy ministers with a 'justification' or 'rationale' for regrading jobs in accordance with their perceived need at that time. What discriminated between jobs was not the *system* but, rather, the *people* within the system. The job evaluation method and criteria are seen to be flexible enough to offer ample opportunity for numerous interpretations. The resistance of most deputies to fundamental change in long-established relativities and the yielding to pressure from women's groups is illustrated in this chapter. The lesson here is that 'he or she who has the power gets the upgrade.'

Chapter 7, 'Pricing the Jobs: The Objective of External Competitiveness,' explains how the point scores obtained by the evaluation committees were converted into money values. As will be seen, the pay division used the 'scientificity' of the job evaluation plan to 'sell' the new pay ranges to the employees within Atlantis. Even though the assignment of pay ranges was ultimately determined by economic expedience, 'ability to pay,' and a host of other factors, the impression was given that the scientific evaluation of jobs and the new pay rates were somehow inextricably connected.

Chapter 8, 'Reaction to a "Rational" System,' reveals how various members of the organization reacted to the outcome of the job evaluation project and how the system was further manipulated and used to meet certain desired objectives. In this chapter, job evaluation is defined as a series of judgments arrived at through a continuous process of negotiations and compromises between various stakeholders and power groups. Job evaluation is inherently a political process, and 'naturally' lends itself to a process of 'give and take,' despite its cloak of rationality. While some researchers have asserted that 'subjectivity' does frequently creep in to *disturb* the job evaluation process (e.g., Thomason 1968, 1980; Livy 1975), I asserted that job evaluation is, *by necessity*, a subjective and political process.

Chapter 9, 'The Failure of Job Evaluation: A Triumph of Political Action over Bureaucratic Logic,' pulls together the case-study chapters and assesses the extent to which job evaluation realizes its practical stated objectives as developed in the job evaluation literature. While the findings of this study might create the impression that inadequate administrative control actually caused the failure of job evaluation, this chapter makes the point that the Atlantis case should not be viewed as a 'failed' job evaluation exercise, but as an indicator of the inherent limitations of the technique itself.

Chapter 10, 'The Success of Job Evaluation: The Creation of an Institutional Myth,' seeks to understand what it is about job evaluation that makes this technique so attractive to organizations. This chapter turns around the traditional perspective from which job evaluation is analysed. The theoretical framework applied in this chapter is social constructionist (Berger and Luckmann 1966). It is suggested, in this chapter, that the real function of job evaluation lies not in the rational claims upheld in the managerialist literature, but rather in the more diffuse area of 'meaning management' and the social construction of reality. From this frame of reference, I define job evaluation as a *rationalized institutional myth*.

Job evaluation is *rationalized* because it takes the form of rules and procedures specifying the means necessary to accomplish the end goal of measuring the value of jobs. Job evaluation is *institutional* because actions are repeated in organizations and given meanings by their participants. Job evaluation is a *myth* because it is a process based on widely held beliefs that cannot be objectively tested. Levi-Strauss (1965) has defined myth as a sacred narrative that resolves the irresolvable. It is argued, in this chapter, that job evaluation functions as a 'myth' (presented in the form of bureaucratic order and logic) that resolves an otherwise indeterminable problem – the determination of job worth. More specifically, job evaluation is the myth that mediates between internal organizational equity and external competitive forces.

Chapter 10 also makes the point that Atlantis was attracted to formal job evaluation, at least in part, because the process has wide organizational and social legitimacy. The 'institutional isomorphism' theory of Meyer and Rowan (1977) is used here to attempt to explain the popularity of job evaluation. It is argued that the spread of job evaluation is an aspect of institutional isomorphism, whereby organizations pattern themselves on each other, incorporating already legitimated evaluation criteria. Further, it is maintained that the way in which job evaluation involves the structuring and transformation of reality has been ignored in the payment-systems literature, thereby restricting the way in which we interpret and see job evaluation. By approaching job evaluation sociologically, through *social constructionism*, we can begin to understand job evaluation in quite new and different ways. Specifically, the book points to the way in which job evaluation 'creates and enacts' social reality, a reality so readily accepted, that its concept is used to operationalize the pay equity movement.

PART I

Job Evaluation: The Debate to Date

2 The History of Formal Job Evaluation:
The Bureaucratization of Job Worth

In this chapter an attempt is made to define job evaluation and to trace its evolution as a formal measurement technique. Fundamental to the search for an acceptable (and current) definition of job evaluation is the need to understand how this increasingly complex and 'scientific' technique has evolved over the years. In many ways, the definition and the history of job evaluation are closely related. Although the basic activity of deciding that one job is worth either more or less than another might be considered to be as old as industry itself, it is maintained that the novelty of job evaluation lies in the intensity and level of formality of the approach. The history of job evaluation is seen to be strongly linked to the logic of 'formalization.' Job evaluation can be seen, in fact, as an important aspect of the 'bureaucratization' of organizational life.

Most of the information gathered for this chapter derives from U.S. sources because formal job evaluation techniques are generally recognized to have originated in the United States (Patton, Littlefield, and Self 1964) and thence to have spread to other countries. The use of formal job evaluation technique in Britain, for example, is said to have been imported from the United States after the Second World War (National Board for Prices and Incomes [NBPI] 1968; Collins 1969; Thakur and Gill 1976). Although the case-study selected for this research is set in Canada, there are sparse data on the particular development of job evaluation in that country. Despite this lack of systematic data, it is fairly clear that the U.S. experience provided the impetus for the spread of job evaluation to Canada and the United Kingdom.

This chapter is divided into six main sections: 1 / the definition of job evaluation as it is known today; 2 / the pre-1930s pioneering work that led to the development of job evaluation in both the public and, later, the private sector; 3 / the rapid spread of job evaluation in the United States during the 1930s and 1940s; 4 / developments since the Second World War that have further served to entrench job evaluation as a major management tool in the operation of payment systems; 5 / the growth of job evaluation in Canada; and 6 / the effect of pay equity on the proliferation of job evaluation in Canada. This account of the history of job evaluation differs from that in any other account in that it pieces together, from a wide variety of primary and secondary sources, the relatively obscure origins of job evaluation. It is hoped that this chapter contributes to our knowledge of job evaluation in relation to the organizational and social context within which the technique has developed in the past and continues to develop today.

The Definition of Job Evaluation

'Job evaluation' is a 'label' applied to a variety of techniques that purport to measure the relative value, or worth, of jobs. The many definitions of job evaluation in the personnel-management and industrial-relations literature are consistent in portraying the key logic of job evaluation as the 'ranking' of jobs within an organization for the purposes of establishing the income hierarchy. Fundamental to the search for an acceptable definition of job evaluation and a framework to organize it, is the idea that 'job evaluation should be a general basis for, on the one hand, setting salary scales for the jobs within an organization, which are felt to be acceptable, relative to each other, by the employees. On the other hand, the resulting salary structure ought to be properly related to the going rates in the labour market in general' (McCormick 1976: 365). The assumption here is that job evaluation establishes pay rates that are both internally equitable and externally competitive.

Indeed, job evaluation, as the term implies, is commonly defined as a systematic method of determining the relative importance of jobs to establish an 'appropriate' rate of pay for each job in relation to the requirements of that job. Treiman (1979: 1), for example, defines job evaluation as 'a formal procedure for hierarchically ordering a set of jobs or positions with respect to their *value* or *worth*, usually for the purpose of setting pay rates.' Thomason (1980: 3) also defines job evaluation as 'a term which is applied to a number of distinct but

related administrative methods which rank or assess the relative value of different jobs or occupations.'

The different types of job evaluation share a similar methodology. For instance, all types require the acquisition of basic information about the job. Therefore, the first step typically involves the preparation of a job description; that is, each job is formally described according to its duties, responsibilities, requirements, and working environment. The job description may be prepared by the job holder, his or her supervisor, a job analyst, someone from the personnel department, or even by a consultant from outside the organization.

The second step involves the actual application of job evaluation standards and measurements to a set of jobs to determine their 'value' to the organization. It is primarily the fashion and manner of carrying out this evaluation process that distinguish one type of job evaluation from another. Moreover, the process of evaluating jobs may be carried out by an individual from within the organization (usually from the personnel department), an outside consultant, or an evaluation committee made up of various members of the organization and/or consultants. It should be noted that the process of job evaluation relies heavily on pooled judgment.

It is commonplace to assert, as well, that job evaluation is concerned with evaluating the 'job' and not with the performance of the individual. Job evaluation takes no account of variations in personal performance or merit displayed by individuals in the execution of their jobs; it is concerned solely with variations in job content.

There are many methods of job evaluation in use. The different methods of job evaluation can be divided into two main categories: non-analytical and analytical (NBPI 1968). These categories are also known as 'quantitative' and 'non-quantitative' (cf. Frank 1982). Non-analytical methods compare 'whole' jobs, whereas analytical methods break jobs down into factors. In recent years combinations of analytical and non-analytical techniques have been developed. These are generally known as 'hybrid' methods and are associated with the growth of management-consultancy services. Many consulting firms, and academics, have devised and marketed their own distinctive brands of job evaluation.

The main types of job evaluation that have been identified in the personnel literature are summarized below. Any one of these may be used for manual, technical, white-collar, managerial, or executive jobs, although some researchers or practitioners may claim, for various reasons, that certain jobs are more suited to certain types of job evaluation.

There are two principal types of non-analytical schemes: ranking and classification.

In *ranking* schemes, jobs in the organizations are ranked from the highest to the lowest, based on the job as a whole and not on a series of compensable factors, such as education, effort, and working conditions.

In *classification* schemes, jobs are divided into 'classes' or 'families' of jobs. Within each class predetermined definitions are prepared, each of which is meant to reflect discernible differences in the level of skill and responsibility required by jobs (e.g., general clerk – grade I to grade VII) that would typically fall into each class. The duties of the job are then compared (usually using a job description) to the set of definitions within a relevant 'class' or family of job, and matched to the 'closest' standard definition. This non-analytical form of job evaluation is most popular in government organizations.

The principal type of analytical scheme is known as points rating. The *points rating* scheme is the most popular method in the United States (Treiman 1979) and the United Kingdom (NBPI 1968; *Industrial Relations Review and Report* [*IRRR*] 1983). Points rating involves choosing 'compensable' factors, such as skill responsibility, effort, and working conditions, and attaching weights to each of these according to their perceived relative importance to the organization. When a job is evaluated, the total sum of points for each job represents the point value of the job relative to other jobs; according to the informing principle of this method, the point value of a job translates, via some internally or externally devised formula, into the appropriate money value for the job.

A number of 'hybrid' job evaluation schemes combining various features of the above types have been developed over the years. Some of the most popular of these include: the Hay-MSL Guide Chart Profile method, the Inbucon 'direct consensus' method, the Urwick Orr and Partners job-profile method, and PA International's page system of job evaluation (all devised by consultants), and Elliot Jacques's time span of discretion and T. Paterson's decision-band theory (both devised by academics).

The relationship between job evaluation and the establishment of the pay structure is of primary interest to this research and will be considered at some length in the case-study. In the meantime, however, for the purposes of deriving an official definition of job evaluation, it is sufficient to note that, according to popular literature on the subject, it is seen to play a major, if not *the* major part in determining rates of pay.

As is demonstrated below, current modes of job evaluation are merely the product of their more primitive historical forms. In fact, there has been, over the years, an increase in the complexity of job evaluation technique, which usually requires, or claims to require, an ever-higher level of expertise and training from those involved in the introduction and maintenance of these schemes.

Early Beginnings: The Public Sector

The concepts of job evaluation were used long before the ideas became formalized into a systematic body of thought. For example, the historical differences between apprentice, helper, journeyman, and master can be seen to reflect the application of such concepts.

The earliest recorded attempt at formal job evaluation took place in the offices of the U.S. federal government in 1838 (Treiman 1979; Shils 1984) when a group of government clerks, upset that clerks in other branches were receiving higher pay, requested that 'an inquiry be made ... into the kind and character of the duties of the several clerks in all the departments and subordinate bureaus, and a general law be passed, apportioning and fixing salaries to duties, so that all clerks performing like duties shall receive like salaries and every clerk (regardless of the department to which the clerk belonged) ... shall receive a salary larger or smaller, in proportion as the duties performed by him may, by Congress, be deemed complex and responsible, or plain and easy' (25th Congress, 2d Session, 1838). In response to this request for equal pay for equal work, the U.S. Senate passed a resolution instructing government department heads to prepare a 'classification of the clerks ... in reference to the character of the labor to be performed, the care and responsibility imposed, the qualifications required, and the relative value to the public of the services of each class as compared with the others' (Sen. Res. 25th Congress, 2d Session, 1838). This resolution represented the first attempt to establish, as public policy, the principle that jobs ought to be paid in proportion to their worth. There was, however, slow progress in administering this resolution. It was not until 1871 that the first use of formal job classification by the federal government actually took place (Patton, Littlefield, and Self 1964). The type of job evaluation known as 'classification' was also spreading to other government jurisdictions. In 1912, for instance, the government of Chicago had developed its own classification scheme (Shils 1984: 8/8).

During the First World War, the Bureau of Labour Statistics prepared a series of 'Descriptions of Occupations' for use in the U.S. Employment Service, for the purposes of selection and recruitment (Federal Board for Vocational Education, Washington, DC [FBVE] 1919: 35). Several civil-service commissions at both state and municipal levels – including those of Ohio, New Jersey, Milwaukee, and New York City – also prepared elaborate specifications during the First World War (ibid: 38). With the standardization of job levels and pay levels in these government organizations came the inevitable discovery of existing inequities. As the 1919 FBVE report points out: 'One of the first and probably the most startling revelations made by job analysis is the inequality of prevailing wage rates. Practically every investigation emphasizes this fact' (50). In other words, various governments expressed surprise over the number of inequities to be found: For example, while preparing a 1917 report entitled 'Standard Specifications for Positions in the Classified Service of the State,' the Ohio Civil Service Commission found innumerable inconsistencies in compensation and claimed that 'the average taxpayer would be dumbfounded if he were fully aware of the many inconsistencies in salaries paid to different employees for the same grade and character of work. Hundreds of inconsistencies could be cited. In one department two typists are seated at the same table and perform exactly the same work. One receives $62.50 per month and the other $100.00 per month' (ibid: 51).

After the First World War, the Federal Classification Act of 1923 introduced pioneer legislation in job 'classification.' Not until that year did the federal government finally manage to prepare the comprehensive program that had been requested by the government clerks mentioned above in 1838. By developing some kind of 'rationalized' system, Shils (1984: 8/8) points out, 'the government was able to persist in its theory of being accountable for the pay of several million federal employees under civil service. There had to be a doctrine of internal equity for the government to document and justify its accountability under the law.' The new principles of centralized financial control in vogue in the early 1900s in the civil service might also be considered an important influence on the development of government classification schemes: 'Uniform accounting required a uniform job terminology in place of the hodgepodge of nondescript and conflicting titles' (ibid).

Over the years, the 1923 Classification Act was amended many times, until finally it was completely replaced by the Classification Act of 1949. Like the 1923 act, this new act articulated a policy for the classification of jobs that was to be based entirely on the goal of internal equity within the federal system; comparing federal pay rates with those in the private sector was not considered to be relevant and therefore the issue not addressed (Treiman 1979: 52).

The 1949 act reduced the vast multitude of job classifications by occupational group down to the two schemes: the General Schedule (GS) and the Federal Wage System. Today these two schemes cover approximately 70 per cent of the non-military civil service. Roughly half of all federal workers are covered by the General Schedule, a system of eighteen grades meant to represent a hierarchy of difficulty, responsibility, and qualification requirements for white-collar jobs. Approximately 20 per cent of federal workers are covered by the Federal Wage System, which applies to trade, craft, and labouring jobs (Jacobson 1977: 450). The U.S. postal service, encompassing more than 25 per cent of federal workers, now utilizes its own separate classification scheme, which is divided into the Postal Service Salary Schedule, the Postal Management Salary Schedule, and the Postal Executive Service Schedule (Treiman 1979: 15). The remaining 5 per cent of federal employees (e.g., those in the Foreign Service and the National Security Agency) are covered by a variety of specialized job classifications (Austin 1977).

Once the early job-classification schemes had been developed and adopted by sections of the federal government and a few key state and municipal jurisdictions, it did not take long for the technique to spread to the rest of the public service. For example, in 1979, at the last known count, it was estimated that almost all the jobs of the approximately 2.8 million civil and federal employees were covered by a job evaluation system (Treiman 1979: 15).

How is it that formal job evaluation first developed in the public sector? It is suggested that certain characteristics peculiar to public-sector employment are likely to have stimulated its arrival. First, it is likely that public interest in comparing government rates of pay with those for similar work in private industry (often attended by the notion that government salaries, set without the competitive pressures of private industry, tend to be overly generous) prompted the practice of large-scale salary surveys. By nature, salary-survey work requires the use of some type of job description that is linked to a form of pay structure.

Another possible stimulus to job evaluation stemming from civil-service employment may be the high profile of government salaries compared to the confidentiality of pay in private industry. It might be said that widespread internal knowledge of salaries could encourage employees in a large civil-service organization to make constant judgment as to the appropriateness of their own pay compared to that of other government employees. Because such comparisons are likely to engender discontent (Daniel 1976), a government might feel the urgency to develop techniques for rationalizing the pay of its employees.

Yet another characteristic associated with civil-service employment that might explain the early use of job evaluation is the very size of the organization. Grouping a large number of office workers, for payment purposes, under the same job title is likely to have led to requests for standardization (as in the case of the U.S. federal government clerks in 1838). Employees carrying the same job title do not necessarily perform work of the same responsibility and complexity. Nor do different job titles necessarily reflect different types of work, especially since it is relatively well known in government that salary increases are usually easier to obtain by changing the title of the job. In the early days, without the benefit of job descriptions, there was little way of checking up (or appearing to check up) on the content of one job compared to that of another.

Apart from the inequities in remuneration caused by misleading job titles, the inherently 'political' nature of government organizations appears to lend itself, as it likely did years ago, to the use of status or rank by superiors to influence decisions about a subordinate's pay. As Dickinson (1937: 188) points out, 'favoritism and differences in aggressiveness in asking for pay increases on the part of the employee or any of his superiors, are potent sources of unequal pay for equally valuable work, or equal pay for unequivalent work.' It might, therefore, be suggested that government organizations believed that the standardization of job content and rates of pay provided a certain protection from such abuses.

Finally, public-sector jobs might be considered to lack an obvious reference point in the labour market (therefore requiring a method to legitimize these pay scales). As revealed below, outside of government organizations, the development of a formal job-measurement device was somewhat slower. It will also be seen that a different set of circumstances influenced interest in job evaluation in the private sector.

Early Beginnings: The Private Sector

According to one historical claim, 'job evaluation has developed as part of the expansion and definition of the staff functions of personnel and industrial engineering' (Slichter, Healy, and Livernash 1960: 560). During the period from the end of the Civil War (in 1865) to the turn of the century, the organizational unit had begun to increase in size, and it was also then that departments devoted to finance and accounting, production, and marketing first appeared in industry; the personnel function, however, did not exist in industry as a distinct management department until the early 1900s (Miner 1969: 19).

Before the turn of the century, and before the advent of the personnel department, the closest thing to job evaluation in most organizations was the 'budget,' which listed arbitrary job titles with their corresponding rates of pay; little was known about job descriptions, uniform job titles, methods of determining job worth, or wage scales permitting progression within pay ranges (Lutz 1969: 608). It seems likely, then, that the growth and development of job evaluation are linked closely to the development of the personnel function itself.

It could be argued that interest in scientific management was an important step towards the development of the personnel function, and eventually to the development of formalized job evaluation systems. As Miner (1969: 20) notes, 'Although Taylor and other industrial engineers of the time such as Frank and Lillian Gilbreth and Henry Gantt, had little interest in the formation of personnel departments as such, they did make a major contribution to that end through their insistence that management must pay attention to such matters as the selection of employees, proper training and methods, and the development of appropriate compensation programs. This was in relation to a predominant concern with how machinery might be used more effectively.'

Livy (1975) claims that interest in scientific management led industrialists to consider 'wider aspects of productivity and related problems of remuneration, particularly for manual workers' (13). By placing considerable emphasis on job analysis, scientific management is likely to have provided useful information for the eventual preparation of the position descriptions that make up such an important part of the job evaluation process.

Referring to the decade preceding the First World War, Lytle (1942: 9–10) points to the role of technological change in encouraging the growth of job evaluation: 'A rapidly improving mechanization plus a widening use of motion study had been changing job methods so radically and frequently that few jobs in one plant remained exactly like similarly titled jobs in any other plant ... Thus the "going rate" for any class of job in a community became less evident, and more undependable, as a basis for informal rate setting. This meant that the management of each plant had to work out its rate structure almost independently of interplant comparisons.' Because employers could no longer rely upon informal methods for pricing jobs, such as 'title matching,' the job description (a more detailed version of the job specification used in recruitment) began to be used for comparing pay for parallel jobs within the organization and within comparable job categories outside it. It was not until such job descriptions were in use that the extent of internal pay inconsistencies came to light, leading employers to depend less and less upon the rate structures of outside companies.

Although the use of the job description as a basis of comparison for the content of jobs and therefore for the pay received for them did open a Pandora's box of wage inequalities, by the same token it was also considered to have had the advantage of providing the means for solving any such problems: 'the first period of real attention to the determination of equitable job rates occurred about the time of World War I ... Job evaluation for the determination of equitable rates of pay began to receive a modicum of attention' (Lanham 1963: 107). The private sector first devised simple 'ranking' systems such as those developed by L.A. Miller and by W.D. Stearns' of Westinghouse Electric in 1917 and 1918, respectively. These ranking schemes placed jobs in order of their relative difficulty or value to the firm (FBVE 1919: 59).

The 'classification' type of job evaluation, so popular with government organizations, was also introduced to private industry. Classification techniques were devised and refined at the Bureau of Personnel Research at the Carnegie Institute of Technology, and this method was reportedly installed in six or seven private companies by 1922 (Kelday 1922: 13).

The first known 'point system' type of job evaluation came into being in 1925–6 after Merrill R. Lott wrote a book entitled *Wage Scales and Job Evaluation* (British Institute of Management 1952: 5). Under that particular point method devised by Lott, each job was broken down into fifteen factors, each assigned point values or weights according to its estimated importance to organizations. This point method has served as a model for many modified point schemes in existence today.

In 1926, E.J. Benge and others at the Philadelphia Rapid Transit Company tried to apply Lott's point method and found that certain aspects of that point system did not suit their needs. They therefore added a 'key scale' of five basic factors to be considered in evaluating jobs: mental requirements, skill requirements, physical requirements, responsibilities, and working conditions. This modified point scheme was entitled 'factor comparison' (Lanham 1963: 108). As Benge (1984: 12/1) states, 'the system was later used and expanded by Samuel L.H. Burk, and Edward N. Hay, and ultimately the three of us coauthored one of the early books on job evaluation.'

The three major types of job evaluation – ranking, classification, and points rating – were in existence by 1926. Job evaluation, as we know it today, had basically been developed. Although the early pioneering work described above did establish the ground rules of job evaluation, and a few companies were experimenting with various plans in the 1920s, the technique was not yet being used on any grand scale. The private sector's apparent lag behind the public sector might be explained by Lytle's observation that 'the use of job analysis to determine rates scientifically did not get so far in the factories during the 1920s because the tendency was toward incentive payment where base rates were then considered incidental' (1942: 9). Patton and Smith (1949: 4–5) also remark that private-sector employers were consumed by scientific management and paid little attention to the notion of job evaluation: 'At that time modern business management was, for the most part, too awe stricken with the possibility of wage incentives to realize that superimposing incentive earnings on maladjusted base rates would multiply the inequalities. Consequently job evaluation remained almost wholly on a flat basis.' It was not until the 1930s and 1940s that the growth and spread of job evaluation took place in the United States.

Large-Scale Expansion of Job Evaluation: From the 1930s to the End of the Second World War

Three influences appear to have contributed the most to the rapid and large-scale expansion of job evaluation in the United States during the 1930s and 1940s, namely: 1 / management response to the growth of industrial trade unionism; 2 / rapid technological change; and 3 / National War Labor Board regulations favouring the use of job evaluation for solving disputes and allowing the introduction of the technique to provide a means of escaping incomes policy.

A crude estimate of the early coverage of job evaluation can be derived by considering a survey conducted in 1940 by the National Industrial Conference Board (NICB) to obtain information on the personnel practices of 2,700 companies in the United States. The NICB reported that 13.3 per cent of companies used points and/or ranking types of job evaluation. A later survey, conducted by the same organization in 1948 and covering 3,498 companies, found the following increase in the use of job evaluation: 59 per cent of the companies surveyed applied job evaluation to nearly all hourly paid jobs; 50 per cent to salaried jobs; 33 per cent to supervisory jobs; and 12.5 per cent to executive jobs (Lytle 1954: 13). By the end of the 1940s, the Bureau of Labor Statistics reported that unions were participating in job evaluation plans at 50 per cent of the plants involved in the metal industry (ibid). From these figures, it can be seen that the use of formal job evaluation had come a long way since the techniques were pioneered in the 1920s.

WARDING-OFF INDUSTRIAL UNIONS: THE 1930S

Until the advent of industrial unionism, the craft unions had dominated the labour scene. Galenson (1961: 14) explains that 'powerful employer opposition and indifference of the crafts held the unskilled in check until the catastrophe of the Great Depression unleashed a flood of organization which carried all obstacles before it.' During the Depression and post-Depression years, certain laws were passed which favoured organized labour and helped to intensify union activity. For example, the Norris La Guardia Act of 1932 drastically limited the use of court injunctions, which, until then, had often been imposed to prevent work stoppages (Miner 1969: 27). Also, having long advocated 'standard rates,' organized labour was successful in obtaining minimum-wage laws on a federal scale, through the National Industrial Recovery Act of 1933–5 (Lytle 1942: 9). Furthermore, another national labour federation was founded in 1935, the Congress of Industrial Organizations (CIO), which was made up of unions that had seceded from the AFL. The National Labour Relations Act

(Wagner Act) of 1935 had a particular influence upon the growth of industrial unions because it officially gave workers the right to organize into labour unions and to bargain collectively. Following the introduction of the Wagner Act, it was observed that 'the CIO was able to increase its membership by large numbers of unskilled and semi-skilled workers and exerted a power never before wielded by American employees' (ibid.).

The new legal environmental thus served to encourage the growth of trade unions in a number of industries – auto, aluminum, and rubber, for example – that had never before been unionized. As Miner (1969: 27–8) notes: 'Increasingly management found itself faced with demands from *industrial unions* that included all types of workers from a given industry, regardless of specific occupation. Almost all unions, previously had been of the *craft* variety and had contained workers in a single occupation irrespective of the industry in which they worked.' Galenson (1961: 13) points out, however, that 'the American "aristocracy of labour" was less than anxious to embrace industrial unionism when craft structure had paid so well.'

The growing union movement also stimulated the expansion of all personnel activities, job evaluation being a central feature of this expansion. As Slichter, Healy, and Livernash (1960: 561) point out, at that time, job evaluation was used by management '(a) partly to deter or prevent unionization (b) partly to rationalize its wage scales prior to unionization and (c) partly to stabilize the wage structure and eliminate continuous bargaining over particular rates after unionization.' It is not considered here to be likely that job evaluation could live up to such claims, particularly that of deterring unionism. It is conceivable that employers considered the introduction of job evaluation to be synonymous with a peace offering to employees, with the ultimate hope of minimizing controversy and disputes over pay and reducing the 'need' for unionization. Slichter, Healy, and Livernash's first claim – that management adopted job evaluation to deter or prevent unionization – is vague and difficult to assess in itself, but it does become plausible if, in fact, an important factor for unionization was perceived injustice in the wage structure. If job evaluation were seen to remove such injustice, then the spread of the technique might have deterred some from unionizing. The second claim, about the reasons for introducing job evaluation at that time, refers to management's desire to rationalize its wage scales 'prior to unionization.' This leads us to consider an important and rarely discussed aspect of job evaluation, that is, its use as a management strategy to 'defend' desired organizational inequality (this feature of job evaluation will be discussed in later chapters). As Barkin points out, 'they [management] wanted to provide a system of rates which could be defended as being a rational and sanctioned by a "superior reasoning". This eliminated, in their opinion, the necessity of considering a system of rates based on their ability to pay' (quoted in Gomberg 1948: 65).

Slichter, Healy, and Livernash's third reason for organizational interest in job evaluation refers to the management belief that the technique would limit the scope and extent of collective bargaining. Employer groups such as the American Management Association (AMA), for instance, claimed that the role of job evaluation was 'both to improve company wage structure and wage administration and to maintain management control of the wage structure under (soon to arrive) collective bargaining' (Slichter, Healy, and Livernash 1960: 561).

The potentially limiting effects of job evaluation upon collective bargaining did not, however, appear to concern trade unions – at least not during the late 1930s. Faced with glaring inconsistencies in pay rates and having recently acquired the means to bargain collectively, unions threw themselves into solving the more obvious problem of chaotic wage structures. As Lytle (1942: 10) notes: 'Feeling their increased power, the union leaders began in 1937, to raise such questions as "Why has job A been paying five cents an hour less than job B?" ... the few plants which had pioneered in systematic evaluation (e.g., National Electrical Manufacturer's Association, National Metal Trades Association) soon acquired renown among the less foresighted. Feverish emulation followed.' Moreover, the desire for systematic methods of grading employees was given an additional boost by the Fair Labour Standards Act of 1983, which, by setting minimum wages for certain groups of employees, highlighted the problems involved in determining wages. For example, the Fair Labour Standards Act made it essential to distinguish between the executive and operating groups for the purpose of determining who qualified for overtime pay, and, as Lanham notes, 'making the distinction necessitated classifying employees correctly according to work functions' (1963: 108).

Generally, management's reaction to the growing and increasingly powerful U.S. labour movement provided a major stimulus to the spread of job evaluation at a time when unions displayed little resistance.

COPING WITH TECHNOLOGICAL CHANGE

The advent of mass production prior to the Second World War led to increased skill specialization in a wide range of industries, especially in metal fabricating, electrical equipment, etc. (ILO 1960). Also, as the needs created by the war accelerated the trend to mass production, the formerly clear line between mass production and craft jobs increasing became blurred and it was felt that a new 'yardstick' was needed to replace the dictate of traditional differentials.

CIRCUMVENTING SECOND WORLD WAR WAGE CONTROLS

The rapid spread of job evaluation in the United States during the Second World War owes much to the attempts of various companies to circumvent the wage controls imposed by the National War Labor Board (Barkin 1946; Slichter, Healy, and Livernash 1960; International Labour Office 1960; Lanham 1963). According to the regulations administered by regional wage and salary boards, increases above the statutory maxima were permitted through upward mobility within a pay 'grade.' In other words, the boards permitted employees to receive the next 'step' in their pay range (if there was a 'range,' not a flat rate) without recourse for approval to the National War Labor Board; only the overall movement in pay ranges remained subject to regulation.

Those organizations which had, up to this time, operated on individual flat rates rather than pay 'ranges' with step increments found themselves with little flexibility. Although employees could still benefit from the occasional inflation-guided rate increases (without knowing if and when these would occur), the advantage of relatively free movement within salary ranges proved an often irresistible attraction, and many organizations set about establishing job grades with pay 'ranges.' As Slichter, Healy, and Livernash (1960: 562) note, 'the increased flexibility inherent in rate-range regulation undoubtedly encouraged the spread of wage and salary evaluation in order to develop appropriate rate ranges.' To satisfy the board that 'appropriate' pay ranges had been determined, however, the organization was required to demonstrate its use of some formal job evaluation technique.

While the introduction of job evaluation benefited the employer in terms of increased freedom and flexibility in decisions relating to pay, it also presented some obvious advantages to employees, as they stood to gain financially from the freedom to move, with relative ease, within the steps of a pay range. Under these conditions, the introduction of job evaluation was not likely to be met with significant resistance, nor was it.

The regulations also permitted 'above the norm' increases to any organization that introduced a job evaluation plan. According to Slichter, Healy, and Livernash (1960: 562), liberal policies regarding pay increases were applied by the National War Labor Board when an organization introduced job evaluation in order to sell the scheme so that an average increase for the pay structure as a whole was granted, regardless of downgradings or 'red-circled' jobs. Such liberal policies acted as an incentive to introduce job evaluation at a time of severe restriction on pay increases.

The National War Labor Board was also responsible for resolving disputes over wage inequities. The third major reason that the Second World War wage regulations encouraged the rapid spread of job evaluation may be the board's powerful belief in the merits of job evaluation for resolving wage disputes. The board often recommended job evaluation as a framework for solving pay problems (Slichter, Healy, and Livernash 1960: 562; Shils 1984: 8/9). Upon 'satisfactory' proof of either internal or external pay inequities, the board would grant corrected increases; once again, however, it was only through an organization's use of job evaluation that such anomalies could be demonstrated to the board in the first place (International Labour Office 1960: 10). The government was not receptive to the notion of granting increases simply on the basis of job-title comparisons that were not supported by job-content comparisons (Shils 1984: 8/9).

Finally, it has been suggested that, even during the war, comparability debates were rife because many employees who were dissatisfied with their level of pay felt powerless to do anything about it. Millions of employees working in defence industries could not leave their jobs without notifying the draft board, and, if they had no dependents, they could not leave their job without the danger of being drafted. For those employees working in the defense industries, 'the pasture was always greener elsewhere. Hence employers, unions, and government were very happy to have a pay rationalization plan to justify wage levels' (Shils 1984: 8/8). Thus it was that, by the end of the Second World War, the use of formal job evaluation technique had spread considerably.

During the rise of powerful industrial unions in the 1930s the unions as well as management sought to introduce order to pay scales and had wage standardization in mind. The 1930s saw little trade union opposition to the technique. As Patton and Smith (1949: 6) point out, 'collective bargaining forced wage levels upwards, but with little thought given to existent misalignment of rates. The result was such a hodgepodge of rates that management and unions alike were without a sound defensible system of wage determination.' In a review of trade union attitude to evaluation in the 1930s, a Princeton University study concludes that job evaluation met with little union resistance: 'For the most part, organized labour readily accepts the the need for sound job evaluation, and is co-operative both in its original development in a company and in its administration if the union is given a voice in all questions which affect the individual rates and earnings of its members. Not infrequently, the union has taken the initiative in requesting a classification of the relative worth of jobs and a regular review to maintain the established relationships' (1941: 8).

The early 1940s also experienced very little trade union resistance to the spread of the technique. The financial benefits that accrued from introducing job evaluation during the reign of Second World War wage controls appear to have gone some way in encouraging trade union support of the technique. One of the earliest recorded objections, however, comes from a 1940 publication of the United Electrical, Radio and Machine Workers (CIO) which had this to say about job evaluation: 'Our members see through the "mumbo-jumbo" of point rating systems and are not deceived by it. The fact that point rating systems can sometimes be used to get more wages should not obscure the important fact that they were invented by management to eliminate collective bargaining as much as possible in favour of a so-called "scientific" method of determining wage differentials' (quoted in Baker and True 1947: 81–2).

Certainly, claims were being made that the unions were being bought off, but, as Slichter, Healy, and Livernash (1960: 563) note, 'objection was not strong enough to turn down evaluation if an increase in the rate structure was also involved. The lack of resistance to job evaluation on behalf of U.S. unions has been explained in a similar way by Barkin, a representative of the Textile Workers Union of America, who was largely opposed to job evaluation: 'the trade unions were not overly sensitive to the shortcomings of these [job evaluation] plans because they wanted to get wage increases through any means ... as a result these plans were more readily accepted than would ordinarily have been expected' (quoted in Shister 1956: 263).

It can be seen that the government wage regulations, by allowing organizations to circumvent wage controls via the use of job evaluation, played a large part in overcoming the possible hurdle of union resistance to job evaluation in the United States. Basically, then, it is suggested that the union position during much of the period in which job evaluation was spreading was one of general acceptance. Moreover, it should be noted that this expansion of job evaluation also took place at a time when the wage level had been almost continuously rising (Moberly and Buffa 1947: 1; Patton and Smith 1949: 6) and this feature alone is likely to have helped rather than hindered union acceptance of the technique.

The Continued Growth of Job Evaluation: From the Second World War to the Late 1980s

Following its rapid spread in the 1930s and 1940s, it is interesting to note, that, at least up to the end of the 1980s, job evaluation has not only remained in the forefront of 'rational' management activity, but grown in its coverage. A study of 1,265 firms conducted between 1950 and 1954 reveals that 322 firms had formal job evaluation plans, 56 were in the process of installing a plan at the time, and 181 were considering installing one (Lanham 1955: 10, 11).

In 1955, a federal Bureau of National Affairs survey found formal job evaluation plans in six out of every seven firms. Another survey, conducted by Scott, Clothier, and Spriegel (1961: 583), uncovers the continued growth of the technique: in 1947, 55 per cent of 325 surveyed companies had introduced job evaluation plans; in 1953, 68 per cent of 780 firms had introduced them; and in 1957, 72 per cent of 852 firms had introduced such plans. A 1960 survey by George Fry and Associates found that 65 per cent of more than 500 responding companies had instituted job evaluation (cited in Patton 1961). A 1968 study of job evaluation stated that 'it is probable that some 50 million American employees – about two thirds of the employed labour force – are graded under job evaluation' (NBPI 1968: 12).

A national survey of job-analysis practices in 1970 reported that 75.8

per cent of organizations used job analysis and that the great majority (95 per cent) of these programs were used in job evaluation (Stone and Yoder 1970: 18–19).

Finally, a 1979 report prepared by the National Academy of Sciences in Washington DC, at the request of the U.S. Equal Employment Opportunity Commission, suggest that, 'first, almost all federal employees, including those in the U.S. Postal Service, are covered by job evaluation plans (Austin 1977). Second, most state governments and most large county governments appear to use job evaluation systems (Craver 1977) ... Third, the best available evidence suggests that the majority of large firms utilize formal job evaluation procedures – although the quality of the evidence leaves much to be desired ... (Akalin 1970)' (quoted in Treiman 1979: 49).

One study also found that large organizations were 'somewhat more likely' to use job evaluation than were small organizations, but that job evaluation plans were found even in very small organizations (Belcher 1974: 93). In a British study, Batstone (1984) also found that job evaluation was more likely to exist in large organizations with a well-developed personnel or human-relations department.

The continued and, indeed, increased interest in job evaluation since the Second World War is surely attributable to a host of factors, but, at least historically, some of the more direct influences are considered to be: 1 / the difficulties of post–Second World War reconversion to civilian production; 2 /automation and the rise of white-collar unions; 3 / the desire to circumvent Korean War wage controls; and 4 / equal pay legislation. The way in which each of these factors is seen to have influenced the use of job evaluation is discussed below.

THE DIFFICULTIES OF POST–SECOND WORLD WAR RECONVERSION

Wage-structure problems continued to generate a high volume of grievances not only during the war years but also during 'reconversion' to civilian production. The difficult problems of reconversion were not dissimilar to the earlier, pre-war production 'conversion' problems. In fact, each adjustment period saw major changes in such areas as job content, labour-market composition, and demand and supply of goods and services. The post–Second World War reconversion scene has been described as follows: 'the no-strike pledge lost all its dwindling effectiveness, the N.W.L.B., its compulsory powers. The federal government found itself embarrassed for lack of wage-price policy, and business and labor squared up for a mighty scrap' (Harris 1982: 112).

The phasing-out of wage and salary controls proved to be of concern to both management and to unions at a time when inevitable confusion lay ahead. During the reconversion, management followed the initial lead of the War Labor Board by holding up job evaluation as a way of minimizing the stress of readjustment to peacetime production. Some indication of the faith in the power of job evaluation is reflected in this claim made by Lytle (1954: 13): '[employers] realized there would be a great commotion wherever management failed to develop a program of job analysis and job evaluation. Much confusion, distress on the part of top management, and in many cases actual strikes were avoided where this preparation took place.' Interestingly, others also attributed conflict reducing powers to job evaluation: 'As the post war years went by internal wage-rate relationships became a progressively less acute labor management problem. In considerable part this meant that job evaluation became an accepted approach to job-rate problems' (Slichter, Healy, and Livernash 1960: 563).

Although it would be difficult to prove that the introduction or existence of job evaluation could actually prevent strikes, it would appear that management turned to job evaluation as a 'strategy' for solving pay-related problems in the belief that the technique would once again justify or rationalize desired income differentials to the unions.

AUTOMATION AND THE GROWTH OF OFFICE UNIONS

It has been said that 'if there is one thing certain under automation it is that the job – even the bottom job – will change rapidly and often' (Drucker 1955: 45). It has also been said that changes in the actual content of jobs can and do affect the method and form of compensation in automated plants and industries (Rezler 1969: 282).

Just as earlier technological advancements, by changing the content of jobs, induced the development of job evaluation in the 1920s and its expansion in the 1930s and 1940s, so this trend continued after the Second World War. With the creation of new jobs that bore little or no historical relationship to other jobs, both management and unions, had to seek ways of rationalizing the wages for them. Both turned to job evaluation as a means to that end. As Stimmler (1966: 594) comments: 'The increasingly evident trend of national legislation toward synthetic solutions to problems of work simplification resulting from technological advancement is forcing industry to explore feasible answers to these problems ... Tireless investigation of means to apply rating methods to new techniques of work performance is ab-solutely necessary for the continued growth of the American enterprise system.'

It stands to reason that changes in automation also had the effect of shifting the extent to which workers could exert control over outputs (Collins 1969: 6). Less control over outputs would have rendered many payment-by-results schemes difficult, or impossible, to operate. Changing from a system of payment by results to a system of payment by time or fixed pay is likely to have generated considerable interest in job evaluation.

With the increase in jobs that are classified as 'service,' 'information,' or 'knowledge,' the use of job evaluation spread to a new and growing group of workers who came to be known as 'white-collar' employees. The increase in numbers of white-collar workers is considered to have been the major growth element in the labour movement since the Second World War, especially in the public sector (Galenson and Smith 1978: 83). Not until after the war did the early classification schemes, originally developed in government organizations, became more widespread. Lutz (1969: 610) differentiates between pre-war and postwar salary administration: 'Formerly there was rarely any organized opposition to or contention with the personnel director's decision as to the grade or pay of a job. He rarely had to justify his judgement except to his superiors. With the advent of strong unions of public employees and the increasing probability of many of these unions actually negotiating individual job rates, personnel directors are now realizing that they must have something more concrete to justify their decision.'

Just as the rise of industrial unions during the 1930s can be seen to have led employees to rush towards some form of job evaluation scheme, the rapid rise of the public-sector unions seems to have further encouraged the use of the technique in the 1950s.

CIRCUMVENTING KOREAN WAR WAGE CONTROLS

During the Korean War, wage controls were once again introduced, operating this time through the U.S. Wage Stabilization Board and the

U.S. Salary Stabilization Board. These boards followed much the same restraint procedures as those employed during the Second World War. Again, those organizations operating (or introducing) job evaluation were in a position to circumvent the statutory maxima set out in the regulations. As Shils (1984: 8/10) points out, 'the government once more honored the criteria it had set up in World War II for relaxing the pay freeze. It permitted many adjustments to firms with rationalized pay and classification plans. By this time, pay rationalization had arrived.' As their counterpart had done during the Second World War, these boards recommended the use of job evaluation to resolve the problem of how to compare one job with another when dealing with disputes brought before them.

EQUAL PAY LEGISLATION

The U.S. tendency use legal enactment in determining conditions of labour in industry is apparent in early federal legislation in such areas as minimum wage, discrimination, pensions, safety, and equal pay. As Galenson and Smith (1978: 83) claim, 'there is hardly a country in the world in which the legal profession plays as important a role in industrial relations as in the United States.'

One of the most widely discussed areas of government intervention in recent years has been the issue of sex-related pay discrimination. The U.S. Equal Pay Act (EPA) of 1963 and Title VII of the Civil Rights Act of 1964, later amended by the Equal Employment Opportunity Act of 1972, by their very language, are grounded in standard job evaluation concepts. The words 'equal pay for substantially equal effort, skill and responsibility, under similar working conditions' (EPA, 1963, section 6[d]) suggest the need for some form of point-rating system that would measure the extent to which each of the four factors is contained in any job.

Faced with increasing numbers of lawsuits brought under the Equal Pay Act and Title VII of the Civil Rights Act (amended), courts and other government, employer, and union bodies have turned their attention to the relationship between an organization's job evaluation system and pay discrimination. Adherence to the acts is monitored by the federal Department of Labor in the case of the Equal Pay Act, 1963, and by the Equal Employment Opportunities Commission (EEOC) in the case of the Civil Rights Act (Thomsen 1978: 14). As Brandt (1984: 2/1) observes: 'now, with the growing numbers of equal opportunity cases and increasing interest of "equal pay for equal work", companies are coming to recognize the need for a document that is a legally defensible basis for staffing actions, job administration, and compensation determinations.'

U.S. interest in the subject of job evaluation in general has increased substantially in recent years, and much time and money is being spent by the U.S. government to develop improved and less 'discriminatory' job evaluation procedures. The EEOC, for instance, initiated its first effort towards producing a 'non-biased' job evaluation method in 1977 (Thomsen 1978: 14). Also in 1977, the EEOC commissioned the National Academy of Sciences (NAS) to review, over a ten- to fifteen-year period, the subject of 'comparable worth' and the effect of job evaluation upon minority members of the workforce (Dertien 1981: 566).

In the United States, equal pay legislation has stressed the importance of job evaluation and has strengthened or augmented government intervention in this area to ensure the existence of 'proper' pay relationships in organizations. As Paton (1978: 28) points out, 'job evaluation has become more credible as a valid tool of work measurement which, in turn, has created the need for professional job analysts to serve as expert witnesses in pay discrimination cases.'

Other countries are also using job evaluation to attempt to resolve equal pay. In Britain, researchers have claimed that 'the application of job evaluation has been intensified by the implications of the *Equal Pay Act*, as modified in 1984, which places as central in assessing equal pay claims the question about whether or not a job-evaluated payment scheme is in use' (Torrington and Hall 1987: 508) and that 'the implementation of the Equal Pay Act between 1970 and 1975 is likely to have stimulated the spread of the [job evaluation] technique' (Brown 1981: 111).

As is the case in North America, in Britain definite attempts are being made to encourage organizations to formalize their job-measurement technique. The more quantitative, or 'analytical' types of job evaluation are considered to be less biased than non-analytical schemes such as ranking or job classification. The British Equal Opportunities Commission (EOC; 1985) argues, for instance, that analytical methods of job evaluation can avoid sex discrimination, while non-analytical methods are particularly prone to sex discrimination. A British study of 106 job evaluation plans operated in 85 establishments concludes that the more formal the job evaluation technique and its method of implementation and administration, the more likely the resultant pay structure is to be free of sex bias (Ghobadian and White 1986).

In summary, it is argued that equal-pay and subsequent comparable-worth legislation have stepped up the use of job evaluation in recent years. Behind such legislation lies the assumption that each job has a certain number of common factors that vary between jobs, and that these factors can be measured in such a way as to produce the 'correct' monetary value for a particular job, or group of jobs. It would appear that state requirements regarding formalization are changing the official definition of what constitutes job evaluation by declaring the older and simpler plans obsolete.

Job Evaluation: The Canadian Experience

The literature is surprisingly silent on the development and diffusion of job evaluation in Canada. A comprehensive history of job evaluation in Canada still needs to be written. In comparison with the U.S. experience with the technique, Canada's displays both similarities and differences. The array of forces I have discussed above to account for the spread of the technique in the United States also has relevance for Canada. The growth of scientific management and the attendant bureaucratization of the personnel function, inducements to further professionalize the personnel function through the various war efforts (with pressure to bring administrative arrangements in line with allied forces), the early growth of large-scale public-sector organizations, and the rapid change in technology doubtless figured centrally in the development and spread of the technique in Canada.

Much of the history and development of the technique in Canada needs, however, to be located within the context of 'institutional isomorphism' and the necessity that such techniques be introduced in order to command organizational legitimacy (as was true of the early U.S. experience with this 'modern' technique). It is also possible to suggest that the early history of job evaluation technique in Canada is linked to the establishment and proliferation of U.S. multinational enterprises within Canadian boundaries. Formalized job evaluation systems are usually associated with large and complex organizational entities and the multinational certainly fits this form.

The chief difference in the U.S. and Canadian experiences of the spread of the technique relates to the pay equity process. Canada has been a recent world leader in pay equity legislation, and job evaluation has proliferated with the enactment of each successive pay equity law. In fact, it is possible to assert that the recent history of job evaluation in Canada is very much the history of the pay equity movement.

Pay equity inducements in the development of job evaluation technique can be traced back to the early 1950s. The 1950s was a landmark decade for the introduction of 'equal pay for equal work' legislation. In the 1950s, such legislation was passed by both the federal and a number of pace-setting provincial governments. This legislation sought to address pay inequities between men and women who were engaged in equal or significantly similar work. The legislation made it illegal to pay lower wages if the jobs were substantially similar in terms of skill, effort, responsibility, and working conditions. Although the legislation did not compel organizations to have formal job evaluation in place (in order to ensure that similar work was paid equally), often formal job evaluation was turned to to make the necessary assessments of job content. Job evaluation became particularly important in the settlement of disputes where jobs were not identical but were 'significantly' similar in content.

The most significant boost for the spread of job evaluation in Canada did not come, however, until the introduction of 'equal pay for work of equal value' legislation. Unlike 'equal pay for equal work,' 'equal pay for work of equal value' allows jobs to be compared in terms of 'composite' value (whether or not jobs are the same is not important). 'Equal value' is based on the composite or sum of skill, effort, responsibility, and working conditions. In other words, pay equity requires thet male- and female-dominated jobs that are different in content but equal in 'composite' value (skill and so on) be paid the same.

By the 1980s, Canada had become a world leader in the area of equal pay for work of equal value. The latter part of the 1980s saw a flurry of pay equity legislation across Canada. The many legislative initiatives are summarized in table 1.

This pay equity legislation had a huge impact on the spread of job evaluation technique across Canada. With the passing of this legislation we have witnessed an unparalleled 'bureaucratization' of the pay-determination process (what may be referred to as the coming tyranny of the professional job evaluator!). The legislation has com-

TABLE 1
Pay equity legislation/initiatives in Canada

Year	Jurisdiction	Title of legislation
1976	Quebec	Quebec Charter of Rights and Freedoms
1977	Federal government	Canadian Human Rights Act
1985	Manitoba	Pay Equity Act
1986	Yukon	Yukon Human Rights Act
1987	Ontario	An Act to Provide for Pay Equity
1988	Prince Edward Island	Pay Equity Act
1989	New Brunswick	Pay Equity Act
1990	Northwest Territories	Compliance under Canadian Human Rights Act will result in pay equity study for the territorial public sector

Source: Weiner and Gunderson (1990: 107)

pelled organizations to have some form of job evaluation in place to make the necessary adjustments in pay inequities. This has meant the introduction not only of job evaluation procedures but also of the organizational infrastructure necessary for the conduct of formal job evaluation (for example, formalized job descriptions and specifications). Ironically, this legislation is being imposed precisely at the time when organizations are attempting to 'de-bureaucratize' and to move to more flexible forms of work (which, in many cases, has implied moving away from the job description – 'doing whatever needs to be done to get the job done'). With the exception of Ahlstrand and Quaid (1992) and Mahoney (1990), this internal contradiction has gone unnoticed in the literature.

The Manitoba, Prince Edward Island, and Nova Scotia legislation require that a single job evaluation scheme be used for all employers. Manitoba itself goes even farther and requires that a 'quantitative' system be used (here there is a belief that a 'quantitative' system is somehow more 'objective' and 'scientific'). The Quebec Human Rights Commission prefers that the point-factor method be used but allows employers to use any job evaluation system that is free of 'gender bias.'

The Ontario legislation requires that a 'gender-neutral job compensation' system be used but does not limit the possibilities to job evaluation. Realistically, however, this provision does not appear to open up possibilities for any device for job-worth measurement other than job evaluation. In fact, any composite comparison of skill, effort, responsibilities, and working conditions could really be classified only as job evaluation. It could be argued that the definition of job evaluation itself is changing. What may have been defined as job evaluation yesterday, does not necessarily meet today's definition criteria. Because of pay equity legislation, simple ranking and classification types of job evaluation are being rejected in favour of supposedly 'less biased' quantitative point schemes.

Since job evaluation is the mechanism increasingly favoured by many Western capitalist governments (e.g., those of the United States, Canada, and the United Kingdom) for resolving claims over pay inequity, it appears that what actually constitutes job evaluation is becoming much more narrowly defined. While common 'qualitative' practices such as job ranking and job classification have always been identified as forms of job evaluation, this chapter makes the point that 'the state' is shifting the definition of job evaluation to include only those schemes that are 'quantitative' in nature.

The impact that the pay equity movement has had on the spread of job evaluation technique in Canada cannot be overstated. By being given a formal legislative stamp of approval it has gained a level of status and legitimacy never before attained. Formal job evaluation is no longer a choice; now it is the law.

Conclusions

This chapter has attempted to trace the origins of job evaluation as a formal measurement technique. This task was made somewhat difficult by the simple fact that the activity of evaluating jobs is basically as old as industry itself. However, it is generally recognized that the United States is the birthplace of formal job evaluation technique (Patton, Littlefield, and Self 1964) and that it spread to other countries from there. Job classification, the first known type of job evaluation, originated in government, and the other two types of job evaluation – ranking and points rating – were developed in the private sector. By the mid 1920s all three techniques were in use, and during the 1930s and 1940s the technique began to spread. In the 1930s, faced with a growing and increasingly powerful (especially industrial) trade union movement, management introduced job evaluation partly to deter or prevent unionization, partly to rationalize its pay scales prior to unionization, and partly to eliminate continuous bargaining over particular rates after unionization (Slichter, Healy, and Livernash 1960). In the 1940s, during the post–Second World War period of reconversion to civilian production (Harris 1982), and subsequently during periods marked by increased automation and the rise of white-collar unionism (Lutz 1969), Korean War wage controls (Shils 1984) and equal pay legislation (Patton 1978), job evaluation continues to thrive in the United States.

Many of the forces that spurred job evaluation in the United States also appeared to be active towards that end in the Canadian context. However, recent pay equity legislation in Canada indicates that the technique has really taken hold there, the legislative stamp of legitimacy having breathed new life into it.

It could be said that, with the increased use of elaborate and quantitative point schemes that give the appearance of 'scientificity,' job evaluation technique has become more sophisticated over the years. As the technique gains relevance within the law (i.e., in terms of legal decisions relating to pay equity), it is likely that the non-quantitative forms of job evaluation will die a slow death. Of the three main types of job evaluation methods identified earlier (ranking, classification and points rating), 'points rating' is, by far, the most popular method used in the United States (Akalin and Hassan 1971; Treiman 1979) and in many other countries, including Canada (Pay Research Bureau 1981) and Britain (NBPI 1968; IRRR 1983). Surveys of job evaluation practices in the U.S. state and county government organizations have demonstrated a definite trend towards greater use of quantitative than qualitative methods (Craver 1977; McConomy and Ganschinietz 1983).

In this chapter I have attempted to provide a 'history' where none existed before. It is far from complete, but through the assembling of disparate data sources I have provided, at the very least, groundwork for the development of a more comprehensive history of job evaluation, a promising area for further research.

It is possible to suggest at least three different lines of inquiry that could be followed by future researchers in developing a comprehensive history of job evaluation (each of these, I believe, flows out of my research). First, it would be fruitful to explore the links between the growth of job evaluation and the growth of formalization and bureaucratization in organizations. Job evaluation might be seen as an important index of bureaucratization itself. Second, this increased formalization could be linked to a wider social context. In doing so, organizational and societal 'crises' would be identified that have necessitated a method and language change in the evaluation of job worth. Finally, it might be useful (at least in the more recent history of the job evaluation) to link the rapid spread of job evaluation from one organization to another to the logic of *institutional isomorphism* itself. Institutional theory tells us that organizations tend to pattern their structures on other socially legitimated structures. My own research suggests that there is good reason to believe that this patterning also takes place for specific administrative interventions such as job evaluation. In turn, this trend suggests the further formalization and bureaucratization of organizational life.

In an early Princeton University study of seventy-six separate job evaluation plans being used in single plants or companies, the authors claimed that 'the older plans were found to have simpler administrative structure' (Baker and True 1947: 28). The British National Board for Prices and Incomes(1968) suggests that the history of job evaluation is really one of substitution of more complex plans for simpler plans.

This chapter has demonstrated that there does indeed seem to be a definite movement in job evaluation from the simple to the complex. Thomason (1981: 491) claims that the increasing complexity of job evaluation is attributable to 'the decline in "whole job" familiarity with technological change and the increase in "new jobs."' The NBPI report on job evaluation (1968: 9) provides different reasons for the increased complexity of job evaluation: 'in general, job evaluation schemes are becoming more refined for two reasons – the recognition of drawbacks in earlier procedures, and the ability to apply statistical techniques with the aid of the computer.' While these explanations undoubtedly have some merit, it is suggested here that, behind the complex language and procedures of job evaluation, lies the belief that the act of 'formalizing' or 'refining' its methods can better, or more convincingly, solve the vexing problem of how to mediate between internal organizational equity, on the one hand, and external market competitiveness, on the other. As Koprowski (1960: 298) claims, 'science is the "golden calf" of Western Civilization ... people have come to identify the "complex" with the "scientific." This has made anything which is complex desirable in terms of our cultural values.'

3 What Is Job Evaluation Supposed to Do?
Some Unexamined Assumptions

What is job evaluation supposed to do? This chapter seeks to answer this question, at least in so far as the literature to date has suggested an answer. I have identified three contributors to the job evaluation debate: the personnel-management school, the industrial-relations school, and the feminist school, and survey the literature under these broad categories.

Conventional personnel-management theorists tend to emphasize the administrative advantages of job evaluation. Within this theory, for instance, the technique is portrayed as providing a rational and scientific method of ranking jobs within the organization, based upon measuring job content, and as determining pay rates that are externally competitive.

The industrial-relations tradition accepts the personnel-management claims about job evaluation, expressing concern over the potentially limiting effects of job evaluation upon collective bargaining. The British industrial-relations 'reform' movement of the 1960s saw job evaluation as a control mechanism that would restore order out of chaos and increase the formality and stability of British industrial relations ([National Board for Prices and Incomes [NBPI] 1968; Brown 1981; Purcell 1983). Job evaluation stood as one of the more promising instruments for industrial-relations reform. Other industrial-relations theorists of a more radical persuasion have seen job evaluation as an important tool for the further subordination of labour to capital (Collins 1969; Crouch 1977).

The growing feminist school on job evaluation and pay equity, interestingly, like the personnel-management school, tends to endorse the technique, sharing a faith in its ultimate rational-scientific powers. In endorsing job evaluation, feminist writers have demonstrated an unabiding faith in the technique to sort out the complex and troubling pay-determination process. For the feminist school, the trick is one of reconfiguring the technique so as to purge existing 'gender bias.' In crude terms, what this means is manipulating the 'weights and factors' used to score jobs so that the technique will 'automatically' yield higher scores for those occupations normally held by 'marginalized' women. To turn the feminists' critique of 'gender-biased job evaluation systems' back on itself, what the feminist school proposes is 'cooking the books' to preordain the valuation process.

In this chapter I argue that an improved understanding of job evaluation can be obtained by examining and reformulating our assumptions. The importance of this chapter lies in making known the various claims that have been made about job evaluation in the literature so that their plausibility may be weighed in the contexts of theory and the case-study findings presented in chapters 4 to 8.

One of the most striking observations to be made about the literature is the virtual paucity of works that cast any doubt upon the supposed powers of the technique. In later chapters, it will be seen that the personnel-management, the industrial-relations, and the feminist school have perhaps oversold and misunderstood the properties of job evaluation.

The Personnel-Management Claims ⚹.

What does job evaluation do? This, question has, for the most part, been posed and answered from a 'how to' perspective. To date, most research conducted on job evaluation has been approached from a managerial frame of reference and has been concerned with the *administration* of the technique, thereby serving to insulate job evaluation from a broader sociological line of inquiry. Although a large number of informative articles and books on job evaluation exist, much of what has been written is intended for the practitioner, for the personnel manager or compensation specialist in charge of managing the salary-administration system. Thus, much of the writing on job evaluation is part of the personnel-management literature. Such accounts of job evaluation are typically structured in a way that describes the various methods in use and the various steps required to implement a successful job evaluation plan (see, for instance, Thomason 1968, 1980; Livy 1975; Treiman 1979). These works also describe the related processes of 'job-description writing,' 'evaluating the jobs' (the objective of internal equity), and 'pricing the jobs' (the objective of external competitiveness).

From this rather technical perspective, job evaluation is seen to constitute a device for the settlement of the troublesome question of how to establish an internally equitable pay structure that is also externally competitive. The basic properties of job evaluation are unquestioned and taken for granted. So far, textbooks have concentrated on the advantages of using the technique and the advantages of using one particular type of job evaluation over another (e.g., Thomason 1968; Treiman 1979). Articles on job evaluation published in specialized journals can be divided into a number of categories: the improvements brought to a particular organization by introducing job evaluation (e.g., Kress 1969; Lutz 1969; Ward 1973; Oliver 1976); the importance of statistical technique in job evaluation (e.g., Foster 1968; Risher 1978); the role of the job analyst or the evaluator (e.g., Kimball 1964; Douglas 1966); the accuracy and validity of job evaluation results (e.g., Fox 1962; Gomez-Mejia, Page, and Tornow 1982; Dertien 1981); the possibility of instituting national job evaluation (e.g., Webb 1973); the effects of new technology upon job evaluation (e.g., Grayson 1982); sexual bias in job evaluation plans (e.g., Johnson and Cooke 1982; McNally and Shimmin 1984; Arvey 1986), and so on.

In the personnel-management literature, the main advantage of using job evaluation is viewed directly in terms of the increased amount of administrative control that accrues to management as a result. This objective implies two separate functions: the establishment of a hierarchy of jobs based on the measurement of job content and the linking of evaluation to pay determination.

Does job evaluation establish the organization's hierarchy and determine what amounts of money will be attached to different jobs? According to the following summary of the popular personnel-management literature, job evaluation does indeed fulfil such functions.

ESTABLISHING THE JOB HIERARCHY

Let us consider some of the claims that, over the years, have depicted job evaluation as a device for establishing the organizational hierarchy:

Job evaluation, through job description, job analysis, and job rating by factors, *creates an hierarchy* of jobs according to skill and responsibility requirements, and according to physical effort and working conditions. (Slichter, Healy, and Livernash 1960: 560; emphasis added)

Job evaluation is a systematic method of appraising the value of each job in relation to others. It provides a rational, consistent approach to the *establishment of a hierarchy of jobs.* (Dick 1974: 176; emphasis added)

Job evaluation is the evaluation or rating of jobs *to determine their position in a job hierarchy.* (U.S. Department of Labor, Bureau of Labor Statistics 1950; emphasis added)

The plausibility of such claims will be discussed later in this book.

DETERMINING PAY RATES

Just as job evaluation is seen to establish the hierarchy, it is also commonly seen to determine pay (either directly or indirectly). For example, an early Princeton University survey on job evaluation states: 'For the purposes of this study, job evaluation is presumed to include any systematic method of determining a logical and consistent alignment of rates' (Baker and True 1947:10). This notion has not disappeared with the years. The following quotes illustrate further the continued belief that, somehow, job evaluation determines pay:

Point plans differ from all others in that jobs are first rated and given a point total. The point totals are then converted into monetary equivalents. (Moore 1950: 325)

By establishing the true relative value of jobs it [job evaluation] will provide a logical structure for promotion. Job evaluation establishes a series of base rates for jobs without reference to personal effort or merit. (British Institute of Management 1952: 8)

You may be overpaying some people in your company (thus adding to costs) and underpaying others (thus running the risk of losing them). The answer to both problems is job evaluation. (Wilking 1961: 38)

The purpose of 'job evaluation' is to set a rate for a job irrespective of the attributes of individual workers who may be employed on the job in order to establish the rate for one job in relation to another. (Stettner 1969: 54–5)

Every organization, large or small, has the problem of determining how much employees should be paid. Over the past few years a steadily increasing number of companies in the United States have been adopting job evaluation plans as a yardstick to replace arbitrary personal judgments. (Kress 1969: 341)

The purpose of job evaluation is to assess the relative money value of jobs. (deJong 1972: 7)

Job evaluation is a complex of job analysis, the study of jobs, job description, the statement of the results of the analysis, upon which follows job grading, the placing of jobs in a sequence or ranking which is the basis of job assessment and the establishment of fair pay. (Paterson 1972: xi–xii)

Job evaluation is a widely used method of determining salaries in industry, government and other sectors. (Curston 1976: 11)

Job evaluation plans come in many different shapes and sizes, but this is a constant objective: to relate job payment to the job demand. (Thomason 1981: 490)

Job evaluation is the most common method used to provide the basis for a rational pay structure. (Torrington and Hall 1987: 517)

A survey of job evaluation practices in fifty organizations in Great Britain was conducted in 1983 by the Industrial Relations Review and Report. This survey drew the following conclusion: 'Job evaluation is now widely accepted as a basis for setting pay rates' (1983: 2).

Related to the power of job evaluation to determine pay rates is the notion of setting pay differentials. Job evaluation is also depicted as determining the appropriate differentials between jobs:

The most fundamental objective of job evaluation is to determine what the job relationships are, considering the requirements of the jobs, and to establish the correct relationships in the job-rate structure. (Moberly and Buffa 1947: 2)

Formal Job Evaluation may be classified as one of the techniques devised to establish acceptable standards for determining wage differentials. (Nicolopoulos 1954, quoted in NBPI 1968: 48)

Job evaluation is the process of determining systematically and as objectively as possible the differential rates of pay for jobs in a prescribed organization. (Merrie 1968: 1)

A job evaluation program shows relationships between jobs in the company and establishes correct differentials between these jobs. An understanding of this fact is extremely important in getting the employee to understand his position on the wage scale. (Bartley 1981: 5)

Such claims will be discussed later in this book.

SUPPOSED BY-PRODUCTS OF JOB EVALUATION

Not only do personnel writers appear to view job evaluation as a panacea for the problem of establishing an equitable and workable pay structure, but they also claim that there is a whole host of personnel related by-products from which management supposedly also benefits as a result of using the technique (e.g., Patton and Smith 1949; International Labour Organization 1960; Kindig 1963; Miner 1969; Dick 1974; Curston 1976; Bartley 1981). It is often claimed that record keeping, recruitment, selection, placement, training, turnover, and below-standard production can be improved through the use of job evaluation (see, for instance, Bartley 1981: 5–7).

Moreover, the increased use of job evaluation in a number of countries in recent years (e.g., Canada, the United States, and the United Kingdom) also suggests a certain belief that the use of job evaluation can prevent pay inequities that are considered to be based on sex discrimination.

Lupton and Bowey (1974: 20) also point out that job evaluation may be used by organizations to solve a variety of problems or considerations, such as labour-market rates, career aspirations, beliefs about fair payment, wage bargaining processes, overtime pay, wage drift, productivity bargaining, age increments, merit payments, length-of-service increments, working-conditions allowances, and attempts to avoid grade distortion and to restore differentials.

An early British Institute of Management report (1952: 12–13) claims the following:

The careful introduction of a Job Evaluation scheme will yield in addition to the establishment of a sound wage structure a number of by-products of value to management ... Much of the information gathered for the preparation of job descriptions and analyses will be of use in drawing up job specifications for personnel recruitment, selection, placement, promotion and training ... Material which can be of help in merit-rating of individual workers can be derived. Organization, functional and promotion charts may be constructed from the job information which becomes available and will help to clarify and resolve lines of responsibility, opportunities ahead, concepts of authority, inter-departmental conflicts and misunderstanding of functions.

SOME PROBLEMS WITH THE PERSONNEL PERSPECTIVE

Critics of job evaluation have traditionally aimed their attacks at specific but avoidable 'technical' flaws. Such criticisms generally point out that improved quality of service could be achieved by 'modifying' existing forms of job evaluation (Spencer 1990) or call into question the accuracy and validity of job evaluation results (Dertien 1981; Doverspike et al 1983; Fox 1962; Gomez-Mejia, Page, and Tornow 1982), among others things. Job evaluation technique has also been criticized because it is a 'subjective' process and is therefore likely to be less than reliable. A number of researchers have focused on the random error of measurement within job evaluation technique; however, research results have been mixed regarding this issue (Arvey 1986). In general, while recent researchers have identified some specific flaws of job evaluation, they seem to have avoided the more fundamental one – that job evaluation does not, itself, evaluate.

Many writers from the personnel-management tradition have made claims about the properties of job evaluation that are seen here to be of doubtful value. Although the case-study in Part II of this book is devoted to the question of what job evaluation actually does do in an organization, some basic theoretical (and practical) points that seriously question these popular claims are raised here. For instance, is it realistic to believe that job evaluation actually positions jobs so as to make up the organizational hierarchy? Job hierarchies existed long before formal job evaluation. Even in those rare cases where a firm finds itself in a position to build a pay structure from scratch, certain external factors must always be taken into account in setting differentials and pay rates (such as minimum-wage laws, union scales, and market rates). Certainly, in established companies where long practice has created well-defined job hierarchies, the introduction of a formal job evaluation scheme can threaten existing relativities. But how often does it really affect them? In any case, the danger of disruption is somewhat limited by the knowledge that the factors and weights typically used to value jobs are usually those already endorsed and built into the organizational hierarchy.

Job evaluation tends to adopt those 'values' that are already understood to be 'important' and builds them into the process of evaluation. It is interesting to note, in this regard, that practitioners frequently advise that job evaluation plans should be 'tailor made' to the specific needs of the organization. Implicit in this suggestion is the idea that the job evaluation plan (including the factors and weights) should be compatible with the existing organizational hierarchy and prevailing notions of fairness. In this way, job evaluation is fitted to particular organizations so that the outcome will be 'acceptable' to all workers alike.

Seen in this way, job evaluation can be understood to be offering a retrospective fit to existing organizational values. This prior matching of 'weight and factors' to organizational values would lead to a minimal disturbance in the organizational hierarchy. Slichter, Healy, and Livernash (1960: 575), for instance, make the following points about an apparently successful joint job evaluation venture between a large U.S. company and a local of the United Steelworkers: 'Whatever weights for the factors and spread of points produced the best fit to the existing structure was to constitute the manual and the point scoring for the jobs ... A very good statistical fit and thus a *minimum of disturbance* to existing relationships was achieved.' While most job evaluation researchers and practitioners suggest that job evaluation creates or establishes the hierarchy, I am suggesting quite the opposite: that job evaluation really serves to both reinforce and endorse an already existing job hierarchy (or a newly desired one). Thinking about job evaluation in this way requires one to locate it in a wider organizational and social context. As Lupton (1982: 13) has aptly suggested, about payment systems more generally, 'it might be enlightening to think of a pay system as embodying certain assumptions about the social context in its rules and procedures rather than to think of it as some separate device having a social context that influences it.'

The role that formal job evaluation plays in ranking jobs on the basis of job content can be further questioned by taking a look at the extent to which the technique has been used in the event of technological change where, as machines are substituted for labour, such change results in the simplification of work. Studies have shown that decreased job content as a result of technological change rarely lowers the actual grade (Baker and True 1947). It was also seen, in the previous chapter, that during the period following the Second World War, unions successfully resisted managerial attempts to use job evaluation to lower pay rates when wartime production was converted to often less complex, civilian production (Barkin 1946). This point is also made by Lytle (1954: 10): 'any improvement in working conditions theoretically should mean a reduction in [a worker's] wage rate. For example, if a worker is located in a poorly heated building and better heating is installed, the installation of the heating equipment, an improvement in working conditions, lowers his job classification. Theoretically, the base rate for the job should be lowered accordingly. Actually, poor working conditions rarely carry high ratings.'

Job evaluation also tends to fly in the face of consistency among a society's pay relativities. As Brown (1979: 119) notes, 'pay structures are remarkably resilient. Despite substantial shortages and surpluses of certain occupations at certain times, their relative pay with respect to other occupations tends to vary little ... The explanation of this rigidity of pay structure appears to lie in the notion of "fairness". The most enduring and widespread basis for assessing the fairness of the rate for the job is simple convention.'

Not only does the personnel perspective generally depict job evaluation as a useful device for constructing the organizational hierarchy, but, as we have seen above, the implication seems to be that job content provides the only relevant factor in the determination of equitable pay structures. Could it possibly be believed that, through the sheer power of the 'scientific' process, a grading of jobs can be obtained that actually reflects their existing value on the market? This is what we are told. Is it logical, however, to assume that formal job evaluation (despite the efforts that have gone into making the factors and weights reflect generally desired levels of social inequality) can take account of all the considerations that go into making up the pay package?

The point must be made that job evaluation does not fix absolute wage levels or, for that matter, the absolute pay differentials between the evaluated jobs. The actual pay rate of a job is determined *after* the measurement or evaluation process has taken place, through a number of activities that are not necessarily linked to the evaluation process.

Whatever type of job evaluation is used – ranking, classification, point method, factor comparison, or a combination of these – none can operate in a vacuum. There are many influences on the actual determination of pay, whether these relate to, among other things, demand and supply, the historical background of a given job, sex differentials, geographical differentials, collective bargaining, or a company's ability to pay.

Although the influence of outside forces is often noted in the literature, at the same time it seems to be ignored. The literature reads as if the job evaluation process flows naturally into the actual wage-determination process; as if job evaluation has the 'magical' powers of determining actual wage levels. There is, in other words, an obfuscation between the setting-out of relativities and the actual determination of pay levels. Implicit here is the point that job evaluation somehow replaces a range of external factors (labour market, bargaining, and so on) in the pay-determination process. Let us, for instance, take a second look at Moore's (1950: 325) language: 'point scores are converted into monetary values.' This kind of language suggests that the pay-determination process is purely a 'mechanical' exercise, a simple matter of 'converting' evaluation outcomes. Thus, it tends to obscure the reality that 'conversion' is never divorced from a mess of external factors, such as market, 'ability to pay' considerations, and bargaining. It is possible to argue that this obfuscation is the same kind that tends to exist within 'work study' – in which the skill, procedures, and the technical jargon of the 'work-study engineer disguise or hide away the bargaining, cajoling, and extorting that go into setting the rate for every job (see Brown 1973).

Frustrated at the reluctance of job evaluation advocates to confront the difficulty of reconciling external pressures with the sometimes conflicting standards of job evaluation, Rossman (1961: 315) exclaims:

there are very definite forces at work exerting external influence on the salary structure. Perhaps the greatest of these forces is the labor market ... It seems unrealistic to eliminate consideration of probably the strongest determinant of pay from the initial set-up of a system to determine pay. Most salary administrators will argue that this is necessary in order to keep the system 'pure' and that only by making the internal comparison under considerations of 'sterility' can the right structure be determined. They seem to regard the labor market as a vulgar influence which would corrupt the new evaluation system, at least until they have to make the system work.

Lawler (1981: 37) also discusses the importance of external forces on the internally derived ranking of jobs, claiming that, 'in most cases it makes sense to focus on external pay comparisons as the major criteria for determining total compensation levels. Both internal and external inequity have serious consequences for the organization. However the consequences of external equity (e.g., turnover, absenteeism) are the most severe for the organization and are the ones that deserve primary attention ... Strategically it would seem to be advisable for organizations to emphasize external pay comparisons.'

Does this mean then that basic wage and salary surveys can be used to set the pay structure and that job evaluation plays no real role in the determination of pay? Not necessarily, particularly where jobs are not easily matched to the external labour market. However, it does mean that caution should be taken when listening to the promises of what a formal system of job evaluation can bring to an organization in the form of establishing fair and equitable rates of pay. As Livy (1975: 130) suggests, 'the price of a job is much like the price of anything else, a subjective evaluation of what a willing buyer is prepared to pay and a willing seller accept.'

The case-study contained within this research itself demonstrates how the results of job evaluation do not readily convert or translate into money values, or, as some have suggested, determine the actual amount of differential between one job and another. It will be seen that job evaluation merely 'suggests' that one job should be paid more, less, or the same amount as another. Determining the precise amount of pay and the differential between jobs lies outside the scope of formal job evaluation.

Why is it that the rational claims are so heavily endorsed? Perhaps it is the scientific aura of this measurement technique that has seduced so many into believing in its questionable powers relating to the construction of the job hierarchy or the establishment of equitable rates of pay. While most writers would agree and, indeed, often admit that job evaluation is not 'totally' scientific or objective (e.g., Moore 1950; Livy 1975; Treiman 1979; Elizur 1980; Beatty and Beatty 1984; Milkovich and Broderick 1982; Arvey 1986), the admission is often couched in terms that leave the impression that the technique is *almost* 100 per cent objective. Moore (1950: 326), for example, makes the following comment: 'After the factors are chosen, they must be weighed according to importance ... Apparently it is all empirically arrived at or, at best, represents the averaging of opinions of several people. It is admittedly impossible to be *truly* scientific in determining these weights' (emphasis added).

It is argued that the personnel-management claims that have been made in the literature have led to a certain amount of confusion in defining the technique and a lack of research interest in understanding the crucial relationship between measurement techniques and the assignment of monetary values to jobs; importantly, these unexamined assumptions encourage others not only to accept such claims as given, but also to build upon them. This result is seen below, where some of the theories about the effects of job evaluation that have been put forward by the industrial-relations tradition are discussed.

Industrial-Relations Claims

Whereas the problem with the personnel-management view of job evaluation is the questionable assumptions it makes about the importance of formal job evaluation in establishing a fair organizational hierarchy and determining pay, the problem with the industrial-relations approach to job evaluation is that it appears to accept the unexamined assumptions discussed above, particularly as these are seen to affect collective bargaining and the balance of power between management and unions.

Certain writers in the industrial-relations tradition make various claims about the way in which the technique affects the incidence and scope of collective bargaining, the number of pay grades, multi-employer bargaining, centralization of bargaining, the bureaucratization of unions and shop stewards, the reform of pay structures and the formalization of bargaining, and the reduction of conflict. These arguments are summarized below.

A certain amount of concern has been expressed by unions over the potentially limiting effects of job evaluation upon collective bargaining. The (U.S.) International Association of Machinists (IAM), probably the most outspoken union against the technique to date, has provided an itemized list of the supposed damage done by job evaluation to the process of collective bargaining:

1. It tends to freeze the wage structure and thereby creates an obstacle to the correction of inequities. It restricts the right of negotiating on a rate of pay for each job year after year. It usually limits negotiations to bargaining for a

fixed amount or fixed percentage for all jobs or establishing rates of pay through some 'predetermined formula' that usually does not result in equitable treatment for all.

2. It fails to consider all forces which determine wages, such as supply and demand, other contract or area rates, etc.

3. It tends to create a barrier between the employee and his understanding of his own job rate, because his rate is set in a manner not understood by him.

4. It tends to disregard the ability of the individual.

5. It places a ceiling upon wages which is contrary to a traditional objective of organized labour.

6. It disregards compensation for loyalty, i.e. years of service, etc.

7. It tends to dilute traditional skills, creating many new occupations and many new classifications and thereby reducing wages.

8. It affects the seniority of employees by the creation of additional classifications.

9. It makes the promotion of employees into higher-paying jobs considerably more difficult because of the limiting characteristic of job descriptions.

10. It provides the company with a tool to downgrade employees during times of cutbacks. (1954: 3–5)

It is useful to warn the reader that it is not the purpose of this research to provide critical analysis of the industrial-relations 'control' implications of job evaluation. Although the case-study undertaken for this research does not involve the introduction of job evaluation to a 'unionized' group of employees, that is not the reason for cutting short further investigation into these claims. Rather, such an analysis is not provided for the simple reason that all industrial-relations arguments use the personnel-management claims as the starting-point of their own assumptions. In other words, they appear to accept, unquestioningly, the personnel-management depiction of job evaluation and all its powers.

While the industrial-relations claims are based upon what is considered here to be false assumptions, they are dismissed as unfounded, at least until they can be substantiated through research in a unionized setting from known factors.

REDUCTION IN THE INCIDENCE AND SCOPE OF COLLECTIVE BARGAINING

As early as 1946, Barkin pointed out that 'these job evaluation programs attempt to establish rigid formulae for establishing job rates and therefore reduce the area for collective bargaining. They limit the considerations which may be raised in the review or the determination of job rates. They definitely are management's tools' (quoted in Gomberg 1948: 66). Collins (1969: 16) also comments on the damaging effects of job evaluation on collective bargaining: 'it [collective bargaining] is definitely restricted where job evaluation operates, as intended by its practitioners ... Stewards and other workplace bargainers thus operate in a straight jacket [sic]. The intention is to reduce the level of day-to-day bargaining and with it the scope for workplace bargainers to obtain improvement for their members.' The IAM (1954: 66) makes the observation that 'there is a tendency on the part of unions and management to refer to, and think in terms of, the *labor grade wage structure* rather than rates of pay for individual classifications ... The importance of negotiating as much as you possibly can for each *individual classification* has become screened and hidden.' Purcell (1983: 10), too, makes a similar point about job evaluation, suggesting that 'taken with changes in the basis of bonus calculation the incidence of bargaining is reduced.'

Although these notions may appear to be quite plausible, they are not supported by any evidence to demonstrate their accuracy. In fact, Batstone (1984) discovered, on the basis of a survey of 133 manufacturing firms, that where job evaluation existed, formal collective agreements played no less of a role.

REDUCTION IN THE NUMBER OF PAY GRADES

Some have claimed that job evaluation tends to reduce considerably the number of pay grades (Cliff 1970: 95; White 1981b: 13; Sisson and Brown 1983: 142). What type of effect can this grade reduction have upon industrial relations?

Cliff (1970: 95) maintains that, by dividing workers into a small number of wage grades, job evaluation makes it more difficult for employees to push wages upward by climbing from one rung of the ladder to another close by. Similarly the National Board for Prices and Incomes (NBPI) claims that a job evaluation structure reduces leap-frogging claims by small groups at the workplace or enterprise level, and imposes a discipline upon ad hoc decisions on pay managers and supervisors (1968: 37). The Institute for Workers' Control expresses much the same opinion as the others, and warns against the technique: 'Why should the unions and workers not resist it [job evaluation] in the interest of obtaining more for workers by a series of "leapfrogging" advances?' (quoted in Collins 1969: 17).

Another possible effect of grade reduction on industrial relations is seen to be caused by a reduced distinction between jobs. Cliff (1970: 95), for instance, claims that job evaluation, while encouraging flexibility in the use of labour, tends to eliminate existing craft and job titles and facilitates the extraction of labour from employees. In this instance, 'workers often become more conscious of skill demarcation – this raises their resentment and determination to defend craft titles.'

It was seen above, in the IAM's list of problems with job evaluation, that job evaluation 'tends to dilute traditional skills, creating many new occupations and many new classifications thereby reducing wages' (1954: 3–5).

SHIFT FROM MULTI-EMPLOYER TO SINGLE-EMPLOYER BARGAINING

In Britain, another aspect of control that has been observed is that multi-employer agreements tend to upset the relativities established by job evaluation. Sisson and Brown (1983: 142), for instance, claim that 'although the combination of job evaluation and multi-employer bargaining is not in principle incompatible, managements have found it difficult to maintain they integrity of their newly-established pay structures if they have to accommodate subsequent increases in the rates of pay arising from multi-employer agreements. Thus the spread of job evaluation has been a stimulus behind the change in this operation of multi-employer agreements.' Brown (1979: 121) notes the same shift, pointing out that 'most job evaluation applies to a single "bargaining unit" ... under a single employer, because otherwise it is difficult to prevent deviant notions of fairness from creeping in and generating discontent.'

In Britain, certain researchers have also claimed that the increased use of job evaluation (see, for example, White 1981b; Brown 1981; Sisson and Brown 1983) has changed the actual location of pay bargaining from one of decentralization to one of centralization. Sisson and Brown (1983: 142), for instance, believe that job evaluation 'centralizes pay bargaining ... it is difficult to continue with fragmented pay bargaining once a job evaluation scheme has been introduced without jeopardising the whole scheme.' Purcell (1983: 10), is of the opinion that since it [job evaluation] creates a structured set of differentials, it is extremely hard for section shop stewards to influence pay levels themselves.' Batstone (1984), however, while agreeing that the ranking of jobs is indeed carried out centrally and that the job reclassifications are usually handled by a central committee, does not agree that this amounts to less worker control. Based on the results of a survey conducted on 133 manufacturing establishments, Batstone found that 'a sense of inequity on the part of groups of workers can still lead to sectional demands and pressures ... aggrieved workers are quite likely to exert sanctions on local management who may be induced to make concessions of various kinds' (1984: 167).

The U.K. Pay Board, after studying a wide range of job evaluation schemes in organizations with both centralized and decentralized personnel practices, concludes 'We have not been able to observe any trend towards either centralization or decentralization in the use of job evaluation schemes' (1974: 20).

Finally, the claim that job evaluation leads to centralization of pay bargaining is not restricted to Britain. In the United States, it has also been claimed (without any stated source) that job evaluation 'centralizes control over the determination of individual job rates' (Slichter, Healy, and Livernash 1960: 560).

Related to the popular opinion that job evaluation centralizes pay bargaining is the view that unions and shop stewards become increasingly bureaucratized – 'sucked into the system' – through participation in job evaluation schemes. The increased trend in participative schemes has been observed by, among others, Treiman (1979) in the United States and the Pay Board (1974) and the British Institute of Management in the United Kingdom (Bradley 1979). Along with the observation that union participation in job evaluation has increased, the Pay Board (1974: 18) also hints at the possibility of trade-union bureaucratization: 'In common with other practices in industrial relations, there appears to be a move towards introducing job evaluation in a "participative" manner, especially where the employees affected have been formally represented by trade unions. It is now more usual for worker representatives to be fully involved in the detailed working of a scheme and the preparation for it – and possibly even in the choice of scheme to be introduced.' Purcell (1983: 10) has made the point far more forcefully:

As the trade unions are often involved in the implementation and maintenance of job evaluation they are encouraged or forced to consider the impact of one sectional claim on the operation of the scheme as a whole. Thus unions can take on a quasi-managerial function of blocking or filtering claims which challenge the logic of the agreed pay differentials. The process of implementation, if undertaken by joint teams of management and unions, is a powerful means of encouraging joint problem solving techniques and a depolarization of industrial relations. The domestic union leadership becomes, along with industrial relations management, the custodians of the scheme ... The bureaucratization of union leadership is encouraged.

A similar view has been expressed, again without any indication of evidence for such claims, by the Institute for Workers Control, which has indicated that 'full-time officials and even shop stewards, in studying a particular technique, may swallow the management values with it, so that the edges of militancy are smoothed off ... thus job evaluation may lead to emasculation by involvement' (quoted in Collins 1969: 12, 17). A Dutch sociologist, Scholten (1979, 1981), also claims that job evaluation is an example of 'regulation' that enables the trade unions to control their members, and the employers their employees.

Once again such bold claims have been refuted by Batstone (1984). On the basis of the same survey evidence of 133 manufacturing firms, Batstone found that 'job evaluation is not related to steward bureaucracy; neither full-time shop stewards nor regular steward meetings are associated with its greater use' (250). Batstone did, however, recognize that in establishments practising job evaluation, senior stewards were more likely to be 'sympathetic' to management, although he pointed out that these features may in fact be attributable to the type of establishment using job evaluation in the first place – for example, larger firms, which may have more sophisticated personnel policies and procedures as well as more money with which to allocate employee benefits and higher pay (251).

THE REFORM OF PAY STRUCTURES AND THE FORMALIZATION OF BARGAINING

A major purpose of job evaluation from the industrial-relations perspective has been to stabilize the wage structure and protect it from pressures of wage drift. This view is particularly evident in the British government's attempts at industrial-relations 'reform' during the troubled years of the mid 1960s. The Donovan Commission, established in 1965, was assigned the task of making recommendations to the then Labour government on methods of improving industrial relations.

This commission, having identified two quite distinctive systems of industrial relations – the formal and the informal – in operation, made recommendations, leaning towards increasing the formal; in doing so, it strongly advocated the use of job evaluation (and productivity bargaining) to restore order to pay structures and formalize collective bargaining (Ahlstrand, 1990). The board also recommended the establishment of the Prices and Incomes Board (PIB, later the National Board for Prices and Income, or NBPI) to investigate and encourage developments in this area.

Flanders (1975: 270) emphasized the value of job evaluation in the reform of British industrial relations: 'The many varied techniques of job evaluation offer methods of grappling with the problems which are associated with the breakdown of normative order. The report of the PIB (Prices and Incomes Board) on job evaluation suggests that companies are turning increasingly to its use in order to secure "the removal of pay anomalies," the "introduction of order out of chaos," the "modernization of pay structures" and the "definition of differentials" – all of them objectives which clearly relate to the search for normative order.'

In a summary of its 1968 report on job evaluation (1969: 92), the NBPI reinforces the use of job evaluation for the purpose of reform: 'It is stressed that job evaluation is concerned with the reform of pay structures, whether associated with managerial, technical, clerical or manual workers. Since it is considered that pay structure reform is an important means of achieving greater economic efficiency and that inadequate payment systems often lie at the root of industrial disputes, the Board favours the use of job evaluation as an instrument of reform.'

The belief that job evaluation is part of a broad management strategy to increase control over workers, under the guise of reform, has been expressed by the Institute for Workers' Control: 'Job evaluation is a technique for reforming pay structures, especially the pay structure of a firm or plant. It goes with productivity deals, work study based incentive schemes and MDW [measured daywork] as part of a strategy to align payment systems with modern technology, and to check "earnings drift" by bringing the various components of the pay packet under strict management control' (quoted in Collins 1969: 3).

Similar beliefs have been expressed by Crouch (1977: 59), who indicates that 'a major development in the managerial counter-attack has therefore been to find alternative forms of payment system that would subordinate the pay structure to managerial control.' Purcell (1983: 10) also appears to make the point that management control is increased through the use of job evaluation: 'Even if implemented unilaterally by management, job evaluation and the "rational" ordering of differentials makes plant industrial relations more controllable.'

Despite the lack of evidence as to the actual impact that the increased use of job evaluation has had on industrial relations in Britain, the conclusions drawn by the 'Warwick' survey of 970 manufacturing establishments in Britain probably sum up the general beliefs of industry: job evaluation methods 'have been a central feature of the reform of payment systems and the formalization of workplace bargaining' (Brown 1981: 111).

In the United States, similar views have been expressed by Slichter, Healy, and Livernash (1960: 560): 'There have been a variety of reasons for management interest in job evaluation. Of course the primary direct purpose was to develop an equitable and simplified job rate structure. In case after case the existence of a more or less chaotic wage structure was given as the basic reason for introducing job evaluation.'

THE REDUCTION OF CONFLICT

Probably one of the most popular industrial-relations claims to be made about job evaluation is that use of the technique reduces conflict. What kind of conflict? Different theoretical perspectives have tried to explain pay-related conflict. To Baldamus (1961: 9–10), for instance, problems over pay stem from an 'imbalanced and variable distribution of effort rewards in the context of employment.'

Reference-group theory (e.g., Patchen 1961; Runciman 1966) points to the problems that arise when an individual compares his or her position with that of membership reference groups, even though, as Runciman (1966: 218) points out, the choice of these reference groups is not usually the most ambitious. In a study of shop stewards, McCarthy (1966: 17) found that their various demands (including job regrading) related to the perceived advantages of 'another individual or group in similar circumstance, or employed on similar work.'

Equity theory (e.g., Homans 1961; Jaques 1958, 1967) suggests that pay dissatisfaction occurs when an individual perceives that his or her input/reward ratio is not equal to that of another. To Jaques (1958: 313), 'all industrial disputes about payments are differentials disputes. They arise over the question of how much one group is getting compared with others.' To White (1981a), conflict over pay is seen to be less a matter of differentials and more a matter of what kind of 'authority' the payment system is seen to stand for. Conflict, in other words, can mean different things to different people, although the claims made in the literature about the conflict reducing powers of job evaluation rarely address the meaning of 'conflict.'

As early as 1941, a Princeton University study of job evaluation practices across the United States (number of companies not indicated) stated: 'Companies have reported that the foremen and supervisors are for the most part enthusiastic about job classification because it gives them a clearer idea of the jobs over which they have jurisdiction and minimizes the number of individual grievances on wage questions' (8). Many others have also stated, albeit with varying degrees of evidence, that job evaluation reduces conflict at the workplace. Let us consider some of these:

Fewer grievances arise concerning relative rates, and grievances cost less financially and from the standpoint of morale. (Moberly and Buffa 1947: 3)

Job evaluation is ... indispensable to the trade union officer as an objective means of resolving conflicting claims of different craft members to various increases to compensate for imagined or real inequities. (Gomberg 1948: 72)

[According to 'users' of job evaluation], ... lost time due to wage disputes was reduced, the number of individual complaints regarding wages was reduced, the number of wage and salary anomalies was reduced. '(British Institute of Management 1952: 8)

Wage rates for new and changed jobs produce grievances, with or without job evaluation, but ... grievances have been reduced in number, restricted in scope, and controlled by agreement on method of resolution ... The spread and acceptance of job evaluation has brought considerable stability to what was formerly a rather turbulent grievance area. (Slichter, Healy, and Livernash 1960: 558 and 592)

Although the method is approximate, it is not worthless as a means of minimizing conflict. (Organization for Economic Cooperation and Development 1967: 83)

We attach a great deal of importance to job evaluation as a means of establishing acceptable pay structures and reducing conflict. (NBPI 1969: 93)

Job evaluation also helps to alleviate dissatisfaction with pay by attempting to put pay structures on a felt-fair basis, which reduces the amount of time spent by company employees in disputes about the grading of jobs. (Burns 1978: 10)

... all forms of industrial action are less common where job evaluation exists. (Batstone 1984: 251)

There have also been views expressing the opposite opinion. The findings of a survey conducted by Daniel (1976), for instance, do not associate the use of job evaluation with a reduction in the level of industrial disputes. In a survey of 250 manufacturing establishments in the United Kingdom, Daniel found that the problem of wage differentials tended to be that much *greater* where job evaluation existed. Issues of differentials, job grading, and comparability were seen to give rise to day-to-day grievances.

Gill, Morris and Eaton's case-study on job evaluation and collective bargaining at ICI led them to declare: 'There is no reason to suppose that employee interest in job evaluation has declined since major changes in job structures have been accomplished. On the contrary, there has been a recent upswing in informally disputed assessments which have sometimes spilled over into the formal grievance procedure despite the evaluation of the majority of jobs in the period 1968–72' (1977: 56). They do suggest, however, that such increased activity may have resulted from the severe curtailment of pay under the incomes policies that were in existence at the time. However, the authors still conclude that 'management justify job assessment not in terms of cost advantages but in terms of its "political" character as an effective conflict resolution device capable of pre-empting local differential wage claims' (57).

Following a survey of payment systems in 400 manufacturing plants, White (1981b: 14) suggests that job evaluation probably facilitates and stimulates pay comparisons, although he claims that there was no definite evidence to be found of a higher incidence of conflict associated with its use. The Warwick survey of 970 manufacturing establishments claims firms found that job evaluation removed resented disparities and obviated disputes (Brown 1981: 129).

In a large-scale 1978 survey of trade-union attitudes of job evaluation carried out in the United States, unions were asked to indicate approximately what percentage of their total grievances concerned 'job evaluation aspects.' The responses were summarized by Janes (1979: 84): 48 per cent indicated fewer than 5 per cent of grievances; 27 per cent, 5–10; 16 per cent, 11–20; and 9 per cent, 21–35. It would appear that the total number of grievances filed did not significantly relate to problems with job evaluation, although, of those that did, Janes found that 15 per cent reached the arbitration stage.

Finally, although there are a variety of ways of approaching the question of whether the use of job evaluation is associated with an increase or decrease in conflict, none of the arguments, at least to date, appears to be terribly convincing.

SOME PROBLEMS WITH THE INDUSTRIAL-RELATIONS PERSPECTIVE

For the speculative nature of the back-and-forth debates we have witnessed above, it is clear that there is a need for further research into the industrial-relations 'control' implications of job evaluation.

My purpose here, however, is not to revive old debates or to enter new ones about whether job evaluation does or does not reduce the incidence and scope of collective bargaining, reduce the number of pay grades, shift bargaining from the multi-employer to the single-employer level, centralize bargaining, bureaucratize unions and shop stewards, reform pay structures and formalize bargaining, or reduce conflict. Despite the plausibility of many of these arguments, I would make the point that there is a need to evaluate the assumptions upon which such claims were made in the first place and that, therefore, a strong case can be made for the need for further research in this area.

As we have seen, the industrial-relations approach to job evaluation aims much criticism at the technique in the belief that it threatens the collective-bargaining process and may even be a substitute for it. However, as soon as it is realized that the measurement of work in terms of job content is a separate function from that of assigning pay rates, there might be a better base for examining such claims more closely, Although this is not what many industrial-relations writers would have us believe, the ranking of points for different jobs in an organization may stress the relative contribution of a worker, but wage levels and the absolute amount of differentials remain to be negotiated.

If the limitations of job evaluation were better understood, the technique might seem less threatening to the institution of collective bargaining. If industrial-relations writers looked more closely into the rhetoric espoused by proponents of job evaluation, the potential effects of the technique upon collective bargaining might end up seeming more imaginary than real.

The Feminist School

Much of the feminist literature on job evaluation is located within larger treatises on the pay-equity problematic itself. In most cases, job evaluation gets 'short shrift' in these works; instead, the pay equity issue is discussed at a general level, divorced from detailed examinations of the job evaluation process. For example, Cuneo's 1990 book, *Pay Equity: The Labour Feminist Challenge,* devotes fewer than fifteen pages to the job evaluation process. Such limited attention appears somewhat odd as job evaluation is the only device used to operationalize the pay-equity issue.

Generally, feminist academics and organizations have endorsed the technique, provided that it has been purged of sex bias. for example, the Labour-Feminist Alliance in Canada has fully supported 'gender-neutral' and 'objective' job evaluation plans. Among feminists (Acker 1987; Burton 1987; Steinberg and Haignere 1987; McArthur 1985), research has been organized around two themes: the identification of hidden gender bias in existing job evaluation systems and the purging of gender bias from existing systems through the development of gender-neutral job evaluation systems.

As a concept, 'gender bias' is difficult. Even though the concept is multi-dimensional and complex, legislators have been not deterred from incorporating it into the concrete world of the law. Gender bias is seen to exist in both the design of the job evaluation system itself and the operation of the system (composition of evaluation committees and so on). With respect to the design issue, two concerns have been expressed: the overlooking or ignoring of skills specific to female-predominant jobs when assigning weights in job evaluation scales and the assigning of low-weights to skills important in female-predominant jobs. The concern that feminists express here is that, because of built-in gender bias, the job evaluation process will simply tend to replicate the existing hierarchy.

In a job evaluation report presented to the Equal Employment Opportunity Commission in the United States, Treiman (1979: 89) makes the following statement: 'The relative weight accorded these factors can have very substantial consequences for the ordering of jobs with respect to their relative worth and hence relative pay. Certain weighting schemes are likely to be relatively advantageous to particular social categories – men versus women, whites versus blacks, and so on.' What feminists want to do in purging sex bias from existing job evaluation systems is to organize the weights and factors in a way that recognizes the importance of certain skills associated with female-dominated work. Practically, what this means for the design of a gender-neutral job evaluation is the identification of female-dominated job skills and the assigning of weights and factors around these skills.

Outside of the 'design' issue, a number of feminist researchers have also identified sex bias in the operation and implementation of the process itself. Steinberg (1991: 195) makes this point in a vivid way: 'Since job evaluation involves hundreds of detailed decisions, each of which has implications for the final estimates of wage discrimination, those who control job evaluation control the outcome. Thus, the tactics for containment generally involve specific ways of maintaining the appearance of full participation of advocates, while minimizing proponent input into the decisions surrounding job evaluation.'

The literature provides a number of examples of 'implementation' gender bias. For example, Arvey (1986: 318) notes that, during job analysis, the stage at which job-related information is collected, bias can infect the process in a number of ways:

First, it is possible that job analysts may perceive and recall differential information, depending on whether a job involves "women's work" or whether the job is performed predominantly by men ... Second, it is possible that analysts perceive similar information but emphasize different things when seeking job information. Thus, male analysts may ask information about working conditions that involve large/gross body movement but neglect aspects such as sitting still for long periods of time, visual strain, etc. ... Third, job analysis information may well be pre-selected when task inventories are used for job analysis purposes ... the inventory item pool may lack sufficient representation from female dominated jobs. Fourth, male and female incumbents may generate different information about a job even when the job is exactly the same.

Areas of sex bias have also been identified within the job evaluation process itself. Remick (1978) suggests that the factors used in the job evaluation plan emphasize aspects associated with male-oriented jobs (e.g., physical strength) and ignore features of jobs traditionally performed by females (e.g., eye-strain).

Sex bias in factor definitions, and anchor points or degrees as areas where sex bias may occur have also been attacked. Arvey (1986: 322) claims that 'the anchor points for factors often do not include examples that include female-oriented work.'

All these studies are based upon the unexamined assumption that, with various 'technical' adjustments, the use of job evaluation can eliminate pay inequities that are considered to be based upon sex discrimination. Burns (1978: 10), for instance, states that 'there is no doubt that systematic methods of job evaluation will play a major part in achieving for women equal pay for work of equal value in Great Britain.' Various governments (e.g., those in the United States, Canada, and the United Kingdom) have begun to incorporate stricter definitions of what constitutes job evaluation in their pay equity legislation, creating more and more opportunity for the technique to be used to resolve cases under dispute. This development would certainly suggest a certain belief in the importance of job evaluation in determining pay equity for women.

Careful and detailed empirical studies of a feminist nature on job evaluation are few and far between. There are, however, two important exceptions here: Clare Burton's (1987) study of the effect of job evaluation on pay equity in Australia and Joan Acker's (1989) study of job evaluation (also in a pay-equity context) in the state of Oregon. Both studies are underpinned by a feminist theoretic and can be said to be directly informed by their theoretical position. Burton confines herself to identifying gender bias in the same type of comparable-worth evaluation system as was used in my own case-study: Hay Guide Chart Profile method. Burton focuses her attention on a single organizational unit, the College of Advanced Education in South Australia. The research concentrates on investigating the potential contribution of a point-rating scheme to determine work of equal value in an organization. In part, the research sought to identify features of job evaluation that may lead to the undervaluing of jobs done mainly by women relative to jobs done mainly by men. What Burton's study does is to attempt to show how these various different biases in the perception, description, and evolution of women's work, skills, and qualities required to do female-predominate jobs are either not acknowledged or undervalued relative to other positions.

On the whole, Burton's work is illuminating, although it is sometimes difficult to separate out from her many citations of the literature. One gets the sense that the feminist literature she cites directs or informs the results of her own empirical work. In any case, as was the case in the theoretical literature cited above, Burton identifies both design (the choice of weights and factors, numerical calculations related to the factors involved, associated documentation and terms) and implementation gender biases. Burton claims that the design of the system will tend to 'mobilize a direction' for implementation. She claims, in fact, to have found both private-sector and managerial biases in the Hay system. She suggests that women's operational knowledge attained directly through their work and other experiences, gains less attention in the job evaluation process than the formally acquired knowledge of many of their male counterparts (Burton 1987: 89). Burton 'uncovered' other ways in which she felt women's work was undervalued: 'Another way in which we felt that women's work was undervalued was in the definitions of *Human Relations Skills*, and what they excluded. We have noted, in passing, that responsibility for people is not as highly regarded as responsibility for material assets, yet it can be highly regarded *if* it involves motivating and controlling other people. In other words, working through other people in the pursuit of organizational objectives is highly valued, but working for people, or contributing to the quality of working relationships in other ways (more typical of female jobs) is not' (90).

Burton also points to bias in the actual implementation and operation of the technique. She refers to a number of biases already developed in both the pay-equity and the job evaluation research literature. These include availability bias (a tendency to describe the frequency of certain job-related activities according to their ease of retrieval from memory (1987: 99); halo-effect bias; and expectancy bias. She also usefully points out that 'familiarity with a job can have contradictory effects on its evaluation. It appears to lead to a belief that some skills are easier to acquire than in fact is the case. Women who have learned keyboard skills, or human relations and other skills, may underestimate not only their value, but the actual training processes involved in acquiring and accumulating them (for example, on the job, or in the "natural" ground of the family)' (103).

On the whole, Burton provides a number of important observations about gender bias in job evaluation. Her works tend to 'flip-flop' between a rational and a political model of organization. The political model is evidenced by her analysis of how the power structure informs value and the rational model by her qualified faith in the job evaluation device, if gender-bias is removed from the technique. In the end she places a stamp of approval on the technique: 'If there were initiatives – either legislative or through rulings within the arbitration system – developed to promote pay equity, and if points-rating systems were regarded as a fair method of establishing the relative worth of jobs, then it is likely pressure would be brought to bear to ensure that gender bias in the schemes be identified and dealt with' (1987: 116).

To be fair to Burton, she does not consider a gender-neutral job evaluation system to be easy to develop. Here she raises the 'bedrock' question – which value system is to be used in the development of a truly 'objective' job evaluation system? Indeed, as she says, 'the mobilisation of groups behind the pay-equity issue makes it clear, too, that there is not a societal consensus about which attributes of jobs should be valued more highly than others, nor that job ranking in pay terms is at present equitable' (1987: 115).

Joan Acker's (1989) study of comparable-worth efforts in the state of Oregon from 1981 to 1987 (roughly the time frame of my own study) represents a significantly more ambitious feminist project than Burton's. The work is self-avowedly feminist ('an attempt to link the work of practical feminist action with the work of feminist theory' [vii]), and the results of the study are predictably in line with this prior theoretic. Job evaluation is seen as a political tool that has been and is used to subordinate women and to justify male domination. Like Burton's and my own studies, Acker is concerned with the Hay Guide Chart-Profile method. Like Burton, Acker attacks job evaluation and the Hay system in terms of both design and implementation. With respect to design issues, Acker argues that managers' values are encoded in the guide charts to such an extent that hierarchy emerges as a predominant value. She argues that the values underpinning the weights and factors in the Hay system are male/masculine. These values serve to reaffirm and reinforce the existing male-dominated organizational hierarchy. She claims further that 'this part of the process accounts for some of the success in using job evaluation to locate and remedy undervaluation of women's work. My observation indicates that, within the confines of the values it represents and replicates, job evaluation is what it purports to be: a systematic, consistent, and open process of applying a set of values in the assessment of the content of jobs. Making qualitative decisions about values is a difficult process, but it can be done. The important question is, What are the values (Remick,1984)?' (83).

She also provides useful insights into political problems associated with challenging the existing weights and factors in long-standing systems, like Hay's. She notes that consultants and management vigorously objected to the idea of adding two levels to the 'Human Relations' skill factor (something that would have automatically boosted the scores of women's jobs). By raising the issue of negotiation over the appropriateness and 'correctness' of the weights and factors she importantly points to the critical link among social values, conceptions of fairness, and the weights and factors that underpin job evaluation and ultimately determine 'value.'

Much of the case detail in Acker's work exposes important sex bias in the Hay system and in the way that the system is presented. Hers is an important book because it is one of few very detailed empirical studies of the introduction of a formal job evaluation system (aimed at purging sex bias). Too many studies have been pitched at a theoretical and general level, and Acker's work represents an important corrective to that tradition. In the end, however, Acker herself places faith in the bureaucratic-rational tool of job evaluation. She feels that job evaluation is the best way to proceed (provided that the system is adjusted to rid itself of gender bias): 'job evaluation seems a more fair and open method of assigning relative value than market or other types of power, such as that related to gender or racial privilege' (1989: 190). She also suggests that 'the job evaluation training and process further assured the replication of a managerially oriented hierarchy in several ways, through operational definitions given to factors, through instructions about avoiding overcounting, through the use of organizational charts, and through insistence on consistent relationships between factors' (83).

While feminist critiques represent the interests of a disadvantaged group and indeed raise a legitimate discussion, I argue that the critique of job evaluation needs to go beyond that. In other words, the recent critiques aimed at sex bias contained within job evaluation have deflected our attention from the real critique. This book makes the claim that those writers concerned with eliminating sex bias from job evaluation plans have failed to grasp the true essence of the technique. It maintains that the crusade to purge sex bias from the weights and factors associated with various job evaluation schemes serves to deflect attention away from the main issue, which is that, in the first place, job evaluation does not and cannot live up to its rational claims (e.g., the establishment of a 'hierarchy' of jobs based on rational criteria and the determination of absolute pay levels). Critiques aimed at job evaluation to date merely reify the technique and reinforce its rational guise.

This book argues that the rational properties of job evaluation have been oversold. Job evaluation does not evaluate. Rather, job evaluation must be seen as a device that disguises cultural values and political action within the context of a rational technique. Despite its objectivist and rational appearance, the relative worth determined by job evaluation is nothing more than the expression of culturally sanctioned pay claims. What this means for hierarchy and pay differentials is that change will take place only if we have a *prior change* to the cultural and political order. Seen in this way, the purging of 'sex bias' from existing job evaluation techniques has less to do with improving the 'objectivist-rational' powers of the instrument than with the adjustment of the technique to ascendant, culturally sanctioned pay claims.

Job evaluation does not clinically determine job worth. Rather, it is a ritual device that is predesigned and prestructured to 'fit' existing cultural values. If job evaluation suggests a change to the existing hierarchy of pay differentials it is not because the technique has the power to discern 'inequities' in the structure but rather because the prior political-cultural apparatus informs job evaluation in one direction and not the other. *Real* evaluation, in other words, takes place in the political and cultural terrain. The way in which the instrument is designed and structured (in the first place) and the way in which the technique is (subsequently) 'used' by its administrators are themselves predetermined by wider political-cultural forces. We know this to be true because those organizations that, for years, have used traditional, formal job evaluation technique are now producing different 'objective' results – that is, women's jobs are suddenly being upgraded even though the technique has remained the same. The case-study presented in this book suggests that this change occurred not because of improved understanding of the technique but rather because of a shift in cultural values that recognizes the value of women's work and the empowerment of women who can now force the technique to produce one result and not another. The purging of sex bias from job evaluation needs, therefore, to be understood as evaluation itself. Once purged (if such a feat is possible), the technique's evaluations are, in effect, 'predetermined.' *Job evaluation does not evaluate – it provides a useful 'rational-objectivist' aura to justify current political-cultural views on what the structure ought to look like.* Seen in this way, job evaluation is a ritual that does little in the way of objectively 'determining' job worth and much in terms of justifying and legitimizing pay structures. To put this argument in its simplest terms, job evaluation is a device that is 'loaded' to predetermine the evaluation. The purging of 'sex bias' is simply another way of 'loading the dice.' The more general powers and basic properties of job evaluation have, for the most part, gone unquestioned and are taken for granted.

I believe that my research has a serious message for this movement. One hopes that it will allow those involved in promoting 'equal pay for work of equal value' to recognize that job evaluation itself, as a technique does not achieve change, but, rather, is a vehicle through which desired change can be achieved.

Conclusions

The personnel-management, industrial-relations, and feminist schools have demonstrated faith in the rational-bureaucratic powers of job evaluation. Indeed, each relies upon the same basic beliefs about job evaluation and takes for granted that the technique actually fulfils its manifest functions. Any consideration of job evaluation at the level of 'control' must necessarily take a more sophisticated approach than studies that treat the properties of job evaluation as given, relying upon largely unexamined assumptions to make even further claims about the technique. Thus, an examination of these assumptions is essential.

The overwhelming commitment on behalf of those engaged in payment-systems research to the 'stated objectives' level of measurement techniques has led to a failure to grasp some of the deeper control implications of both work study and job evaluation, from the level of both the organization and the society. In many ways, the claims made by the industrial-relations and feminist schools about job evaluation appear to be more realistically critical and more sociologically aware than those of the personnel-management literature. It might even be said that the industrial-relations claims made about job evaluation are rather reminiscent of Braveman-type claims made about work study and the function of 'scientific management' in increasing management control over workers. Each, however, builds a case without examining the actual properties of the measurement technique (whether work study or job evaluation) upon which these interesting theories are founded.

This chapter has argued that the nature of job evaluation has been disregarded or neglected for too long, especially by those involved in advocating its wider use. Little or no research has been conducted into the real meaning of job evaluation. The common error of taking any 'rational' or stated-objective level for granted has been observed by Meyer and Rowan: (1977: 342) 'Prevailing theories assume that the coordination and control of activity are the critical dimensions on which formal organizations have succeeded in the modern world. This assumption is based on the view that organizations function according to their formal blueprints: coordination is routine, rules and procedures are followed, and actual activities conform to the prescriptions of formal structure.'

By approaching the issue of job evaluation and 'control' through the particular language and rituals associated with the technique, I hope to uncover layers of meaning beneath the surface claims about job evaluation that have been summarized in this chapter. The case-study presented in Part II describes the introduction of formal job evaluation to a group of 1,200 non-unionized employees in a government organization and is devoted to answering the question 'What does job evaluation really do?'

PART II

Job Evaluation in 'Atlantis':
A Case-Study

4 Why Job Evaluation?
The Case for a 'Rational' System

The Case-Study Background

In this and the next four chapters I provide a detailed account of the introduction of a formal job evaluation system in a typical civil-service organization in a Canadian province, which I call 'Atlantis.' It is a long story, but the details of it are important to the arguments that I will subsequently develop. I ask readers to persevere in reading it. I hope that the case provides, for Canada, the same kind of detailed empirical analysis that Acker's study (1989) provided for the U.S. context.

The time frame for analysis for this research is five years, from the time the government originally approved the plan, in March 1980, to my return to the site for field-work in the winter of 1985.

I was directly involved in the introduction and implementation of the job evaluation plan for a two-and-a-half-year period, that is, from April 1980 to September 1982. During this time I was one of four 'pay analysts' within the government's central personnel agency, the Civil Service Commission. This position was normally charged with the responsibility of operating the compensation system for both unionized (10,800 employees) and non-unionized (1,200) employees within Atlantis. Each of the four analysts was drawn directly into the introduction of the new formal job evaluation plan and acted as the front line of communication between employees and the Civil Service Commission.

The introduction of the formal job evaluation plan consisted of a major-change project in Atlantis. During the two years of implementation, a considerable number of person-hours were devoted to carrying out the different phases of the plan. Apart from the six pay-division staff (a director, a manager, and four analysts) and various clerical support who were mobilized, almost exclusively, for 'Hay' work, twenty-one deputy ministers (the senior administrative level of government) also invested a great deal of time. Three evaluation committees, each composed of seven deputy ministers, held two-day meetings every second week for six to eight months to evaluate the selected 'benchmark' jobs of 350 employees.

Committees made up of three or four senior directors (the administrative level below deputy minister) per government department (twenty-one departments) each spent an average of about ten days evaluating the remaining jobs of 850 employees. Finally, the time of the employees themselves was taken up, not only attending training and briefing sessions held throughout Atlantis, but also in having to write job descriptions in the 'strict and demanding' Hay format. The Hay consultant warned that it might take as long as twenty hours to write the job description 'properly,' but it soon became clear to all involved that this was a conservative estimate of the time required, especially as employees were trying to present themselves and their jobs in such a way as to benefit from the most 'evaluation' points.

The job evaluation plan selected by the government of Atlantis is called the Hay Guide Chart Profile method. This particular plan, a type of points-rating scheme, is well known in many countries. The Hay consulting firm, based in Philadelphia, is the largest compensation consulting firm in the world. In Britain, Incomes Data Services (1979: 30) says the following about the Hay job evaluation plan: 'The Hay-MSL Guide Chart Profile has become one of the most popular package schemes available. Some of the top 200–300 firms quoted by the Times Index have now introduced the Hay-MSL system for their employees. It is generally regarded as a scheme for senior managers or specialized technical staff. More recently, however, ... the consultants have found a rapid increase in the use of the guide chart profile method for white-collar, and skilled and semi-skilled manual jobs.'

Some idea of the popularity of this particular type of job evaluation plan may be gleaned from table 2, which summarizes Hay Group growth charts published in two 1980s Hay annual reports. The 1991 Hay Group annual report reveals the continued growth of this successful organization. In outlining the 'vast resources' available to the Hay Group, the report cites 'the broad array of analytic tools, methodologies, and databases that we continue to develop; our accumu-

TABLE 2
Growth of the Hay Group

Year	Offices	Countries	Revenues ($ millions)
1984	94	27	108
1982	80	25	104
1980	78	25	85
1978	65	19	46
1976	37	17	25
1974	28	13	17
1972	19	10	8.3
1970	14	8	5.5

SOURCE: Based on data from Hay Group annual reports

lated insight and experience with more than 10,000 clients; our nearly 50 years of operation; and an unrivaled 32 country network of over 1,000 top professionals.'

In the position of pay analyst, I worked closely with the consultant from Hay Associates. The analysts played a key role in each of the phases of the introduction of the plan (assistance and control activities on the job-description-writing phase, oral presentations to employees on the nature of the new system, recording information in evaluation committee meetings, and so on).

While some of the information gathered for the case-study relies upon my experience as an 'innocent observer-participant,' it should be pointed out that I already had a Master's degree in Industrial Relations and Personnel Management and, certainly during the last year in which I was involved in the project, the 'critical social-science observer' emerged.

My research on job evaluation as an academic at Oxford commenced some three years after the introduction of the plan (and one year after I had left employment with this government agency). I returned to Atlantis to carry out field-work, which extended over a three-month period, from January to March 1985. This period of field-work involved a number of discrete activities. First, I administered a structured survey questionnaire (see Appendix G) to a population of 230 employees whose jobs had been selected as benchmarks. (Although 230 jobs had been selected as benchmarks, these jobs represented a population group of 350, since, in some cases, more than one employee held a 'benchmark' job. The questionnaire was administered to only one person per job title.) Out of the 230 people who received the questionnaire via internal mail, at their work stations, 134 (or 58 per cent) returned completed questionnaires to the researcher. In the interest of confidentiality, respondents had been asked not to put their names on the response sheets. The questionnaire posed fixed-response questions as well as open-ended questions. Many of the responses to this questionnaire were not used in this research, how-ever, because it became clear that job evaluation had variable sets of meanings not possible to discern from a survey questionnaire. Still, the questionnaire is used selectively as supporting evidence.

Second, semi-structured interviews were held with each of the deputy ministers who had been part of the Atlantis administration when the job evaluation plan was introduced (nineteen of the twenty-one deputy ministers). Each of these deputy ministers had belonged to one of three evaluation committees charged with evaluating the 'first round' of positions, the benchmark jobs, using the Hay method. They were asked fewer, but similar questions to those asked in the survey, most of these relating to their experience as evaluators and to any changes that might have occurred in the department since the introduction of the formal job evaluation plan.

Further semi-structured interviews were held with a total of ten professional personnel people within the central personnel depart-ment. In addition, a random number (about fifty) of employees (whose jobs had been either benchmarks or non-benchmarks) were inter-viewed less formally during the researcher's visits to departments, particularly the personnel officers. Finally, the Hay consultant as-signed to the project was interviewed.

To supplement the information gathered from the interviews and the questionnaire, I also had full and complete access to all Civil Service Commission documentation on this change project. Perhaps not surprisingly (given that this was a government bureaucracy that I was studying), documentation was comprehensive and voluminous. The researcher was given permission to photocopy any and all documentation and to remove these copies from the premises.

It is not possible, within the scope of this research, to detail all the steps taken to install and maintain the job evaluation plan, so it has been necessary, at times, to omit lengthy instructions and procedures on the operation of the scheme. The case-study is presented in se-quence, in as complete a form as the limitations of space permit.

Although the material is interlaced with comments that point out certain key observations, much of the data should be seen as 'artefacts' to be examined later on, when the picture is more complete. Presented in such a manner, this case-study may also serve as a source for other researchers interested in exploring the meaning of job evaluation. It is my understanding that a number of interpretations could flow from the case-study that differ from those drawn out here.

The book makes a number of methodological contributions. First, it represents a development of the 'case-survey' approach (as developed by White [1981a]). The research combines a longitudinal case-study with a structured survey questionnaire. The case-study is used in an 'interpretive' manner and provides a 'narrative' account of the job evaluation process (used principally to uncover its political aspects), whereas the survey is used to determine how much values are shared (i.e., to demonstrate to what extent reality has been 'created' and 'enacted'). The research findings could not have been obtained through either a survey or a case-study alone. The case-study 'narrative' is itself offered to other researchers as an artefact and is considered to be open to further interpretation. One hopes the research has been able to demonstrate the further viability of this case-survey method.

The research also provides an example of a 'practitioner-academic' mode of analysis. In this respect, the research highlights the elements of a 'moral career' (innocence–awareness–critical awareness).

This book also makes a practical contribution by providing an account of the 'administrative phases' of the job evaluation process. Detailed historical job evaluation case-studies are rare. My case not only offers the 'practitioner' an appreciation of the sequence of events typically involved in the implementation of a job evaluation program, but also sets out this sequence within the context of *people*. In this way it attempts to put some 'life' into the otherwise dry accounts of job evaluation offered within the managerialist literature. It could also be said that this research has served to sensitize managers to the reality of a non-rational and political approach to job evaluation.

Finally, the case can also be seen to have implications for 'implementation' research – an area much discussed but rarely studied (the shortage of studies on implementation has been lamented by Pressman and Wildavsky [1973]). The case clearly highlights problems associated with the implementation of a major organizational change. In particular, I have shown how an organization, at the time of implementing a job evaluation plan, strives to balance the integrity of a rational approach against such pressures as internal traditional differentials and external market forces.

Why Job Evaluation?
The Case for a 'Rational' System

How does formal job evaluation come to exist in organizations? It is suggested here that the introduction of formal job evaluation formed part of a highly visible 'efficiency strategy' on the part of the government of Atlantis, which was newly elected to power. The consultants brought in by the government to look for efficiency improvements recommended the replacement of existing practices with a 'systematic job evaluation' scheme. The notion of job evaluation was sold by the consultants as a 'modern' and 'rational' technique for determining (and defending) rates of pay. A formal job evaluation system represented one way for the government to make its new efficiency policy concrete. Thus, the job evaluation scheme stood as an important symbol of change.

While the introduction of a job evaluation system might have stemmed principally from the need, or desire to project an image of efficiency, this did not mean that the consultants had not identified problems with the existing method of grading jobs. From a rational perspective, the introduction of job evaluation can also be attributed to the efficiency consultants' identification of a whole host of problems associated with the existing classification practices in Atlantis. Indeed, when a comprehensive audit of existing practices was conducted, these were condemned as 'ad hoc' and 'personality based.'

The problems identified by the consultants were not unlike those commonly raised in standard personnel textbooks in making the case for the introduction of a job evaluation system. The introduction of a formal job evaluation plan to Atlantis stands as an important case for analysis, especially since Atlantis appeared to possess many of the problems that job evaluation had the power to solve or rectify.

THE 'EFFICIENCY' STRATEGY

In 1978, the government of Atlantis, one of the ten provincial governments of Canada, voted in a new provincial government. Speaking from the throne, on his election to office, the new premier pledged to 'increase the effectiveness of government operations' and to 'engage in rigorous, rational and instrumental change.' A few months after this speech, the premier announced the immediate formation of a cabinet committee to improve government efficiency and management.' This committee was made up of six cabinet ministers hand-picked by the premier.

The first step taken by this committee was to engage the services of a well-known, prestigious management-consulting firm based in one of the larger provinces. This consulting firm was also known to have supported the political party at both the federal and provincial level. Two consultants were sent to Atlantis in response to the government's request for assistance and were charged with investigating the government's existing management practices and procedures and making recommendations for improvement. Specifically, the consultants were asked 'to review government departments and agencies to identify':

- illogical groupings of functions, services, or skills;
- plans for improving effectiveness and efficiency;
- any gaps or overlaps in the existing structure; and
- any constraints or impediments to improving efficiency due to present policies. (internal document)

To provide the two 'external' consultants with inside knowledge of the organization during the time of their research, two senior administrators from within the civil service were selected by the cabinet committee (as per the recommendation of Treasury Board executives) to work alongside the consultants. One of these administrators, MacRae, was then a director in the central personnel department, the Civil Service Commission. The other, Jamieson, was then a director in the Department of Social Services. As recounted to the researcher, MacRae claimed that he and Jamieson had been chosen because 'we must have been considered, by the powers that be, to be "reliable" and "forward thinking."' The two external consultants and the two internal civil servants made up what came to be known as the 'efficiency' group.'

To begin the collection of information, the efficiency group of four divided into pairs, each made up of one external consultant and one civil servant. The teams interviewed all fourteen ministers and twenty-one deputy ministers. Some idea of the scope of this information-gathering activity may be gleaned from the organization chart of the Atlantis government depicted in figure 1.

Each government department is headed by a minister to represent the political level (some ministers are responsible for more than one department). The top administrative position of each department is that of deputy minister. While it is fairly common for ministers to change portfolios at different times and for different reasons, those holding the position of deputy minister rarely change departments. Deputy ministers provide consistency of operation and sometimes specialist knowledge of departments, for example, Agriculture or Mines and Energy. Deputy ministers are not officially civil servants because they are paid directly by cabinet as 'order-in-council' appointments. This mode of payment would suggest that the position of deputy minister is somewhat less secure and more vulnerable to the caprices of politicians than civil-servant positions might be.

The organizational layer beneath that of deputy minister is the 'director' level (usually two to five per department), followed by a management and/or specialist level, under which would normally be a supervisory level. Supervisors (and some managers) would oversee the work of unionized employees in any of a number of job groups, including technical, maintenance, educational, and clerical.

During the time that ministers and deputy ministers were being interviewed, the efficiency group also met, both formally and informally, with civil servants from lower levels of the organization. Over the six months of information gathering, the efficiency team also met, every couple of weeks, with one or more group members of the cabinet committee. MacRae, one of the efficiency-group members, told the researcher that these meetings were called by the efficiency group in order to 'feel out the reaction' to any preliminary findings.

Finally, on the basis of interview data, old consultants' reports (some implemented, some not), and a comparison of Atlantis operations with those of other Canadian government organizations (a more recent consultants' report), the efficiency group made its recommendations to the cabinet efficiency committee. The consultants, aided by the two civil servants, had agreed upon the identification of four problem areas. It is notable that each of these areas is described in terms of rational images, accompanied by a specific recommendation for resolution. The findings of the report to Cabinet can be summarized as follows:

FIGURE 1

Organization chart of the Government of Atlantis

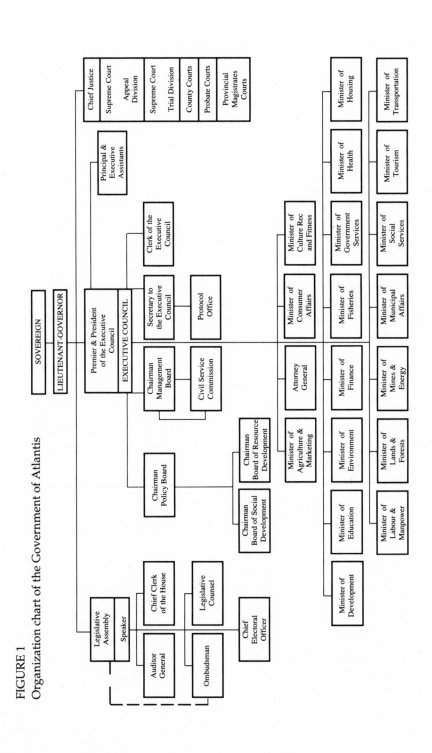

1 *Legislation*
   Problem: legislation outdated
   Action: establish mechanism for regular review
2 *Communications*
   Problem: organization structure between Cabinet and civil service
   prevents effective communication between the two
   Action: create Executive Council to link both bodies
3 *Finance*
   Problem: absence of financial objectives
   Action: introduce 'Zero Base Budgeting' technique with the help
   of outside consultants
4 *Human Resources*
   Problem: outdated and inequitable classification practices
   Action: (a) introduce formal job evaluation plan (preferably that of
   the Hay Associates consulting firm) and (b) reorganize Civil
   Service Commission, particularly classification division, to restore
   competence and credibility of department and ensure success of
   job evaluation plan.

The cabinet committee, already informally in agreement with the
recommendations above, formally approved them. Although action
was soon taken on all these recommendations, the following research
is concerned only with the 'Human Resources' action. Why is it that
formal job evaluation was chosen as a recommendation by the efficiency group? Clearly, the apparent lack of a formal job evaluation
system was identified as the core of Atlantis's human-relations problems. Did the existing classification practices present such a vulnerable target to the 'rational'-minded consultants? What was to be
gained by introducing the technique? Let us take a brief look at what
was going on in the classification division of Atlantis at that time.

WHAT WAS WRONG WITH THE 'OLD' WAY?

MacRae, who was the director of classification research (before his
promotion to director of pay), told the researcher that when the consultants found out about the Atlantis salary-administration procedures, 'they didn't like what they saw. They seemed to dislike the fact
that we apparently had no rules or guidelines for grading the jobs.'
    To understand the practices that disturbed the efficiency consult-
ants, a brief description of the 'old' system is provided. The researcher

is familiar with, and, indeed, operated the 'old' system, so this description represents first-hand knowledge. Information on the evolution of this system, however, was derived by talking to senior Civil Service Commission employees.

The particular way of grading jobs in Atlantis prior to the introduction of the Hay job evaluation plan had apparently evolved (or degenerated?) from an old classification system installed in the 1950s by a U.S. consulting firm. By the 1950s the U.S. Civil Service Commission's classification scheme, known as the General Schedule (GS), had reached beyond the U.S. border into Canada, to both the private and the public sector. The Canadian federal government and a few of the provincial governments were already using the scheme by the time Atlantis called in the firm of Jerome Barnham and Associates to introduce the same type of classification system.

'Classification' is a non-quantitative type of job evaluation whereby a job, or group of jobs, is matched to the written class definition that best describes the level of complexity, responsibility, and skill required to perform it. At the time, the notion of grouping jobs into 'classes' was considered to be popular, especially in government organizations (Lutz 1969).

Little is known and no records remain in Atlantis about the introduction of the GS system. Some people in the Civil Service Commission do remember that it was made up of twenty grades into which the jobs of all 1,100 civil servants were sorted. Everyone, from manual and clerical workers to the administrative level below the deputy minister, was slotted into one of these grades. Although the exact definitions that made up the hierarchy of job grades in Atlantis in the 1950s have been lost or destroyed, the scheme upon which these were patterned still remains in use in the U.S. federal government (the extant scheme uses eighteen grades). The difference between a GS-1 and a GS-2 is outlined below to provide an example of the type of scheme upon which the Atlantis practices were based:

1 / Grade GS-1 includes those classes of positions the duties of which are to perform under immediate supervision, with little or no latitude for the exercise of independent judgment –
  (a) the simplest routine work in office, business, or fiscal operations; or
  (b) elementary work of a subordinate technical character in a professional, scientific, or technical field.
2 / Grade GS-2 includes those classes of positions the duties of which are –

(a) to perform, under immediate supervision, with limited latitude for the exercise of independent judgment, routine work in the office, business, or fiscal operations, or comparable subordinate technical work of limited scope in a professional, scientific, or technical field, requiring some training or experience: or

(b) to perform other work of equal importance, difficulty, and requiring comparable qualifications. (United States Code [1976], Title 5, section 5104: 434)

It is obvious that one of the problems of job 'classification' is the very fine nature of the distinctions between one grade and the next. Each of the grade definitions in Atlantis carried an associated salary range. Each salary range contained a progression scale of four to six steps, or increments, through which the employees were meant to progress annually, until the last increment, contingent upon satisfactory performance in the job. Having reached the last increment, the employee would thereafter receive only the annual range adjustment, unless he or she moved to a job in a different grade. The responsibility for the classification of jobs lay with the Civil Service Commission, although the departments, through the offices of their deputy ministers, held the initiative for proposing changes in the classification of civil servants. No system of 'appeal' was ever introduced. The Civil Service Commission was officially considered to have the last word in classification matters.

The classification plan introduced by Jerome Barnham and Associates began to change in the 1960s when the Atlantis civil service grew, not only in numbers but also in the variety of services offered to the public. As new types of jobs were created, some employees complained that their jobs did not fit as neatly into the twenty general class definitions as did other jobs, because of specific or 'unique' job requirements (e.g., health services or educational services). The classification division was finding it more and more difficult to operate using a single twenty-grade classification scheme.

In 1967, in response to the demand that greater sensitivity be shown to certain groups of employees, the pay division separated the 'one grand classification scheme' into the ten following satellite schemes: Clerical, Educational, Health Services (nursing services), Health Services (technical), Maintenance and Operational, Medical Services (doctors), Dental Services, Professional and Related, Institutional and Related, and Technical. These schemes existed until the introduction of the new Hay job evaluation plan in 1979.

The number of grades in each of these new satellite job 'classes' or 'families' varied anywhere from fifteen to thirty, depending on the number of perceivable differences in skill and responsibility between the top and bottom jobs in each group. According to the theory of classification, a grade 'standard' or definition should have been written for each of the new grades in each of the ten new job families, but this was never done. Officially, such definitions serve as the standards against which jobs are compared. However, the only written rules in place were now merely those dictating the criteria for belonging to a particular job family. The criteria for classifying a job by grade within these families were no longer specified.

The classification division carried out its grading functions using what staff called 'general comparison' with other positions both inside and outside the civil service. The control mechanism appears to have shifted at this time from one of bureaucratic dependence upon what the 'book' says to one of blind trust in the classification officer's 'general comparison' findings. The method of slotting jobs within the job hierarchy without reference to any formal criteria continued to be known as classification, even though a formal, rule-based system was no longer in place.

Thus, after 1967, the classification scheme installed by Jerome Barnham no longer depended upon any written standard or grade definitions that described or explained how or why a job was slotted into a certain grade. Considerable emphasis was placed on memory and informal exchange of information, particularly since each of the then six classification officers was assigned only to three or four departments and many jobs – for example, clerical, technical, and maintenance – were common across all departments.

In 1975, when the government workers of Atlantis became unionized, the same classification practices continued, with the Civil Service Commission formally retaining all rights relating to the classification of both unionized and non-unionized positions. Each of the job families was now made up of two groups, one unionized and one non-unionized. This doubled the number of grades with which the classification staff had to deal.

If a job included responsibility for supervising employees, or for maintaining confidentiality (as would jobs in personnel), it was classified as non-bargaining. All other civil-service jobs, including professionals such as lawyers and engineers, became part of the union.

Although the union and the management pay scales for each class of jobs started out as equivalent, it eventually became the tradition that the management or supervisory scales of each pay category were fixed at a slightly higher (2–3 per cent) level than those secured by the union at the bargaining table. This relativity soon became accepted practice and was commonly attributed to 'status' differences. Bluntly stated, the appearance of a clear differential symbolized the superior status of the non-unionized category. Under this 'old' system non-unionized staff had the smug assurance that their union counterparts were always paid slightly less. (Once the Hay plan was introduced, the ready availability of the union pay scales provided a reminder to newly graded jobholders of what their salary 'would have been' under the 'old way.' This added an interesting dimension to the case-study: the union pay scales acted as a constant reference point, a blatant measuring rod to which employees could point if dissatisfied.)

The typical steps involved in classifying or reclassifying all civil-service jobs in Atlantis *prior to* the introduction of the new Hay plan in the early 1980s are outlined below.

1 / The personnel officer in one of the client departments prepared a new or 'revised' job description (signed by the incumbent and his or her superiors, up to and including the deputy minister) and completed a 'justification for reclassification' form. All requests had to originate from client departments and could never be initiated by the Civil Service Commission. Often a specific grade was requested, whether the job was newly created or merely being considered for reclassification.

2 / The department's request was forwarded from the office of the deputy minister of the department to the office of the deputy minister of the Civil Service Commission. From there it travelled to the desk of the director of classification who then forwarded it to the manager. Once the director and the manager had each seen the request, it was then forwarded to the classification officer assigned to that particular department.

3 / The classification officer visited the department in question (if the officer deemed it necessary) to interview the incumbent, his or her supervisor, and sometimes the department's personnel officer. In the event of a request for reclassification, the officer was meant to be looking for any 'significant' change that might have occurred in the job as such a change is the only recognized reason for recommending alteration of a grade. The difficult task of defining 'significant change' was the subject of many discussions between officers and their client departments.

4 / At the Civil Service Commission, the classification officer searched through the directories of job titles and grades to identify any job descriptions that might prove to be useful comparisons. If there was found to be 'significant change' and higher grade did not seem to disturb existing relativities across government, the officer would likely recommend to either the classification manager or the director that the job changed (usually upwards) to a certain grade. The department in question would then be notified. If there was no change found in the job, or the officer was unwilling to move the job for reasons of comparability (or some other reason), the department was then notified that its request has been denied.

5 / Departments responded in any one of a variety of ways if they were not satisfied with the classification division's decision: They may have reluctantly accepted the ruling; begun to prepare a stronger case (some classification battles were found to have been going on for years and one was found to have been challenged annually for ten years); arranged to have the departmental deputy minister pressure the deputy minister of the Civil Service Commission; or enlisted support at the political level, depending very much on whose job was under discussion. As Roberts, the previous classification director (who lost his job in the reorganization), commented to the researcher: 'When the politicians got involved, we gave them what they wanted. They never heard a peep out of us!'

6 / If, however, the classification division decided in favour of the department's request, or if some satisfactory compromise had been reached (e.g., 'to split the difference' between the requested grade and the grade selected by the classification officer), the department prepared the appropriate change-of-pay forms to move the job to a new grade.

Basically, these grading practices were, in 1979, considered by the 'efficiency' group to have fallen into disrepute. According to the 'efficiency consultants,' the existing 'classification' scheme was considered to have a number of interrelated problems.

Inequitable rates were found to exist throughout the civil service. Under different job titles, the same basic jobs (e.g., jobs within accounting or personnel) were paid at different rates of pay in different departments of Atlantis. Individuals and groups were considered to have, over the years, taken advantage of the absence of written rules to press home their claims for upgrading, thereby upsetting internal equity. As described above, practices were criticized as 'ad hoc' and 'personality based.' In fact, the efficiency group did not consider the existing classification practices to make up a 'system' at all. Because there were no established evaluation criteria, gradings were seen to depend on a combination of personal judgment, precedent, often lethargic comparison with other jobs, the seriousness of market problems, and the influence or 'clout' of those trying to get their way. 'Haggling' over grades was found to be commonplace between the Civil Service Commission and its client departments.

The search for the cross-departmental comparisons was not found to be standardized and was seen to depend on the amount of effort that the classification officer was willing to put in on a given day. Although consistency of gradings between the then six classification officers was meant to be achieved by verifying all new gradings or grade changes with either the manager or the director of classification, there were considered to be too many jobs across the civil service for these two individuals to monitor the process adequately.

The existing method of grading was also criticized because employees could not understand it. According to the efficiency team, such an informal method of comparing jobs made it difficult to justify the Civil Service Commission's rulings to client departments. There was no written record of how or why a job was slotted into a certain grade. The government was also warned that the lack of any administrative machinery for evaluating the content of jobs left the organization particularly vulnerable in the event of someone's lodging an equal pay or pay equity complaint.

The job descriptions used in Atlantis were also considered to be too brief and not sufficiently detailed for informed grading decisions to be made. Both job descriptions and organization charts in Atlantis were found to be out of date, with no procedures in place for their updating. Moreover, the job-description format was found to be of little value for other 'long-term' human-relations programs, such as merit-pay schemes, training, and management-succession plans. It was maintained that 'utilization and productivity of staff could be improved; training is inadequate, particularly at senior levels; no established system of attracting, identifying and grooming future Deputy Ministers and senior staff' (Report to Cabinet, June 1979). The poor job-description format and the out-of-date job descriptions also made the efficiency group question the reliability of the salary information obtained in the market survey conducted by MacRae's classification 'research' division every two years. The consultants wondered how the classification staff could be certain of comparing 'like with like.'

A string of other problems was identified: 'too many job classifications (500 job classifications, 3,000 job titles for a staff of 12,000 – every 3rd or 4th person has own title); system is outdated; classification system 20 years old; personnel are not rewarded on the bases of merit and performance' (Report to Cabinet, June 1979). The efficiency group also found that the Civil Service Commission (CSC) had an 'image' problem. Although the two other divisions of the Civil Service Commission (staffing and industrial relations) were also criticized for being 'slow,' 'arbitrary,' and 'generally unprofessional,' the classification division received the most complaints.

The efficiency group claimed that departments often viewed the classification division as an obstruction, a roadblock to accomplishing an objective. Because of so many harangues between the CSC and client departments, deputy ministers had apparently indicated to the interview teams that they often sought ways of either circumventing the classification officers or outsmarting them. Circumventing the officers usually meant either 'going over their heads, to the director or straight to the deputy minister' or 'going the political route,' whereas outsmarting them usually involved 'trumping up' the job description or 'digging up our own comparisons in government to prove our point.'

By describing the already existing salary-administration practices of Atlantis, it might be suggested that conditions were probably ideal for those charged with the task of making 'rational' recommendations to cabinet. The efficiency group made it clear to the politicians that, by introducing formal job evaluation (and a certain Hay system at that), inequities in the civil service could be redressed and other related human-resource deficiencies could be gradually resolved.

The rationale of 'efficiency' associated with the introduction of a formal job evaluation plan seemed to fit in neatly with the government's overall 'efficiency' project, and the politicians readily accepted the proposal.

THE DECISION TO CHOOSE THE HAY SYSTEM OF JOB EVALUATION

While the four members of the efficiency group were finishing up their overall investigation, they were also giving some thought to different types of job evaluation systems. Very little consideration was given to the notion of developing a job evaluation plan 'in house.' At that time, the efficiency group was finding that most members of the classification division were 'incompetent,' had little 'professional expertise,' and 'lacked credibility with their client departments' (it will be remembered that one of the conclusions drawn by this group was that a 'reorganization' should take place in the classification division before job evaluation was introduced). Therefore, under the circumstances, the possibility of developing an in-house job evaluation scheme was barely given any thought.

The job-classification practices that were criticized by the efficiency group related to both unionized (10,800) and non-unionized (1,200) employees, since exactly the same procedures were applied to both groups. While the introduction of a formal job evaluation plan to the non-unionized group was considered a relatively unproblematic undertaking, the consultants were told by their two civil-service assistants that the introduction of such a plan might not be acceptable to the union. It was agreed that the government would use the 'best job evaluation plan available' for the non-union employees, that is, for professional, supervisory, and managerial employees, and 'just hope that the union will want to adopt the same plan down the line.' (As it happens, the union was not interested 'down the line.')

Two other points-rating plans were given brief consideration, but, according to MacRae, the group's greatest interest lay in the plan known as the Guide Chart Profile method of the firm of Hay Associates. After a successful meeting with a consultant from the out-of-province firm of Hay Associates, the efficiency group eventually recommended this particular plan to the Cabinet Committee for Efficiency. When asked to explain the group's attraction to the Hay plan at that time, MacRae recalls that

the two consultants were really keen on the Hay plan, and so was I. Jamieson, from Social Services, didn't really care, although he thought the Hay plan looked 'pretty impressive.' As far as I was concerned I saw that Roberts's days were numbered as director of classification. I knew that, as director of classificatrion research (the neighbouring division), and as a member of the 'efficiency' group, I had a good crack at that job. You see, I knew, from all the survey work that my old division did, that a lot of organizations in the public and the private sectors were using the Hay system. The chance to get to implement the Hay system here would make me 'golden' on the job market.

By the time that the efficiency recommendations were presented to the cabinet committee, MacRae was, indeed, already in place as the new 'director of pay.' His new division – the pay division – encompassed both his previous 'classification research' division and those few who had escaped the sack in the 'classification' division itself. (The previous director, Roberts', had been relocated to administration, but the manager of classification was allowed to keep his job. Four of the six classification officers were eventually dismissed, in preparation for the Hay plan, and two more hired – the researcher was one of these two newly hired pay analysts.)

Although the expensive and time-consuming Hay plan was heavily endorsed by the consultants and by the pay division, it could not be adopted without the approval of the Cabinet Committee for Efficiency. The same Hay consultant (Burr) who had travelled to Atlantis earlier to make a presentation to the members of the efficiency group was invited back to make a presentation to the Cabinet Committee. This presentation, like the one made in the Atlantis earlier, outlined the basic operation of the Hay Guide Chart Profile method of job evaluation and the advantages of using this particular plan. Burr, the Hay consultant, was asked to study the organization and, based on his findings, to write up a report stating what exactly could be offered to Atlantis and how much this would cost.

After Burr left Atlantis, a Hay 'letter of interest' was soon received by the government. Some passages from this letter are reproduced here because they provide interesting insights into claims that are made about the Hay system and the promises that are made to clients. The 'Introduction' section of this letter, for instance, states: 'In some cases it is 20 years since certain jobs were first evaluated and you are presently considering the re-evaluation of all jobs to ensure internal equity within the government. In addition you are concerned with ensuring externally competitive renumeration in order to attract and retain qualified and experienced personnel within the [Atlantis] Civil Service.' The 'letter of interest' also explained the Hay philosophy:

Hay's philosophy is based upon the following premise: 'The amount of money devoted to salaries and benefits represents a significant cost to every government. A rational, systematic means for ensuring that the right amount in the right proportions is allocated to the right people for producing the right things is the goal of every manager.'

We offer a process which will allow you to do this on an effective and continuing basis. Our approach is designed to meet these fundamental criteria in your compensation administration and to produce a system that is:

* Internally equitable, both vertically and laterally throughout the structure of the Government.
* Externally competitive with other public and private sector organizations, particularly in the neighbouring provinces ...
* ... and to which pay can be related to performance ... (Hay Letter of Interest, June 1979)

Another feature of the Hay plan lay in the assurances provided for 'defensibility' and 'protection' against challenge. The use of such a quantitative plan, combined with the participation of senior management personnel on evaluation committees, 'ought to meet the test of any challenge on the basis of equal employment opportunity ... The Hay Guide Chart Profile Method conforms to all United States Equal Employment Opportunity Commission guidelines and in the United States has often been used in court proceedings, and labour relations arbitration cases to determine job content value and prove or disprove the existence or absence of internal equity of salary administration.' The letter also pointed to the 'qualifications of Hay Associates' as an advantage of using this plan over others available on the market:

Our firm is the world's largest human resource management consulting firm with some 400 professional consultants operating in nineteen (19) countries through thirty nine (39) offices. The firm is in its 35th year of operation and over sixty (60) percent of its services are in the field of managerial, professional, and clerical job evaluation and related compensation plans.

... Hay has worked with over 4,500 industrial and commercial companies and hundreds of organizations in the public sector in the specific area of managerial job evaluation. In Canada we have worked with over 550 organizations in the public and private sector. In the private sector, a list of our clients utilizing the Hay Guide Chart Profile Method would include well over one-third (indeed almost one half) of 'Fortune's' 500 companies and one half of the Financial Post's 200 companies in Canada. [A list of such companies accompanied the letter.]

... In recent years Hay has become increasingly involved in job evaluation within the Canadian public sector (including three other provincial governments) and are presently spearheading a major project to develop compensation standards within the Federal Civil Service. (Hay Letter of Interest, June 1979)

The Hay fees were not specified in the letter, but the procedure of paying consultants 'by the day, plus expenses,' was mentioned.

THE NEW HAY JOB EVALUATION PLAN

The consulting firm of Hay Associates was founded in Philadelphia in 1943, and it was in 1951 that the now-famous Hay Guide Chart Profile method was conceived by the Hay Group, out of their experience in performing job evaluations for numerous clients. Edward N. Hay, the firm's founder, developed ways to define his own particular concept of job evaluation. He recommended that an organization's representatives be asked a series of questions if they were planning to use an outside firm to handle their job evaluation program. This question format, still in use today, was used in the province of Atlantis:

1 / Will the program give management new insights into individual positions or into its organization?

2 / Are the criteria to be used realistic for management positions?

3 / Will certain management positions, such as those in research and development, have to be handled separately?

4 / Does the measurement device demonstrate the difference between jobs?

5 / Can the program be explained and justified to employees, to stockholders, to a board of trustees or to some other group?

6 / Is the program flexible enough to cross department and division lines?

7 / Is it flexible enough to cover future growth and expansion, even into new areas?

8 / Does the program contain checks on itself to reveal evaluation errors or to prevent the evaluations as a whole from going off in a biased direction?

9 / In the future, will it be possible to look back and see why and how any single position was evaluated as it was?

10 / For the external comparisons of salaries, how accurate and complete are the surveys? How often will they have to be repeated? How expensive will they be? Are they based on job titles or job descriptions?

11 / How will the information be presented to management?

12 / Finally, will the program provide information that can be used for purposes other than base salary information, such as organization analysis, extra compensation, performance appraisal, selection, development or management continuity? (quoted in Doyen 1967: 63)

According to its originators, the Hay system has been designed to meet needs and solve problems identified in these questions. The system involves comparing jobs with respect to three factors – Know-How, Problem Solving, and Accountability – considered to be common to all jobs. Here it is useful to recognize that, while Hay's concept of job evaluation appears to be technically uncontroversial, it is pervaded with rhetorical claims.

The evaluation of jobs is carried out by using three 'guide charts' each of which measures one of these factors. A guide chart is defined as 'two or more evaluation scales brought together in one sheet, or chart. Each scale is defined in a general way and each level or step of each scale is further described, or defined, in detail' (Atlantis/ Hay *Position Evaluation Manual*). The numbering system used in the guide charts is a geometric scale with a ratio of approximately 15 per cent between terms in the series. In other words, the value of each amount listed grows in 15 per cent increments, i.e., 50, 57, 66, 76, 87, 100, and so on. According to the Atlantis/Hay *Position Evaluation Manual*,

the selection of a geometric rather than an arithmetic scale is justified by empirical considerations and also by the fact that salary changes from jobs of low content to jobs of high content are geometric in character ... there seems to be a similarity between this characteristic of measurement and Weber's Law [footnote cites *Great Experiments in Psychology* (New York: Century 1930), 268 – 74] in psychological measurements. Weber put it this way: 'in comparing objects we perceive not the actual difference between them but the ratio of this difference to the magnitude of the two objects compared.'

It is important to note that, since 1951, the Hay Guide Charts have been refined in language and in application. Also, guide charts are tailor-made to each organization, reflecting guide-chart 'sizing', which relates to such activities as adjusting the length of the scales to each different client and modifying the scale language relating to the organization's character, structure and type of work (Hay Group pamphlet, undated).

The first guide chart (see figure 2) measures the know-how required to perform the job. This guide chart is supposed to measure the sum total of three types of knowledge and skill: specialized and/or technical, managerial, and human relations.

The second guide chart, 'Problem Solving' (see figure 3) is meant to measure the intensity of the thinking required to solve problems and meet challenges. Because it is assumed that 'one thinks with what one knows,' the Problem-Solving point score is taken as a *percentage* of whatever points were obtained earlier for Know-How.

The final guide chart, 'Accountability' (see figure 4), claims to measure the effect of the job on end results. (In Canada, at this time, Hay was in the process of refining a fourth guide chart, 'Working Conditions.' According to Burr, the reason for adding this fourth dimension was based on the then Canadian pay-equity legislation, which demanded that jobs under dispute be measured against all four factors – skill, effort, responsibility, and *working conditions*.) The 'Working Conditions' guide chart is now selectively used in some jurisdictions to comply with evaluation-criteria requirements of pay-equity legislation. Since the use of this chart has become more prevalent in recent years, it is shown, for illustrative purposes only, in Appendix A.

Even when a total score has been obtained by adding up the Know-How, Problem Solving, and Accountability points obtained, the evaluation of a job is still not complete. The next step in the process is to check the 'profile' of the evaluation (hence, the name Guide Chart Profile method). This activity involves making sure that the 'appropriate' relationship exists between the Problem Solving and the Accountability point scores. A research position, for example, might be expected to produce a higher score in Problem Solving than in Accountability. Similarly, a production manager's job might be expected to score higher in Accountability than in Problem Solving. There are, of course, exceptions to these rules, but, after a job has been evaluated, if the relationship between these two factors is not deemed to fit the nature of the job, the committee is meant to be alerted to a possible 'error' in the evaluation of that particular job.

A further cross-check, called the 'Sore Thumb' process, is then evoked as a way of making certain that the job evaluations are correct. This test requires the evaluators to analyze a chart depicting the detailed point scores of several already evaluated positions, in descending order, to see if any scores in any of the three dimensions

FIGURE 2 Guide chart for evaluating know-how

		N. NONSUPERVISORY Performance of an activity as an individual (not as a supervisor or professional).			I. MINIMAL Performance or direction of activities which are similar as to content and objectives with appropriate awareness of other activities.		
		1	2	3	1	2	3
PRACTICAL PROCEDURES	A BASIC UNDERSTANDING: Familiarity with simple work routines; work indoctrination.	38 43 50	43 50 57	50 57 66	50 57 66	57 66 76	66 76 87
	B ELEMENTARY SKILL AND/OR KNOWLEDGE: Capable of carrying out uninvolved, standard procedures and/or using equipment or machines which are simple to operate.	50 57 66	57 66 76	66 76 87	66 76 87	76 87 100	87 100 115
	C INTERMEDIATE SKILL AND/OR KNOWLEDGE: Experienced in applying methods or procedures which generally are well-defined and straightforward but with occasional deviations. Skill in the use of specialized equipment may be needed.	66 76 87	76 87 100	87 100 115	87 100 115	100 115 132	115 132 152
SPECIALIZED TECHNIQUES	D EXTENDED SKILL AND/OR KNOWLEDGE: Accomplished in implementing practical procedures or systems which are moderately complex and/or specialized skills which require some technical knowledge (usually non-theoretical) to apply.	87 100 115	100 115 132	115 132 152	115 132 152	132 152 175	152 175 200
	E DIVERSE OR SPECIALIZED: A sound understanding of and skill in several activities which involve a variety of practices and precedents, OR a basic understanding of the theory and principles in a scientific or similar discipline.	115 132 152	132 152 175	152 175 200	152 175 200	175 200 230	200 230 264
	F SEASONED, DIVERSE OR SPECIALIZED: Extensive knowledge and skill gained through broad or deep experiences in a field (or fields) which require a command of EITHER involved, diverse practices and precedents OR scientific theory and principles OR both.	152 175 200	175 200 230	200 230 264	200 230 264	230 264 304	264 304 350
SCIENTIFIC DISCIPLINES	G BROAD OR SPECIALIZED MASTERY: Mastery of theories, principles and complex techniques OR the diverse, cumulative equivalent gained through broad seasoning and/or special development.	200 230 264	230 264 304	264 304 350	264 304 350	304 350 400	350 400 460
	H PROFESSIONAL EMINENCE: Externally recognized expertise in a complex scientific field or other learned discipline.	264 304 350	304 350 400	350 400 460	350 400 460	400 460 528	460 528 608

••• HUMAN RELATIONS SKILLS
1. BASIC: Ordinary courtesy and effectiveness in dealing with others.

DEFINITION: Know-How is the total of every kind of knowledge and skill, *however* acquired, needed for competent job performance. Know-How has three dimensions – the requirements for:

• **Practical, Technical Know-How** Practical procedures, specialized techniques, or scientific disciplines.

•• **Management Know-How** Planning, organizing, integrating, coordinating, staffing, directing and controlling the activities and resources associated with an organizational unit or function, in order to produce the results expected of that unit or function. This knowledge and skill may be exercised either consultatively ("thinking like a manager") or directly.

••• **Human Relations Skills** Active, face-to-face skills needed for various relationships with other people.

FIGURE 2 *(continued)*

•• MANAGERIAL KNOW-HOW											
II. RELATED Direction of a unit with varied activities and objectives OR guidance of a subfunction(s) or several important elements across several units.			**III. DIVERSE** Direction of a large unit with functional variety OR guidance of a function(s) which affects all or most of the organization.			**IV. BROAD** Direction of a major unit with substantial functional diversity OR guidance of a strategic function(s) which significantly affects the organization's planning and operations.			**V. TOTAL** Management of all units and functions in the organization.		
1	2	3	1	2	3	1	2	3	1	2	3
66 76 87	76 87 100	87 100 115	87 100 115	100 115 132	115 132 152	115 132 152	132 152 175	152 175 200	152 175 200	175 200 230	200 230 264
87 100 115	100 115 132	115 132 152	115 132 152	132 152 175	152 175 200	152 175 200	175 200 230	200 230 264	200 230 264	230 264 304	264 304 350
115 132 152	132 152 175	152 175 200	152 175 200	175 200 230	200 230 264	200 230 264	230 264 304	264 304 350	264 304 350	304 350 400	350 400 460
152 175 200	175 200 230	200 230 264	200 230 264	230 264 304	264 304 350	264 304 350	304 350 400	350 400 460	350 400 460	400 460 528	460 528 608
200 230 264	230 264 304	264 304 350	264 304 350	304 350 400	350 400 460	350 400 460	400 460 528	460 528 608	460 528 608	528 608 700	608 700 800
264 304 350	304 350 400	350 400 460	350 400 460	400 460 528	460 528 608	460 528 608	528 608 700	608 700 800	608 700 800	700 800 920	800 920 1056
350 400 460	400 460 528	460 528 608	460 528 608	528 608 700	608 700 800	608 700 800	700 800 920	800 920 1056	800 920 1056	920 1056 1216	1056 1216 1400
460 528 608	528 608 700	608 700 800	608 700 800	700 800 920	800 920 1056	800 920 1056	920 1056 1216	1056 1216 1400	1056 1216 1400	1216 1400 1600	1400 1600 1840

••• HUMAN RELATIONS SKILLS	
2. IMPORTANT: Understanding and influencing people are important requirements in the job.	**3. CRITICAL**: Alternative or combined skills in understanding and motivating people are important in the highest degree.

MEASURING PRACTICAL, TECHNICAL KNOW-HOW: This type of knowledge and skill may be characterized by breadth (variety), or depth (complexity), or both. Jobs may require some combination of various skills, some knowledge about many things, a good deal of knowledge about a few things. Thus, to measure this kind of Know-How, the evaluator has to understand WHAT SKILLS ARE NEEDED AND HOW MUCH KNOWLEDGE IS NEEDED ABOUT HOW MANY THINGS AND HOW COMPLEX THEY ARE.

FIGURE 3
Guide chart for evaluating problem solving

	1. REPETITIVE Identical situations requiring a simple choice of known things.
A HIGHLY STRUCTURED: Thinking within every detailed and precisely defined rules and instructions AND/OR with continually present assistance.	10% 12%
B ROUTINE: Thinking within detailed standard practices and instructions AND/OR with immediately available assistance or examples.	12% 14%
C SEMI-ROUTINE: Thinking within well-defined somewhat diversified procedures: many precedents covering most situations AND/OR readily available assistance.	14% 16%
D STANDARDIZED: Thinking within clear but substantially diversified procedures; precedents covering many situations AND/OR acces to assistance.	16% 19%
E CLEARLY DEFINED: Thinking within a well-defined frame of reference and toward specific objectives, in situations characterized by functional practices and precedents.	19% 22%
F GENERALLY DEFINED: Thinking within a general frame of reference toward functional objectives, in situations with some nebulous, intangible, or unstructured aspects.	22% 25%
G BROADLY DEFINED: Thinking within concepts, principles, and broad guidelines towards the organization's objectives or functional goals; many nebulous, intangible, or unstructured aspects to the environment.	25% 29%
H ABSTRACT: Thinking within organization philosophy AND/ OR natural laws AND/OR principles governing human affairs.	29% 33%

STEP VALUES (• THINKING ENVIRONMENT):
2432, 2112, 1840, -1600-, 1400, 1216, 1056, 920, -800-, 700, 608, 528, 460, -400-, 350, 304, 264, 230, -200-, 175, 152, 132, 115, 100

STEP BELOW 100%:
▽- ▷100-, 1- 87, 2- 76, 3- 66, 4- 57, 5- -50-, 6- 43, 7- 38, 8- 33, 9- 29, 10- -25-, 11- 22, 12- 19, 13- 16, 14- 14, 15- -12-, 16- 10, 17- 9, 18- 8, 19- 7, 20- -6-

Hay Group

DEFINITION: Problem Solving is the amount and nature of the thinking required in the job in the form of analyzing, reasoning, evaluating, creating, using judgment, forming hypotheses, drawing inferences, arriving at conclusions, and the like.

Problem Solving has two dimensions:

• The environment in which the thinking takes place — the extent to which assistance or guidance is available from others or from past practice and precedents.

•• The thinking challenge — the novelty and complexity of the thinking to be done.

N.B. The evaluation of Problem Solving should be made without reference to the job's freedom to make decisions or take action: decision-making is measured on the Accountability Chart.

FIGURE 3 *(continued)*

•• THINKING CHALLENGE				
2. PATTERNED Similar situations requiring resolution by discriminating choice of known things.	**3. VARIED** Differing situations requiring search for solutions within area of known things.	**4. ADAPTIVE** Variable situations requiring analytical, interpretive, evaluative, and/or constructive thinking.	**5. UNCHARTED** Novel or nonrecurring path-finding situations requiring the development of new concepts and imaginative approaches.	
14% 　　16%	19% 　　22%	25% 　　29%	33% 　　38%	**A**
16% 　　19%	22% 　　25%	29% 　　33%	38% 　　43%	**B**
19% 　　22%	25% 　　29%	33% 　　38%	43% 　　50%	**C**
22% 　　25%	29% 　　33%	38% 　　43%	50% 　　57%	**D**
25% 　　29%	33% 　　38%	43% 　　50%	57% 　　66%	**E**
29% 　　33%	38% 　　43%	50% 　　57%	66% 　　76%	**F**
33% 　　38%	43% 　　50%	57% 　　66%	76% 　　87%	**G**
38% 　　43%	50% 　　57%	66% 　　76%	87%	**H**

MEASURING PROBLEM SOLVING: All thinking requires the presence of knowledge in the form of facts, principles, procedures, standards, concepts, etc. This is the raw material to which the thinking processes are applied. Problem Solving measures the degree to which thinking processes must be applied to the required knowledge in order to obtain the results expected of the job.

To the extent that thinking is limited or reduced by job demands or structure, covered by precedent, simplified by definition, or assisted by others. Problem Solving is diminished and results are obtained by the automatic application of skills rather than by the application of the thinking processes to knowledge.

FIGURE 4
Guide chart for evaluating accountability

		(M) MINIMAL Up to $10M				(1) VERY SMALL $10M - $100M	
•• IMPACT		A	C	S	P	A	C
R RESTRICTED: These jobs are consistantly subject to explicit, detailed instructions AND/OR constant personal or procedural supervision.		5 6 7	7 8 9	9 10 12	12 14 16	7 8 9	9 10 12
A PRESCRIBED: These jobs are subject to direct and detailed instructions AND/OR very close supervision.		8 9 10	10 12 14	14 16 19	19 22 25	10 12 14	14 16 19
B CONTROLLED: These jobs are subject to instructions and established work routines AND/OR close supervision.		12 14 16	16 19 22	22 25 29	29 33 38	16 19 22	22 25 29
C STANDARDIZED: These jobs are subject, wholly or in part, to standarized practices and procedures, general work instructions, and supervision of progress and results.		19 22 25	25 29 33	33 38 43	43 50 57	25 29 33	33 38 43
D GENERALLY REGULATED: These jobs are subject, wholly or in part, to defined procedures AND/OR clear precedents and past practices. There is supervisory review of results which are well defined and expected in the short term.		29 33 38	38 43 50	50 57 66	66 76 87	38 43 50	50 57 66
E DIRECTED: These jobs are subject to broad practices and procedures AND/OR functional precedents and well defined policies. There is managerial direction toward achievement of specified results which are limited to a function or unit and are expected in the medium term.		43 50 57	57 66 76	76 87 100	100 115 132	57 66 76	76 87 100
F GENERAL DIRECTION: These jobs are broadly subject to defined functional policies. There is a managerial direction of a general nature toward unit goals or pervasive functional objectives which are realized in the longer term.		66 76 87	87 100 115	115 132 152	152 175 200	87 100 115	115 132 152
G GUIDANCE: These jobs are subject to the guidance of the organization's policies and general directives from top management.		100 115 132	132 152 175	175 200 230	230 264 304	132 152 175	175 200 230
H GENERAL GUIDANCE. Subject to the guidance of braod organization policies, community or legislative limits, and the mandate of the organization.		152 175 200	200 230 264	264 304 350	350 400 460	200 230 264	264 304 350

••• MAGNITUDE (annual basis)

• FREEDOM TO ACT

GENERAL: Accountability is related to the opportunity a job has to bring about some results and the importance of those results to the organization. Tied closely to the amount of opportunity is the degree to which the person in the job must answer for (is accountable for) the results.There are three components in Accountability in the following order of importance.
- • Freedom to Act – the degree to which personal or procedural control exists as defined in left-hand column.
- •• Impact – as defined at upper right.
- ••• Magnitude – the size of the unit or function (as indicated by the dynamic annual dollars) most clearly affected by the job.

N.B. Magnitude and impact must fit together, neither can be final or meaningful without being related to the other.

FIGURE 4   *(continued)*

(1) VERY SMALL $10M - $100M		(2) SMALL $100M - $1MM				(3) MEDIUM $1MM - $10MM				(4) LARGE $10MM - $100MM			
S	P	A	C	S	P	A	C	S	P	A	C	S	P
12 14 16	16 19 22	9 10 12	12 14 16	16 19 22	22 25 29	12 14 16	16 19 22	22 25 29	29 33 38	16 19 22	22 25 29	29 33 38	38 43 50
19 22 25	25 29 33	14 16 19	19 22 25	25 29 33	33 38 43	19 22 25	25 29 33	33 38 43	43 50 57	25 29 33	33 38 43	43 50 57	57 66 76
29 33 38	38 43 50	22 25 29	29 33 38	38 43 50	50 57 66	29 33 38	38 43 50	50 57 66	66 76 87	38 43 50	50 57 66	66 76 87	87 100 115
43 50 57	57 66 76	33 38 43	43 50 57	57 66 76	76 87 100	43 50 57	57 66 76	76 87 100	100 115 132	57 66 76	76 87 100	100 115 132	132 152 175
66 78 87	87 100 115	50 57 66	66 76 87	87 100 115	115 132 152	66 76 87	87 100 115	115 132 152	152 175 200	87 100 115	115 132 152	152 175 200	200 230 264
100 115 132	132 152 175	76 87 100	100 115 132	132 152 175	175 200 230	100 115 132	132 152 175	175 200 230	230 264 304	132 152 175	175 200 230	230 264 304	304 350 400
152 175 200	200 230 264	115 132 152	152 175 200	200 230 264	264 304 354	152 175 200	200 230 264	264 304 350	350 400 460	200 230 264	264 304 350	350 400 460	460 528 608
230 264 304	304 350 400	175 200 230	230 264 304	304 350 400	400 460 528	230 264 304	304 350 400	400 460 528	528 608 700	304 350 400	400 460 528	528 608 700	700 800 920
350 400 460	460 528 608	264 304 350	350 400 460	460 528 608	608 700 800	350 400 460	460 528 608	608 700 800	800 920 1056	460 528 608	608 700 800	800 920 1056	1056 1216 1400

•• **IMPACT** – The degree to which the job affects or brings about the results expected of the unit or function being considered.

P – PRIMARY: Controlling impact – the position has effective control over the significant activities and resources which produce the results and is the sole position (at this level of Freedom to Act) which must answer for the results.

S – SHARED: Equal and joint control, with one other position, of the activities and resources which produce the results, OR control of what are clearly most (but not all) of the variables which are significant in bringing about the results.

C – CONTRIBUTORY: Providing interpretive, advisory or other important support services for use by others in achieving results.

A – ANCILLARY: Providing information, supplementary assistance, or a required auxiliary service in support of others.

are either very high or very low compared to those of similar jobs, i.e., to see if any scores stick out 'like a sore thumb.'

Finally, after all the jobs have been evaluated in any one organization, the 'Correlation' process takes place. A more detailed explanation of this process can be found in Appendix B. This activity basically involves bringing a selected sample of job descriptions, and the point scores obtained in evaluation, to the (in this case, Canadian) Hay head office, where these are measured for bias (committee generosity or tightness) by a senior consultant, referred to as the 'guru.' This 'guru' works out a confidential 'conversion' formula that would allow an organization 'to plug into the Hay data bank' and more equitably compare salaries with those of other Hay clients, many of which are 'well known.'

CAPTURING THE INTEREST OF POLITICIANS

When the researcher asked MacRae for his impression of the politicians' reaction to the presentation, he said that 'the politicians didn't really understand it, but they thought it made good sense' and went on to say that

in a way I was a little bit puzzled with their reaction. They were given a half-day presentation on the system ... what it was plus how it worked ... and they were given some papers on it. But when I talked to them about it, they didn't seem to know what was going on. When I told them that we might have trouble with specific accountabilities ... it appeared that they weren't even aware that this was one of the three factors. They just kept talking in generalities ... like, we need a system and Hay is the system we need. In the end I felt a little bit pissed off. It was like telling me I didn't have a system.

It was pointed out to the researcher by the new director of pay that the politicians of Atlantis were less interested in the technical needs of the pay division than in adopting a system that was already being used by so many other well-known organizations.

The desire to bring 'rational' management techniques to bear upon the civil service generated an interest in job evaluation. Although they 'knew' that pay problems existed, the politicians, with their vastly varying backgrounds, apparently had a little idea of the specific nature of these problems. This conclusion was confirmed by MacRae, who said that 'all that was ever said ... was that the old system was either out of date, old, or a political smash and grab.' The high status of the organizations listed as Hay clients apparently did much to impress the politicians of Atlantis; especially significant was the recent introduction of the Hay system to the federal government and to three large and wealthy Canadian provincial organizations. Faced with proof of such widespread use of the technique, the government of Atlantis appeared to pay little attention to the complex logic of the actual evaluation criteria described in great detail by the consultant. They seemed more than willing to accept the externally legitimated weights, factors, and rituals at face value. There was never, for instance, any debate about the appropriateness or validity of the 'weights and factors' associated with the system. These were taken as 'givens' and as constituting part of reality.

MacRae told the researcher that the Cabinet Committee for Efficiency was attracted to the notion of using the same pay-related language as that employed in other larger organizations. As a matter of fact, MacRae indicated that he had told Burr to 'play up the idea that other provinces were using this plan so that the politicians would go for it.' Indeed, much of the Hay 'sales pitch' is directed at stressing the idea that other progressive organizations (e.g., those belonging to 'Fortune 500') use the system. It could be argued that the Hay firm itself builds a logic of 'conspicuous consumption' into its sales pitch.

From the complexity of the technique as demonstrated by the consultant, not only did 'job evaluation,' as the politicians knew it, provide the scientificity and objectivity that the government appeared to need, but it also appeared to act as a rite of passage into an élite club of successful and, to all intents and purposes, well-managed organizations. The Hay consultant appeared to recognize the needs of a new government eager to be seen to be efficient. By emphasizing the popularity of this 'rational' means of determining the value of jobs, the consultant reinforced the government's stated objective of efficiency, without overlooking its hidden need for recognition, achievement of 'observable' results, affiliation with status, and, because of the organization's political dimension, low risk.

Conclusions

This chapter has led us to question whether the expensive Hay job evaluation package received cabinet approval in Atlantis because of the politicians' interest in eliminating classification 'problems' (of which political intervention was, and still is, a prime example) or because the technique appeared to provide Atlantis with a modern management technique that was already being used by many successful and well-known organizations.

Despite this question, it must be recognized that certain 'real problems' were identified with old salary practices by the efficiency group. The lack of rules and procedures was found to have permitted numerous anomalies to creep into the system over the years. Existing practices were criticized as being 'ad hoc' and 'personality based.' The traditional salary survey (conducted every two years) was proclaimed 'narrow and unsystematic.' Because the steps or increments in the pay ranges had lost their incentive value, there was no way of rewarding performance. Job descriptions were outdated, and their format was dismissed as 'merely a list of duties,' of little service to either job classification or any other human-resource endeavors. As well as promising a sound pay structure, the introduction of a formal job evaluation plan was meant to form the basis of a number of 'desirable' by-products, such as human resource forecasting and organization development.

For rational-minded consultants charged with the task of making rational recommendations to the Cabinet Committee for Efficiency, it was necessary to criticize existing practices, and, it might be said, conditions in the classification division proved an ideal target. As Trice and Beyer (1984: 659) point out, 'consultants' status as outsiders and whatever credentials they possess symbolize their supposed objectivity; their activities actually are rituals designed to produce a needed artifact – a report "that demonstrates to all concerned the error of the decisions that were made" (Pfeffer 1981b: 216).' Like many other organizations before it, Atlantis was engaged in an activity designed to accomplish the extraordinary task of mediating between internal equity within the organization and external competitiveness. It is suggested here that the pay-related problems that were found to exist in Atlantis could be found, in varying degrees, in almost any organization, whether in the public or the private sector.

Atlantis was not unusual in its reasons for adopting a job evaluation plan. Many similar reasons have long been cited by organizations over the years. As discussed in chapter 3, there were many instances of organizations wishing, among other things, to 'rationalize' the pay structure. More recently, various studies and surveys have started to ask why organizations use formal job evaluation. Thomason (1968: 25), for instance, names some practical reasons that have been given by 'managers and others' for introducing a job evaluation program: 1 / it 'replaces a chaotic jungle of anomalies produced by haggling in the market with a rationally-derived structure based on job content' and 2 / it 'yields a structure which is more equitable – at least on the assumption that rewards for work should be equated with job content.'

In another study, Dick (1974: 177) claims that many experts named the following as their basic objectives in using job evaluation:

- To provide a functional internal wage structure to simplify chaotic wage structures due to chance, custom or favoritism.
- To provide an agreed upon method for setting rates for new or changed jobs.
- To provide a means for realistic comparisons between wage and salary rates of employing organizations.
- To provide a basis upon which individual performance can be measured.
- To reduce grievances over wage and salary rates.
- To provide incentive values to employees to strive for higher level jobs.
- To provide documentation for wage negotiations.
- To provide data on job relationships for use in selection, training, transfers and promotions.

Incomes Data Services (1979: 1) reports that the reason cited most frequently by organizations for introducing or amending a job evaluation plan is 'the demand for a rational grading structure.' A 1976 British Institute of Personnel Management study showed that the 'establishment of a fair pay structure was the most commonly stated reason for adopting job evaluation (Thakur and Gill 1976). Again, similar reasons were cited by the British Institute of Management (BIM). In 1979, the BIM conducted a survey of 236 organizations, and found that 151 were using job evaluation. Those companies using job evaluation were asked to state the 'intended objectives' of their scheme. The most common replies were (in order of frequency): the establishment of a fair and equitable pay structure, the provision of an objective and consistent method of grading jobs, and the more effective implementation of personnel (Bradley 1979).

Atlantis was not alone in its quandary. It would appear that many organizations feel anxious about not having what would be considered (by efficiency consultants, for example) to be an orderly, systematic structure of jobs and pay rates. The absence of such a structure might be said to result in such characteristic symptoms as those found in Atlantis: pay inequities, haggling over rates, unreliable survey data, and so on. The tremendous growth in the use of job evaluation suggests that organizations have become uneasy with informal means of assigning pay rates to jobs. The introduction of a formal job evaluation plan, particularly that of the widely accepted Hay plan, allowed Atlantis to believe (as did the many organizations mentioned above) that a more systematic and rule-based means of assigning pay rates would be not only more equitable but also more manageable.

How can we not believe what so many appear to believe? The job evaluation literature is uncritical of the technique and takes many conclusions for granted. Although certain political and symbolic functions of job evaluation have been signalled in this chapter, a fuller discussion of these is provided in Part III. The remainder of this case-study is devoted to finding out what job evaluation really does, at least in one organization. I begin with an analysis of the first phase of the process, the 'job description' writing phase.

5 Preparing for a 'Rational' System: *Job-Description Writing and Employee Socialization*

A largely new pay-division staff (of which the researcher was a member) conducted briefing sessions throughout Atlantis for the purposes of explaining the objectives of the job-evaluation project and teaching employees how to write a job description in the required Hay format.

This chapter demonstrates the tremendous efforts that went into the job-description writing process in Atlantis. Great emphasis was placed upon the need for 1,200 job holders to write their job descriptions in a new 'results-oriented' format that would permit the evaluation committee to gain a far better understanding of their jobs than they would have under the existing 'list of duties' type of job description.

In chapter 6 it will be seen how these job descriptions were actually used, and sometimes misused, by the members of the evaluation committees. The job-description writing process was by no means, however, a futile exercise. Other meanings surface throughout the case-study to demonstrate the hidden value of drawing employees into the language of their own evaluation.

Reorganizing the Central Personnel Agency

Following the efficiency committee's decision to adopt the Hay Guide Chart Profile method of job evaluation, the premier called together all the deputy ministers of Atlantis to inform them of this decision. At this session, the Hay consultant gave another presentation and the premier explained to the deputies the extent of participation that would be required of them (among other things, they were to make up the benchmark evaluation committees). The deputies were also informed that all civil-service supervisory, management, and professional employees would be writing their job descriptions under the new Hay format.

In between the premier's announcement to the deputy ministers and the first official step of the project, that is, the writing of job descriptions, the staff reorganization recommended by the efficiency group was being carried out at the central personnel agency.

It will be remembered that the report submitted to the Cabinet Committee for Efficiency had not only recommended the introduction of formal job evaluation but also indicated that there was not sufficient skill, competence, or credibility within the Civil Service Commission to carry out a project of this scale, even with the help of a purchased plan such as that of Hay Associates.

The investigation carried out on the Civil Service Commission was accorded the same profile and ceremonial status as the earlier study of overall government efficiency. The review of this department received considerable publicity both within and outside the government, largely because of the high profile of the Civil Service Commission vis-à-vis all government departments and the general public.

Over that four- to six-month period, the division that suffered the most anxiety and the greatest loss of jobs was, as expected, the job 'classification' division. Although the existing deputy minister of the Civil Service Commission was relieved of his duties, the other three divisions reporting to the deputy minister, that is, 'recruitment and training,' 'industrial relations,' and 'payroll,' basically remained intact.

One of the many changes made in the classification division was to rename it 'pay division.' Although this painful reorganization, which involved several sackings and demotions, was officially geared to improving the acceptability and the credibility of the division that would be responsible for selling and administering the new plan, it also provided a highly visible message to all client departments that the government meant 'business.' In symbolic terms, the job-classification division provided the sacrificial lamb for the new efficient order.

Training the Trainers

Unless there are very few jobs to be evaluated, it is customary for organizations using the Hay plan to have employees write their own job description under the guidance of trained internal staff. Before becoming the custodians and disseminators of the Hay system, the members of the pay division themselves needed to learn the required language and procedures. The Hay consultant therefore conducted a two-day training seminar on how to write a job description in the Hay format. This seminar, attended by the director, the manager, and the four pay analysts from the pay division, was devoted to the need for and value of well-written job descriptions. The rationale for the particularly 'rigorous and demanding' job-description format devised by Hay was linked to the evaluators' need for this particular information in this particular format when measuring each job against the multidimensional guide charts.

PROJECT OBJECTIVES

Once the director, manager, and four analysts had written the 'perfect' job description and completed their training, they formed teams and held briefing sessions across the province to explain the objectives of the project to employees and to describe what individuals would be required to do in terms of preparing their new job descriptions. Although all affected employees had received a brief memo announcing the project, along with a manual entitled *How to Write Your Own*, the early briefing sessions were to be attended only by those employees whose jobs had been selected as benchmarks.

The benchmark jobs had been chosen in private meetings of the Hay consultant, the director of pay, and each deputy minister. The consultant explained that a number of jobs should be selected (ten to twenty per department, depending on size) that could be seen as 'benchmark,' that is, typical or representative of jobs across government. These jobs were to have well-defined responsibilities and already be 'correctly' paid. Ideally, benchmarks were to be well-established jobs, of which there would not be either an oversupply or an undersupply on the job market.

Because the briefing sessions conducted by the pay division represented the first face-to-face contact with employees about the project, an attempt was made to allay some of the expected employee fears and suspicions. Pay division staff tried to convince employees that changing to a formal system of job evaluation would eliminate existing pay inequities across Atlantis and result in more rational and objective pay structures. Existing 'classification' practices were discredited as 'arbitrary' and 'outdated'; the names of large, prestigious Hay clients were listed; and the objectives of the project – internal equity, external competitiveness, and pay for performance – were specified:

Internal Equity
To develop a sound and equitable system of classification of all management and professional jobs (non bargaining).

External Competitiveness
To establish externally competitive levels of remuneration to attract and retain qualified and competent personnel throughout the civil service.

(Eventually) Return on Salary Investment
To ensure that staff are rewarded at levels in their salary range consistent with their overall performance. (displayed on a view-graph)

Employees were also presented with overhead-projected slides of the actual 'custom-made for Atlantis' guide charts that would be used to determine the value of their jobs ('custom made' did not mean much more than the replacement of 'company' with 'government'). As discussed in chapter 4, guide charts are the three evaluation sheets describing the breakdown of factors, weights, and assigned point values. Copies of the three guide charts were *not* distributed to employees, and the audio-visual presentation was the only (official) time that employees were to view the criteria and scoring method to be used in grading their jobs.

It was explained that three evaluation committees had been formed to evaluate approximately 230 benchmark jobs held by some 350 employees. These committees were to be composed entirely of deputy ministers. The non-benchmark jobs were to be evaluated at a later date, within departments, by two, three, or four senior administrators, using the evaluations obtained from the benchmark jobs as points of reference. (As the project developed, it somehow began to be perceived in the organization that these benchmark jobs were more important than the non-benchmarks, that is, that there was an 'élite' group of 350 employees selected to be evaluated before the remaining 850 employees.)

Employees were also told about the various cross-checks built into the plan, namely, the 'profile,' the 'sore thumb,' and the eventual out-of-province 'correlation' that would be carried out on the point scores obtained in the evaluation committees. The pay division also gave reasons for adopting the Hay Guide Chart Profile method over any other method of job evaluation. These reasons were documented in a pamphlet prepared by the pay division and the Atlantis public-relations agency entitled, *An Introduction to the New Management Compensation Program*:

It's been more than 20 years since the existing classification system for government managerial staff and non-bargaining professionals was reviewed. During that time, numerous anomalies have crept into the system. Until now, there was also no effective way to reward merit or to provide incentives to retain or attract competent employees. Now, a new management compensation program is being introduced which deals with these problems by ensuring internal equity, external competitiveness, and salary based on performance.

This program is based on the *Hay* system of job evaluation – one which has proven valuable in the private and public sectors. Hay Associates are leading consultants in management compensation and have over 300 major organizations in Canada as clients. In recent years, they have worked with various Canadian provincial governments and with the federal government. The Hay system provides a standard means of classifying positions (ensuring internal equity). It also provides access to information on compensation programs of any other group using the system (making it easy to determine current pay practices of other potential, comparative employers.

Finally, before employees were trained in job-description writing, they were assured that they would not lose money as a result of any possible downgrading, although they were told that the precise way in which the government would handle 'overgraded' jobs had not been fully finalized. Although their rates of pay were 'protected,' so to speak, it was evident at the training sessions that the majority of employees viewed the undertaking as a threat. Suspicions manifested themselves in the often-asked question: 'What are you guys really up to with all this stuff?'

HOW TO WRITE A JOB DESCRIPTION

A substantial literature exists describing the importance of job descriptions vis-à-vis the job evaluation process (e.g., International

Labour Office 1960; Thomason 1975; Bartley 1981). There is probably not a personnel-management book or article available on job evaluation that does not show reverence for the job description. Roeber (1975), for instance, emphasizes the point that the process of working up a job description and assessing it gives a rational basis for relating work to reward. 'No single instrument is as important to effective wage and salary administration as the job description' (Brandt 1984: 2/1). 'Job descriptions are crucial to evaluation' (Torrington and Hall 1987: 519).

The system of job evaluation selected by the government of Atlantis also stressed the importance of job descriptions. These were to be prepared in a prescribed format, in sufficient detail to provide a 'factual' basis for the evaluation of any job against the three factors of Know-How, Problem Solving, and Accountability. Subsequently, it will be revealed that this is a core ritual of job evaluation.

The job-description manual distributed to Atlantis employees makes the following statement: 'A good position description is the foundation of the classification program being developed. It permits a clear evaluation by the Evaluation Committee of the scope and responsibility of an employee's job. This leads to the establishment of a classification level and a salary range for the employee' (*How to Write Your Own* 1980:). This manual also claims that there are certain other advantages to a good job description: 'The description clarifies that which you are paid to accomplish. It is a basis of agreement between you and your superior about work goals and objectives. It is a means of communication for improved work planning and feedback. It gives to a reader who may not be familiar with your job, a clear and understandable picture of the job's nature and scope' (ibid: 2). Such theories need to be tested against real job-evaluation experience.

When the job-description training part of the presentation began, the pay division representatives first criticized the old job-description format, in the language of the efficiency consultants, as 'merely a shopping list of duties and functions,' compared to the new 'results-oriented' format. The 'old' job-description form, which had been rejected by the efficiency consultants and was now being replaced, is depicted in figure 5.

The 'old' form was usually completed, in point form, either by the employee or by his or her supervisor. The new job descriptions were to be written in full-sentence form by the employee. The pay analyst listed the main headings of the new job-description format on a blackboard and carefully described how to respond to the requests for information under each heading. An outline of the new job-description form is reproduced in figure 6.

As can be seen from figure 6, the job outline has five major components. The resulting job description was not to exceed three written pages (exclusive of the organization chart). The longest part of the job description is the section entitled 'Nature and Scope,' usually taking up about one and a half to two pages. Although the job-description headings did not match those used on the guide charts, it was explained to employees that the information that they would provide in the job description related closely to the factors and weights used by the evaluators.

Employees were told that each of them would have a scheduled meeting with the pay analyst assigned to their department to ensure some consistency of quality in job descriptions. It was recognized that not all employees had the same writing abilities, so pay analysts had been assigned to try to minimize these differences before the approved job descriptions were forwarded to the committee for evaluation. At the end of each briefing session (all of which were held over the period of a year), individuals were asked to return to their departments and begin the preparation of their job description.

THE WRITING PROCESS

That part of the job-evaluation project that was most detailed and required the most person-hours was the writing of job descriptions by each of the 1,200 employees (because some job titles applied to more than one employee, either each individual wrote a description of the job and the 'best' one was submitted or employees with the same job collaborated to develop a 'model' job description).

Employees appeared to experience enormous difficulty writing their job descriptions to the required format. On average, the four analysts estimated that only about 5 per cent of all benchmark and non-benchmark job descriptions written did not require some revision. The balance required at least one 'extra' session, in addition to the first planned session with the analyst. Of these, the analysts estimated that about 50 per cent required a total of three or four sessions. Although the Hay consultant had warned that it would take approximately twenty hours to write a job description under this format, and the pay division staff had, in turn, warned the employees, the

FIGURE 5: Format of 'old' job-description form used by Government of Atlantis

Form CSC 10 A

TO BE COMPLETED IN QUINTUPLICATE
WITH ORIGINAL AND THREE COPIES TO
BE FORWARDED TO THE CIVIL SERVICE
COMMISSION

Province of Atlantis

POSITION SPECIFICATION

Position Title	Alternate/Recommended Title		No. of employees
Department	Division	Section	Location

Position Scope

List of duties*

Approximate
percentage of
total time

Lease head up, Daily Periodic or Occasional   ALL FORMS ARE TO BE SIGNED & DATED.

This specification represents a reasonable and accurate statement of the current possition requirments.

This specification was prepared in consultation with the employee(s) Yes ☐   No ☐

Specification Prepared By: Specification Approved By:

.... Dept. Official .... Deputy Head ....

FIGURE 5 *(continued)*

Factors

Alternate headings to be followed where applicable

Minimum education requirements

Special knowledge and skills required or manual skill required

---

Nature & amount of experience required

Judgement and initiative required

Type and level of supervision exercised

Responsibility for decisions affecting costs or responsibility for tools, equipment and materials

(a) Direct responsibility

(b) Indirect responsibility

Nature and extent of contacts or responsibility for safety of others

---

Physical demand

Mental and visual demand

Working environment

Unavoidable hazards

Additional information

FIGURE 6
The 'new' job-description format

SKELETON OUTLINE – POSITION DESCRIPTION

POSITION:

INCUMBENT:

DEPARTMENT:

DIVISION:

LOCATION:

DATE:

GENERAL ACCOUNTABILITY
This position is accountable for _____

STRUCTURE
1 Reports to _____
2 Others reporting to the same superior.
3 Capsule description of each position reporting to you,
  outlining primary purpose and number of staff.

NATURE AND SCOPE
1 Environment paragraph.
2 Functions performed by yourself personally.
3 Major challenges faced.
4 Controls on freedom to act and problem-solving.
5 Contacts inside and outside the government.
6 Any additional pertinent information.

DIMENSIONS (examples)
Number of people
Budget – annual, approximate operating and capital figures shown separately.
Other – annual, approximate.

SPECIFICATION ACCOUNTABILITIES
Usually 4 to 7 statements describing the key result areas of your job. Attempt to list them in order of importance as you see them.

Approved by:

Incumbent _____   Date _____

Supervisor _____   Date _____

Deputy
Minister _____   Date _____

analysts found that, in the end, individuals had spent much longer than that. One analyst claimed that 'some employees simply cleared their desks and spent literally weeks working on their job descriptions. I think their whole work lives were consumed with it. It was like they had nothing else to do at all. It was like their lives depended on it' (analyst interview). My own experiences as 'analyst' indicated a similar slavish attention to the process.

The greatest difficulty employees seemed to have in writing up their job descriptions was in categorizing their jobs under the specific headings required by the Hay format (according to the shared assessment of four analysts). Rather than thinking and writing in terms of 'accountabilities' and 'challenges,' employees were told, they were reverting to the previous style of listing duties. Moreover, it was not uncommon for the analysts to encounter job descriptions that were as long as twenty pages, and these required considerable effort, on the part of both analyst and employee, to reduce to the required three pages. Fearing a 'downgrading' or just trying to maximize opportunities to score the highest possible points for their jobs, employees were often reluctant to leave out any task, however menial. The propensity to write more than was specified came to be known by the analysts as the 'Tolstoy Syndrome.'

There also appeared to be a propensity among employees to write within the 'language of Hay' in the belief that using or 'mimicking' that language would reflect well on their evaluation. Although the guide charts were shown to employees only once per training session, the word passed quickly from one employee group to another to bring a pen and paper to the briefing and to record as many of the evaluation criteria as possible. Accumulated 'bits' of guide charts were exchanged with as much seriousness as trading cards of sports heroes in childhood with the similar aim of collecting a reasonable 'whole.' In one department, a group of engineers even sought out library books on the subject, and distributed copies of various related articles among other engineers. One employee reported to me that 'it turned out to be a bit of a dark comedy. We used to pass our jobs descriptions back and forth to each other ... each one of us trying to fit in the biggest words. One fellow got all the job factors into one sentence. We gave him a prize at the end ... a paper airplane made out of Hay job description paper. It wasn't funny, our job was at stake.' One of the analysts claimed that she was aware of 'at least three informal groups which met after work to try to figure the system out and work up the best possible job descriptions.' Another analyst claimed that some groups 'were meeting in local bars. If I came in they would call me over and try to pump me.' An employee reported that 'our lunch-hour cribbage game was turned into a Hay gab fest. It was all Hay, Hay, Hay.'

The job-description writing exercise was far from light-hearted. Indeed, the whole experience appeared to be met with great trepidation and fear. One of the analysts told me: 'personally, I often found the whole experience quite embarrassing. It was embarrassing because men and women twice my age and experience were trembling when they came to see me. It was like I was a Doctor with a last-known remedy. I didn't like their nervousness.' Another analyst put it in a different way: 'it was like the first time I got any respect around here. Suddenly I had power where I had none. To tell you the truth I kind of liked it. For once people were looking up to me.'

Subsequent analysis of the job descriptions revealed startling variations in writing skills among individuals and among departments. Some departments, such as Economic Development and Education, accustomed by the nature of their work to producing clear and concise reports, showed great talent in the art of job-description writing. Others, such as Lands and Forests or Agriculture, were less accustomed to expressing abstractions and showed great difficulty with the concepts and language required. Among those at supervisory levels in the organization, many had come from the ranks of manual labour (e.g., lumberjacks, farmhands, and maintenance workers) and, sadly, some were discovered to be unable to read or write at all. The assistance provided by the analysts was, in large part, meant to reduce any such variations in individual writing capability.

Complications soon arose over the actual advantages of having been assigned one particular pay analyst over another. The 'jungle telegraph,' as it was called, began to declare the energy and writing capabilities of two of the four analysts to be 'superior' to the services provided by the others, creating discontent and petty jealousies in a number of quarters. One deputy minister openly admitted that 'there were some analysts who were better than others. I told MacRae that I didn't have one of those who did ... and I didn't want my employees' descriptions to suffer. He told me I couldn't change analysts.' Nevertheless, and despite the great frustration expressed by employees during rewrites, most were very eager to accept any advice given by the analysts, in the belief that the analysts 'knew what the committee would be looking for.'

In a review of the job descriptions, it was common to find that employees still mentioned their formal qualifications, despite having been told not to include details of formal education unless it had direct applications in the job, as, for example, in the case of medical doctors. Many were reluctant to remove any such data. A few managed to get their educational accomplishments across, not in the body of the job description, but in the preliminary material, with their names, (e.g., 'John Doe, BA').

Another problem commonly encountered was that of 'freezing' jobs in time. One employee noted, for example:

As you may recall, the Deputy Minister during the time of our Department's involvement had just returned from an extended sick leave and he was torn between the desirability for a 'flatter' structure of organization and the need for someone with authority and responsibility for day to day operations to relieve him so that he could spend his time on policy and other considerations suitable to the Deputy's position. As a result, all job descriptions, as written at that time did not clearly define responsibilities.

A subsequent reorganization followed by a later reassignment of responsibilities has resulted in a significant disparity (in my favour) between myself and other directors. This may not be a fault of the Hay system but is a recognition of practical realities that time changes all things. (From employee questionnaire)

Having finally written and rewritten their job description to the satisfaction of the pay analyst (at least in terms of format), some employees then encountered problems in gaining their superior's approval of the job description. New job descriptions, like the old, required the signature of the incumbent and any superiors, up to and including the deputy minister.

To say the least, this particular 'approval' stage was characterized by a considerable amount of fighting and squabbling over precisely who did what. Earlier attempts to include as many responsibilities as possible had led, in certain cases, to encroachment upon the job territory of others. This problem was particularly acute in director/ assistant director, manager/assistant manager, supervisor/assistant supervisor situations, although there were even some battles between directors and their deputy minister. Often superiors re-claimed responsibilities that had, over time, fallen to subordinates. One employee claimed, for instance, that, 'for the first time in my job, my boss wanted all his jobs back. He shoves all his work on me so he can spend more time up the Valley at his hobby farm. As soon as we had to do our job descriptions he tells me that all my jobs were his jobs. What did he do ... just lend me these jobs? I got burned because he's still up the Valley and I'm still working his job. That's the thanks you get.' Another employee expressed similar sentiments: 'We don't work as individuals around here ... we help each other out. That's the way we do things in these parts. We're a friendly bunch. Telling us to pick out who did what was a stupid thing. I didn't want to steal anyone else's job. You just can't say who does what around here.'

Yet another employee who had been asked to delete some responsibility from his job description felt angered by this, claiming that it was as though money were being taken straight out of his pocket. The pay analysts indicated that some employees told them that they would now 'work to rule,' but since so many employees received hefty increases as a result of the project, it is hard to know how long these feelings lasted.

The responsibility-overlap problem was compounded by the fact that it was difficult for individuals working in a government organization to fill in the job-description section entitled 'Freedom to Act.' Unlike much of private industry, a bureaucratic government organization is characterized by extensive apparatus of approval forms and processes that cover anything from the purchase of a pocket calculator to deciding the fate of a bankrupt fish-processing company.

In this area, even more emphasis was placed upon the language used to describe an activity. Superiors and subordinates each struggled to describe the precise impact that they had upon the same activity. Whenever the pay analysts detected a duplication of function between jobs they merely pointed it out to the employees concerned. The Civil Service Commission did not become involved in the various 'tugs of war' that occurred over specific job content. It was held that this was a matter for departments themselves to resolve. Of the nineteen deputy ministers interviewed by the researcher a couple of years after the project, ten indicated that they had known of, or were required to arbitrate in, cases of job overlap in their departments. In the researcher's questionnaire for those in benchmark jobs, 28 per cent of respondents said that there was an overlap in responsibility between their job and that of a superior or a subordinate.

Likewise, departments had to deal themselves with deliberate attempts at exaggeration or 'empire building' on the part of job-description writers. Although the analyst was in a unique position to detect job descriptions that might have strayed beyond the limits of reality, the departments themselves had to be relied upon to eliminate misleading claims.

One by one, the job descriptions were signed by the incumbents and made their way upwards through the required approval processes, until all had reached the deputy minister's office. The extent to which the job descriptions were scrutinized by deputy ministers varied from department to department, according to a variety of factors (interview with director of pay). Some deputy ministers claimed to have received the job descriptions 'very late in the game' and hadn't had time to go over them closely. In some cases, the deputy minister's existing knowledge of the department and sense of confidence in relaying (to other deputy ministers on the evaluation committee) what his or her employees were actually doing were factors. One long-standing deputy minister declared: 'What do I want to read through all that garbage for? I know what my people do!'

Each deputy's overall interest in the job-evaluation project also affected the amount of time spent on the job descriptions (interview with director of pay). Some deputies spent a great deal of time poring over the details of each job description, others gave the descriptions only a cursory look while signing them. Some conducted 'spot-checks,' while others took the time to read only those descriptions submitted by a much-liked (to make sure that the description did justice) or a much-disliked employee (to make sure that the individual had not exaggerated his or her importance or 'overwritten').

One employee claimed that his job description had been sent back to him from the deputy minister's office with the following words scrawled across it: 'I didn't know that God himself worked in my department!' In another department the deputy minister made his own personal changes to job descriptions (making deletions and additions as he saw fit) and had these changes grafted onto the signed job descriptions by his secretary before forwarding the stack of job descriptions to the Civil Service Commission for photocopying for the evaluation committee. Many months after the evaluations (and regardless of how the employees had fared under the evaluation), employees were furious to discover this 'tampering,' and many telephoned their pay analyst to report this departure from the rules (based on evidence from the department to which the researcher had previously been assigned). The analyst could only 'sympathize,' claiming that the deputy had ultimate responsibility for departmental activities.

It was through the approval process that the Civil Service Commission tried to make certain the deputy ministers were in agreement with the content of the job descriptions that they would shortly be presenting to other deputies in the evaluation committees.

Conclusions

Although the job-description-writing phase of the project was carried out in stages, it represented a major effort in terms of time and commitment from various levels of the organization. It will be seen later that the concern of employees about using just the right words and in rewriting their job descriptions over and over played an important part in drawing them into the language of their own evaluations, even if this language was sometimes used by employees to challenge or exploit the system. It is, in fact, suggested that, by engaging in the job-description-writing process, employees signed an agreement binding them to the 'logic' of the process. In trying to learn the new language, employees conspired to retrieve, collate, and exchange information, and used the pay analysts as official interpreters. It will be argued that, at this level, the job-description process plays its greatest role, and not at the level of its stated objective of providing the 'factual basis' for the evaluation of jobs. The following chapters reveal why.

6 Evaluating the Jobs:
The Objective of Internal Equity

A review of the conventional personnel-management literature reveals two main reasons for using an evaluation 'committee' when installing and/or maintaining a job evaluation plan. First, a committee brings to bear the points of view of several people who are familiar with the organization and the jobs in question; second using a committee can help to ensure greater acceptance by employees of the results of the job evaluation (e.g., Dessler and Duffy 1984).

The job evaluation plan selected by the government of Atlantis also points to the importance of evaluating jobs by committee:

Although it is possible that a skilled specialist in the personnel department could make these evaluations, the results would inevitably be viewed with some reservations. With an evaluation committee there is a greater assurance that each position has an advocate for its day in court, and that all facets of the position receive thorough examination. The whole process is understood better by managers other than those in the personnel function and can gain acceptance more easily ...

The vast majority of organizations using the Hay Guide Chart Profile method do utilize evaluation committees and this is an important ingredient leading to credibility and acceptability. (Atlantis/Hay *Position Evaluation Manual*, 1980: 45)

The evaluation of jobs by committee certainly does bring the background and experience of many to bear on the evaluations and, as later chapters reveal, it can provide the impression that the plan is endorsed by a variety of organizational members (in this case, top executives). This chapter, however, points to other important activities that were taking place through the use of evaluation committees. One was the socialization (through language and culture) of people who were going to play a major part in the maintenance of the plan. Another was the provision of a medium through which important political process takes place. Deputy ministers sought to secure (through whatever means) a higher or lower score of jobs if they considered that a job in their department was not well placed in relation to other evaluated jobs. Much 'haggling and trading' went on over a one- or two-step difference in scores. Political process had, in other words, not gone away; it simply lay hidden behind the technical jargon of the new system. While one or two steps seemed to make all the difference at the time, it turned out to make very little difference in the long run.

It is argued that job evaluation committees provide a powerful political arena, which allows the evaluators to believe that they are having significant effect on how the organization will look. In Atlantis the use of evaluation committees allowed deputy ministers to believe that they could organize their own departments to look the way they wanted them to, that they could indeed gain control of the system. In this case, 'control' meant using the Hay plan to maintain the 'status quo' rather than to tackle the 'internal relativity problem' identified by the efficiency consultants.

Three committees of deputy ministers met over the period of a year and a half to measure the value of 230 'benchmark' jobs (representing approximately 350 employees). This chapter describes what went on behind the closed doors of these evaluation committees.

Why Evaluation Committees?

The early decision to use the twenty-one deputy ministers as members of the benchmark-evaluation committees satisfied the Hay consultant's criteria for choosing evaluators. Ideally, they were to be: 1 / from diverse line and staff departments; 2 / of roughly equivalent level within the organization; 3 / holding positions somewhat higher than those to be evaluated; and 4 / relatively familiar with the operation of the organization and its values.

How many evaluators are needed to produce 'reliable' ratings? There is no concensus in the job evaluation literature on the ideal number. Thomason (1968: 36) finds that 'experience on this varies but the committee is usually quite small – up to about half a dozen.'

Belcher (1974: 95) claims that 'job evaluation committees should be kept small to facilitate decision making – five members may be optimal, ten too many.'

Atlantis chose to have seven evaluators per committee. This number was not particularly unusual. The twenty-one deputy ministers were allocated to three 'benchmark' evaluation committees, each consisting of seven members, with the purpose of evaluating approximately 230 jobs (held by approximately 350 individuals). The pay division had divided the deputy ministers up into three committees for the purpose of convenience and efficiency. By setting up three committees (instead of one large committee of twenty-one deputy ministers), person-hours could be minimized, while still maintaining a broadly representative sample of Atlantis departments on each committee.

Each committee was called upon to meet for two days, Wednesdays and Thursdays, every other week, for a six-month period. (The non-benchmark jobs were to be graded later, by committees of senior administrators from each department.)

TRAINING THE COMMITTEES: THE RULES OF THE GAME

MacRae (the new director of pay) informed the researcher that a lot of care had gone into presenting the job evaluation plan to deputy ministers. Not only were they required to commit considerable time and effort to the evaluation of jobs, but their support was considered to be crucial to the installation and maintenance of the plan.

At the first presentation given by the Hay consultant to the deputy ministers, it was stressed that job evaluation would not strip this senior executive group of their power to influence gradings. They were asked to view themselves as 'key evaluators' who would be in possession of the factual data about how the plan operated. Job evaluation was presented as a way of helping them in that it would provide benefit of the pooled judgment of a competent group of peers. It was also suggested that new 'rational' evaluation criteria would make the well-known power struggles between deputy ministers and the Civil Service Commission a thing of the past.

The same project objectives were stated in all Atlantis presentations: the development of a pay structure that provided internal equity, external competitiveness, and pay for performance. According to

MacRae, this last objective most interested the deputy ministers and 'sold' them on the job evaluation project (no formal system of performance appraisal was in effect in Atlantis).

Several months after this initial presentation, the first evaluation committee (A) was called together. Seven deputy ministers gathered to evaluate approximately one hundred jobs, under the guidance of the Hay consultant. The role of this consultant has been described by a general partner of the Hay Group as follows: 'The benchmark evaluation committee is led by a Hay consultant who acts as a combination teacher and coach. Initially, the consultant teaches the methodology in a learn-by-doing framework, then fades back as coach as the committee develops proficiency' (Bellak 1984: 15/8). Pay division staff were present on the 'side lines' to act as a general resource at meetings and to record the details of the point score allocated to each job.

The Hay consultant devoted the first meeting of committee A to a detailed explanation of the rules of evaluation. The three guide charts – Know-How, Problem Solving, and Accountability – were distributed to participants (for reference see figures 2, 3, and 4, in chapter 4) along with a manual (Atlantis/Hay *Position Evaluation Manual*) that explained how to use these charts to score the jobs. The consultant also explained the cross-checking methods of 'profiling,' 'sore thumbing,' and 'correlation' (for correlation reference see appendix B).

The consultant pointed out that it was indeed possible to obtain more than one correct score, but that consensus still had to be reached by committee members within the discipline of the guide charts.

Throughout the training of deputy ministers, the consultant made constant reference to the value of the job description. As it states in the Atlantis/Hay *Position Evaluation Manual*, 'a position description becomes the formal device for informing the Evaluation Committee in factual, concise and unambiguous form about the nature of the position: why it exists, what results must be accomplished and how results are achieved' (1980: 4). The objective of the committee was to reach consensus. If consensus could not be reached, the job description was blamed: 'If no consensus can be attained, it usually indicates a deficiency in the position description, i.e., different committee members are getting a different view of the position' (ibid: 45).

Evaluators were instructed to ignore any information outside of that provided in the job description – no additional duties or functions could be added by a deputy minister to sway the committee's evaluation. Furthermore, any claims made in the job description about an individual's accomplishments, such as the knowledge of an additional language, had to be specifically used in the job before they could be taken into consideration in the scoring. Similarly, the committee was warned against being influenced by the mention of formal qualifications, or university degrees, that may have made their way into the job description without being an absolute requirement of the job.

Like any job evaluation committee in any organization, the evaluators in Atlantis were also instructed to overlook any knowledge of the current jobholder's performance, and to assume that all jobs were being performed to 'satisfactory' standards. They were also asked to disregard any knowledge of either the jobholder's relative position in the existing departmental hierarchy or the jobholder's current pay status. Likewise, deputy ministers were told to ignore any market fluctuations taking place in the demand for or supply of a certain job.

The 'pay analysts' whose assigned department was under review had two jobs in the committee. One was to act as 'watchdog' for any statements made in the job description that might have required greater clarification than the deputy was able to give. Although it is common for those in analyst-type jobs to assist evaluation committees, their role is not that of evaluator. As du Pont (1960: 22) points out: 'The analyst should take care not to relate facts to the criteria of the evaluation system ... If, in their final decision, the committee wishes to give away their dowry or rob widows, such is their prerogative. But do not let it result from faulty presentation of facts by the analyst.' The analysts' other job was that of information recorder. The analyst was meant to be recording the committee's stated reasons for choosing each and every dimension of a score, on what was called a 'rationale' sheet. The 'rationale' sheet, part of the Hay evaluation process, was meant to provide records and back-up information to justify or explain why a job had been awarded certain points for each subfactor on the guide charts. Rationale sheets could be used in 'sore thumb' meetings, or, later, as reference points when evaluating new jobs or re-evaluating 'changed' jobs. It will be seen, in chapter 9, that the 'rationale' sheet also allowed the Civil Service Commission to claim that 'documentary evidence' existed to prove exactly why the committee had scored the job in a certain way (these rationales were kept confidential and not shown to employees).

However much care may have been taken in training committee members in the rules of job evaluation, in many instances, as we will see, the rules became a veneer for much the same political activity that informed the old system. The rules of the game either were used to justify action (to make the subjective look objective) or were manipulated and tampered with. As the three committees move through the evaluation of 1,200 jobs, it becomes clear that the various stages of the process permit evaluators to 'use' the system to 'arrange' certain desired scores. It is suggested that this political process is a *necessary* aspect of job evaluation (regardless of the system used), given the context and nature of the decision-making process, namely, its diverse goals, uncertain outcomes, and disagreements over cause-and-effect relationships.

THE EVALUATION: ATTACHING POINTS TO JOBS

After a day spent training the evaluators in the operation of the guide charts, Committee A began evaluating jobs. The deputy minister of Agriculture was asked to make a brief presentation depicting his department's organization chart and describing its major functions. Following this presentation, the pay analyst distributed a copy of the first job description to the deputies seated around the table and to Burr and MacRae, seated at the head of the table.

The seven evaluators were asked by the consultant to study the job description in silence for a few minutes, making sure that everyone had finished reading before asking questions. Any questions that committee members may have had about the job were to be addressed to the deputy minister of the department in question. The job descriptions, about three to four pages in length (not counting the page for the organization chart), were studied for about fifteen minutes (at least in the early days of the three evaluation committees). When the evaluators were satisfied that they had all the information needed to grade the job, each deputy (including the deputy of the department in question) was asked to score the job, writing down the details of the evaluation as it related to each of the dimensions and subdimensions of Know-How, Problem Solving, and Accountability.

While the deputies were rating a job, the consultant and the director of pay were drawing up, in hushed tones, an 'ideal' evaluation for the same job. When all the deputies had indicated that their evaluations were complete, each deputy, in turn, called out the details of his score to the consultant who wrote these on a board, under each committee member's name. To demonstrate the new language in

TABLE 3

Sample scoreboard

	K–H	PS	Acc.	Profile	Total	Consensus
Harold	E113 304	E3 (38%) 115	D3C 115	flat	534	
Arnold	F 13 304	E3 (38%) 115	E3C 132	A1	551	
Brian	E 13 264	E3 (38%) 100	D2P 152	A3	516	?
William	F113 350	E4 (43%) 152	E3C 132	P1	634	
Dack	D113 230	E3 (33%) 76	D3C 115	A3	421	
Drew	F113 400	E3 (38%) 152	D1P 115	P2	667	
Gerrard	E113 304	E3 (38%) 115	E3C 132	A1	551	

SOURCE: Civil Service Commission internal document

which evaluators conversed in these committees, a scoreboard for one of the departmental personnel officers is reproduced in table 3.

When all the scores had been copied onto the board, the consultant asked those individuals who assigned the score of a particular dimension higher or lower than the others to explain or justify his choice of score to the other committee members. In the case shown in table 3, the consultant asked Dack why he scored a personnel officer a 'D' for specialized Know-How. Sometimes many long hours were spent on just one dimension of the evaluation. In these cases, other dimensions sometimes received short shrift, in order to expedite the evaluation of a job.

In the evaluation of this job, as with others, the evaluation quickly slipped into the realm of the political or subjective. Central to much of the evaluation was a 'flip-flop' between the rational and the political; it could be said that this 'flip-flop' pervaded much of the language employed within the committees. I present now, as an artefact, some of the 'language' used by the committee to evaluate this job (language taken from notes for 'rationales'). I also discuss the 'bias' contained within these rationales.

On Know-How

DREW: 'I think I've gone short on this. I don't think F113 is high enough. Four hundred may be high in your minds, but not mine. There's more technical knowledge than you think. You need to understand personnel management and know all the government's policies and procedures. It's not all about making people happy. It's a tough job. I did it once and I know. You're off base here.'

D A C K : 'These guys are paper shufflers. D 113 is high enough for those guys. You could do the job with grade-2 education.'

Bias These two 'rationales' juxtapose seemingly technical consider-ations (knowledge of policies and manuals) with personal biases: specifically the bias of 'past experience' ('I did it once and I know') and the bias of 'education' ('You could do the job with a grade-2 education'). In many cases, it was not uncommon to hear how 'lucky' a department was to have an employee with a Masters' degree or Doctorate carrying out a job (educational bias).

On Problem Solving

D A C K : 'Anyone could do this job. It's a clerk's job. I would have gone lower, but Harold told me I was off. What do they do, anyways? This one says that they do organizational development. What's that, anyways? It's all airy-fairy stuff to me. I do the developing around my department!'

W I L L I A M : 'They may have a book and rules. But I work with him closely. He helps me think. We sit together and, I can tell you, some of the bigger decisions come through him. He advises me.'

Bias In the first of these two quotes, we can see the identification of a 'rational' criterion, i.e., 'organizational development.' This criterion does not, however, stand free and is not untouched by bias. In this case, an apparently rational criterion is interpreted by Dack within a personal frame or bias. 'Organizational development' is 'airy fairy'; this can be said to reflect a 'soft science' versus 'hard science' bias. This bias was reflected in other evaluations. For instance, one em-ployee stated in the questionnaire: 'Deputy Ministers can maybe set the tone for an evaluation by their philosophy, beliefs, mood, etc. The human element enters here and some [deputies] may unfairly be of the opinion that some jobs are much easier or of less importance than others without really understanding. For years, the department of Transportation was considered an engineering department and the Deputy Minister was always an engineer. People in the accounting section had problems obtaining adequate classifications' (employee written response to question 9).

The second quote once again juxtaposes (supposedly) rational criteria ('a book and rules') with personal-political criteria ('he' helps 'me' think). In this case the 'individual' intrudes into the job; the individual is being evaluated, and not the job. In the 'political' sense, the 'individual' helps the deputy (and therefore needs to be helped).

On Accountability

H A R O L D : 'These guys shake out on the low end of my chart. Anyways the CSC [Civil Service Commission] tells them what to do. Plus, we can't have him having more freedom to act than his boss.'

D R E W : 'They have freedom. I know. I did it.'

Bias In the first quote we see evidence of the bias of 'hierarchy.' Accountability is defined by direct reference to the (existing) hierarchy itself. The 'mental map' used to define accountability is that carried around with the deputies on a daily basis – namely, the existing organization chart. Moreover, the idea that a subordinate 'can't have ... more freedom than ... his boss' is also highlighted (this point was made many times by the consultant). The basic point observed here is that it is impossible to have more freedom to act than one's own superiors. Organizational layers can be said to sustained and reproduced through such logic (through a bias of existing hierarchy).

In the second quote, we once again have the bias of 'having been there.' It should, perhaps, not be surprising that the highest score for this personnel position was given by 'Drew' who had a past history in personnel management.

The deputies appeared to be quite fascinated to hear how their colleagues in other departments viewed the same or similar positions that existed in their own departments. In this evaluation of personnel officers, for instance, one deputy claimed, 'Mine is definitely nothing more than a man-secretary – and a stupid one at that!' Another deputy explained how his personnel manager 'is brought into all senior departmental meetings and his advice is treated with great respect by the directors and the rest of the staff.' Some went into great detail about all the 'human relations' activities carried out by their personnel officer, to the dismay of other deputies, e.g., 'Does your guy *really* do manpower planning? Jeez, our guy wouldn't know what it was!'

The objective of creating order and grade standardization for the same jobs being performed in different government departments became more difficult than the efficiency consultants could have imagined when they originally recommended that job evaluation be introduced to 'eliminate pay anomalies.' The rational objective stated that there should be standardization.

In an attempt to create order where it did not exist before, Burr tried to encourage the deputy ministers to have a common job description drawn up for the twenty-one personnel-officer positions across the different departments. Burr claimed that performance appraisal and training seminars could be used to bring the less competent personnel officers up to a standard level of 'professionalism.' The way it stood, some were clerks and others were senior administrators.

The evaluation committees were, however, reluctant to have the status of their personnel officers either raised or lowered by any such attempts at standardization. Deputy ministers indicated that they could clearly see the point that Burr was trying to make – that is, that job evaluation had the power to create order and make things clear-cut. However, they did not want to standardize these (or any other, e.g., accounting) positions.

Despite the training session received by the deputy ministers, they still managed to continually work in and around the rules. For example, progressively less attention was paid to the job descriptions that had been prepared specifically for the evaluation process. At about the midway point of the evaluation of benchmark jobs by each of the three committees, the new job descriptions that had been distributed around the room at the beginning of each evaluation basically remained unread (except for reference to the numbers in the 'dimensions' section used to score the Accountability guide chart). Instead of reading the job description, it became accepted practice for some committee member to call out to the deputy minister of the department in question: 'Tell us about this one. Now, how does it fit in with the others?'

In interviews conducted with nineteen of the twenty-one deputies some four years after the evaluation process, they were asked to judge the number of job descriptions that had been read from beginning to end by their benchmark evaluation committee. All indicated that, as the evaluation process progressed, more attention was given to the deputy minister's presentation than to the job description, acknowledging that, after the first few sessions, job descriptions were largely ignored.

One deputy claimed that 'people were impatient and wanted to talk before there was a chance to read the job description.' Another commented that 'it might have been better to get the job descriptions before the meetings because you couldn't read when people were talking.' Two deputy ministers who acknowledged their committee members' lack of interest still claim to have read them all. Generally speaking, the attitude of the evaluators to the job descriptions could probably be summed up by the following words of one deputy: 'In the beginning we read them religiously – by the end, the damn things weren't read at all!'

When the Hay consultant was asked, in a interview conducted by the researcher some four years after the evaluations, to describe the extent to which he believed that the job descriptions had been read, he admitted, with seemingly little concern, that probably fewer than half were read. The consultant made the point, however, that arguments among committee members often resulted in their 'quoting' from the job description.

The evaluation committees' progressive disregard for the job description indicates that this tool may not have the use-value many would suggest. I argue in chapter 9 that there may have been a good reason for the job descriptions' not always being used religiously by the deputies. It is suggested that the function of the job description in the evaluation process may not have been as 'critical' as employees had been led to believe during the detailed job-description training sessions or the painstaking writing process. When the evaluation committees' actual practices are considered, it seems ironic that so much attention was focused upon the new job description. The constantly stated need to move away from the old ('list of duties') job-description format so that the job could be presented in its full light appears to have been somewhat exaggerated.

It is important to note, as well, that the way in which the deputy minister described a job often affected the committee's ratings. If, for instance, a deputy stated, 'This is my top man!' the other committee members were usually inclined to oblige without too much resistance, perhaps bearing in mind that their turn was soon due (Pay analyst assessment).

In one case, the members of Committee A were experiencing difficulty in allocating higher points to a 'top man.' After two attempts at grading a director of administration, the evaluation was still not high enough even to match the scores given to other directors in the same department, let alone surpass them. Committee members claimed that they could not see this job as that of a senior director; it was considered more that of an administrative assistant. The deputy minister of the department (Agriculture) began to supplement the job description with claims that this individual was his 'right-hand man,' 'I tell him all my secrets,' 'I couldn't run the department without him,' and so on. The committee eventually did manage to 'find' the Hay points that were needed to allow this position to retain its existing relativity. The claims put forward were not exactly attributes that were required by the job itself, and one deputy minister joked at the coffee break that he gave in because the deputy minister of Agriculture was a 'likeable sort' who had given many of the deputies advice on gardening and even, on occasion, had had their back-garden soil analysed (for free) in the government laboratory.

There were many other examples of this type of influence being exerted on the scoring of jobs. Thus, a deputy's comment relating to organizational ranking, such as 'the highest,' 'the lowest,' or even 'in between' played a definite part in determining the point scores. In another instance, when a deputy minister was asked to tell the committee about a job, he described it this way:

D E P U T Y : 'Right now this job is two grades lower than the one we just scored at 654. But I kinda always thought they should probably be graded the same. This fella's a darn good worker!'
C O N S U L T A N T : 'How would you justify giving the same evaluation to this job?'
D E P U T Y : 'We could say that this job has one step less in a "specialized" Know-How than the other job, but a broader "managerial" Know-How.'
C O N S U L T A N T (to analyst): 'Okay, same score, but instead of F13, give it an E113 for Know-How, same score in box, total 654 ... What's the next job we've got?'

The evaluators' use of guide-chart criteria to justify or rationalize a desired score became even more evident when it came to addressing jobs that were common across all departments (but not necessarily graded at the same level in all departments). It will be remembered that the efficiency group had reported to cabinet that a number of pay anomalies existed throughout Atlantis (personnel and accounting jobs were cited as examples). The government's stated objective of 'internal equity' applied particularly to the similar jobs that were being performed in different departments of government. The way in which these jobs was graded can be summed up in the words of one deputy: 'I could have sat in the meeting listening for hours to what an accounting officer does, but I don't give a damn! If the deputy minister tells me that he's number two, then that's his business. In my department, I can assure you, he's number 10 and I told the committee that!'

One senior deputy minister of a large department (who, it must be said, did not express support for the project from the start) could be seen at each meeting with a list of the current salaries of his employees slipped under the Hay guide charts. Although the monetary value of the points had not yet been discussed, this deputy made sure that the relativities remained exactly as they appeared on the salary sheet. Although he is the only one of the deputies to have been seen doing this, six other deputies admitted, in a latter interview with the researcher, that they checked the relativities out quite closely throughout the project. One deputy said: 'I had a good look at the "lay of the land" before going over to the commission to "make Hay."'

Another deputy minister also indicated that, in the committee meetings, 'the opinion of some deputies in Atlantis appeared to carry more weight than the opinion of others.' This view was shared by most deputies. Those considered to have had the most influence were deputies in central departments who had regular dealings with all Atlantis departments (e.g., Treasury Board, Department of Finance). It was not only the much-mentioned (by themselves) superior knowledge of these deputies that led others to fall in with their decisions; the dependence of the operating department deputies (e.g., Treasury held the purse strings of government) can also be considered to have played a part. These deputies proved to be of valuable assistance to the consultant. In fact, in a later interview with Burr, he claimed: 'You always know who the big men are and you use them. You get close to them.'

The Hay consultant also claims to have relied upon the help of two other deputy ministers, both from small departments, 'they understood how to use the guide charts so much better than the other deputies. Some of those guys wouldn't have been able to tie their shoes!' These two deputy ministers (one from Committee B and one form Committee C) had learned the Hay system to an extent that elicited awe and admiration from other deputies. The consultant claims that he asked them to explain 'the rules' when the committees got out of control.

Deputy ministers who did not know their departments well were clearly at a disadvantage. Newer or less-experienced deputies appeared to have more faith in the supposed 'objectivity' of the system and allowed more relativity changes to occur through the evaluation process. Even the consultant told a couple of the newer deputies to make sure their relative scores 'looked okay.' Their lack of confidence seemed to make them more vulnerable, and they later complained of having felt 'bullied by the other deputies.' As one of the newer deputy ministers put it, 'I got a little carried away with it. It looked all right at the time, but it turned out wrong. I should have paid more attention.' This 'lack of attention' appears to have had less to do with the deputy's competence in the operation of the system (he was considered to have had the best knowledge of the system) than with the 'give and take' latitude found in the Hay guide charts by other deputies.

Sometimes deputies made a 'deal' if each of them had the same or similar jobs in his department. When the first deputy to present the job of urban-planning supervisor was struggling to have the evaluation raised, he solicited the aid of two other deputies who would soon be evaluating similar jobs in their own departments. According to one deputy who was asked to help in this endeavour, the decision to collude took place in the washrooms at coffee break: 'We just wanted to make sure they didn't come out too low, you know.' Thus, to a certain extent, the evaluations also reflected the power of the parties to gain the informal cooperation of others.

Other 'reciprocal' relationships occurred. Arrangements were made to help out 'someone who had helped me out.' All the deputies interviewed claim to have remembered when someone had done them a good turn during a difficult evaluation; likewise, they all claim to have remembered when a committee member opposed them in what they clearly indicated was an important evaluation. Whether the memory was good or bad, all deputies interviewed acknowledged that there was an element of reciprocity in their attitude to those who had done them either a good or bad turn.

Deputy ministers also admitted to having allowed the performance or personality characteristics of jobholders to affect the ratings, as had become plain in the committee meetings. About half-way through the meeting period of Committee A, the consultant and the director of pay sought to diminish the extent to which evaluation discussions had evolved into 'gossip sessions.' They announced that they were having the names removed from the job descriptions, organization charts, and sore-thumb sheets. The committee members, aware of their repeated offences, reluctantly agreed that this was probably the best thing to do.

The names were duly removed for the next evaluation meeting. The session was thrown into chaos: 'But whose job is this, then?,' 'I thought we already just did some economist!,' 'Well then whose job was the last one?' After two days of this type of session, the deputy ministers requested that the names be put back, 'because we're lost without them.' The names were reinserted on all the documents, and the committee reverted to its earlier ways. Even the consultant and the director of pay expressed relief at going back to the personality-based system. As MacRae pointed out to the analysts at the time: 'When the names were off, it just takes a lot longer for the committee to extract the information that they wanted on the job holder in the first place. They want to know whose job they're grading, whether it's so and so's cousin, whether the guy's any good at his job, all those things.'

Discussions continued on the outstanding performance of some and the total incompetence of others. Although the term 'halo effect' is often used to refer to the effect of a jobholder's above-average performance on the score allocated to the job, there was also what might be termed the 'horns effect' in operation. This occurred when the poor performance of an individual resulted in some penalty in the scoring. This 'horns effect' was reflected in this deputy's comment: 'Maybe if we give him a low score he'll finally get the message and move on!' To allow performance characteristics to enter the evaluation process not only affects the scoring of the job but rewards or punishes the individual twice – first, in a higher or lower evaluation of his or her job, and later in the amount of money awarded for performance.

Economic considerations such as the supply and demand for certain types of jobs also made their way into committee discussions. Despite committee agreement not to consider monetary issues in the evaluation sessions, market realities were often brought up, particularly when dealing with jobs in high demand at the time, such as computer specialists or offshore oil and gas engineers. One deputy minister, trying to get the highest score possible for one of his jobs, exclaimed, 'Do you know how much it costs to get one of these guys ... Let's make sure we don't lose him because of this' (of course, there were attempts to convince the committee that some jobs were harder to recruit for than they in fact might have been).

It is difficult to estimate the extent to which the mention of a professional qualification or university degree influenced the scoring of jobs. At least one of the deputies must have thought that formal qualifications had 'some' bearing on the evaluations. This deputy admitted that, in evaluating a senior officer's position in his department, he deliberately selected the officer with the most education to be put forth as 'representative' of the background required by the other jobs. Months later, at a sore-thumb session with all three committees together, committees B and C expressed surprise at the high scores that had been granted by committee A to this deputy's senior-officer position. It was explained by Burr that the scores obtained by the senior officer had been allocated because of the 'specialty and expertise' required of the position. Surprisingly, the pay division itself employed a similar tactic when their own jobs were evaluated.

It can be seen that many influences, outside of job content, affected the evaluation of the 230 benchmark jobs evaluated by the three committees. The lack of attention paid to the job description created many administrative problems for the pay analysts who were assigned to record the specific reasons for the committee's consensus score on the 'rationale' sheet. Because consensus scores were, so often, achieved on the basis of factors outside of job characteristics, there was very little verbal explanation given to justify why the committee had awarded a certain point score for each and every one of the sub-factors on the guide charts. Why, for instance, was an 'F' assigned for Know-How, instead of an 'E'? More often than not the committee would skim over the uncontroversial scores to focus on an area where disparity appeared to exist. More often than not, points awarded for each subfactor were merely taken for granted by the committee, leaving the analyst without anything to officially record on the 'rationale.'

As the three committees progressed through the evaluations, the analysts had to leave more and more blanks on the 'rationale' sheets. Even when there was discussion over the choice of one score over another, the reasons for finally reaching the consensus frequently related to factors 'outside' of job content, making it difficult to write the official 'rationale.' Consequently, in each of the three committees, the writing of 'rationales' broke down in no time at all. Analysts were taking home stacks of job descriptions in the evenings and on weekends, especially before the 'sore-thumb' sessions at which they risked being called upon to read aloud the 'rationale' for a particular job, to 'remind' the committee of why a certain score had been awarded.

Using passages from the job descriptions, the analysts would fill in the required sections of the 'rationale' to justify the score given by the committee. In some 'sore-thumb' meetings, if the 'rationale' to explain the committee's decision was requested, but had not yet been written up, the analyst made it up on the spot, or read out passages from the available job description prefaced by: 'The evaluation committee gave this position an 'F' in technical Know-How because ... a II in managerial Know-How because ... , a 3 in human-relations Know-How because ... '

THE SORE THUMB: A CHANCE TO REARRANGE

It was during the confusing 'sore-thumb' process that many of the deputies took the opportunity to have certain scores changed that had been 'bugging' them or that they had not been 'quite comfortable with' over the previous few weeks of evaluation. According to the Atlantis/Hay *Evaluation Manual*, the 'sore-thumb' process is 'a vertical analysis of plotting to identify pattern deviations. It does not by itself indicate an improper evaluation, but it does tell us to take another look' (1980: 41). In the Atlantis case, the deputy ministers considered it much easier to 'slip' desired changes through as the 'sore-thumb' sessions grew longer and longer, incorporating more and more jobs. One deputy minister said, for instance, that 'the chaos of the sore-thumb meetings, with everyone yelling about different jobs from different evaluation committees, helped me get the adjustments I needed.' In some meetings, as many as half the jobs would have been changed in some way or other, leaving the pay analysts to rewrite the same number of rationales, once again supposedly 're-cording' the committee's reasoning.

At the sore-thumb sessions, the consultant sometimes requested that the 'rationale' sheet of a certain job be read out. Once again, not only would the 'rationales' provide a valuable service later when it came time to defending certain evaluations, but they also served the more immediate purpose of projecting the image to the evaluators themselves that all was proceeding in a highly professional manner. Deputy ministers always expressed great admiration at the care and attention that they, as evaluators, had apparently put into the scoring of each and every factor on the guide charts. The pay analysts appeared to have consensus that 'most of the information written onto the blank rationale sheets had to be fudged at the last minute.'

The Correlation Exercise: Did Atlantis Get It Right?

Throughout the evaluations, the consultant tended to give the evaluators a lot of scope, always insisting, however, that their decision be justifiable according to the guide-chart material. His role could probably best be described as 'diplomatic.' According to Cobb and Margulies (1981: 53), the diplomatic role required of consultants has been much ignored in the literature. They claimed that the purpose of this political role is 'to communicate the vested interests of one party to another in a language that can be fully understood. The diplomat then seeks to integrate these interests when possible and when not, to reduce the friction caused by competition by negotiations, trade-offs, and the like.'

The consultant was popular and highly respected by the deputies because of his technical skills and his apparent sensitivity to the ranking 'quirks' of each department. He gained even higher regard after the excellent 'report card' that Atlantis was given by Hay's Canadian head office following the evaluation of benchmarks. Based on the correlation exercise, Atlantis had been given a 'gold star.' The correlation process illustrates yet another ritual involved in the evaluation of jobs.

One of the well-known attractions of the Hay Guide Chart Profile method of job evaluation is that the plan provides 'external competitiveness' with selected markets. Torrington and Hall (1987: 519) have described this feature as one of the greatest advantages of the Hay system: 'The proprietors have available a vast amount of comparative pay data on different organizations using their system, so their clients can not only compare rates of pay within the organization (differentials and relativities); they can also examine their external relativities.' The key, however, to comparing the pay of jobs in one's own organization against that of other organizations lies in the 'correlation' exercise. Because different organizations will assign different points to the same job, correlation was designed to permit the Hay clients to use the same 'language' when comparing salary levels (for reference, see appendix B).

The correlation exercise is the procedure by which an organization's scoring pattern is measured against the more or less 'ideal' scoring pattern that would have been obtained by a Hay specialist. Absolute scores are not as important as *relative* scores. Correlation seeks to determine the exact amount of deviation between typical Atlantis scores and the scores that would have been obtained if the entire exercise had been carried out solely by a Hay specialist. The client is informed of the exact extent to which its evaluation committee(s) has (have) deviated from the 'Hay Control Points.' This information is given to the client in the form of a mathematical formula with which to evaluate how well his or her organization performed in evaluating jobs, using the Hay plan, and obtain a 'conversion' formula to access the salary survey information in the 'data bank.'

The Hay consultant told all the deputy ministers and the pay division staff that the correlation exercise would let everybody know how well the committees had performed – in other words, how the evaluations of committees A, B, and C compared with those that would have been assigned to these jobs in a 'sterile' setting.

In Atlantis, there was great excitement over this exercise, primarily because of the mystery that shrouded the activity. First, the process required various Atlantis representatives and the Hay consultant to travel to the out-of-province Canadian head-office location of Hay Associates. Two senior deputy ministers, the manager of pay, and the director of pay accompanied the consultant.

According to the director of pay, the morning that the group arrived at Hay Associates, they were ushered into a large office resembling a boardroom and seated at one end of the conference table, to await the arrival of the 'correlator.' This senior Hay executive was known informally as the 'guru.' He arrived on time and, after brief preliminaries, requested silence while he pored over organization charts and descriptive material on the government of Atlantis. As the day progressed, he read each one of the eight job descriptions and evaluated them, using the guide charts. Finally, he plotted his evaluations against those of the Atlantis committees. These Atlantis job descriptions had been chosen to represent a fairly random sample of the evaluated benchmarks, and also included a couple of 'problem' evaluations.

Five pairs of eyes watched the correlator at work. No one was allowed to leave the room in case the correlator needed to ask a question. Sandwiches were brought into the room for lunch. At the end of the day, the 'guru' made the announcement that they had all been waiting for (much like those awaiting the oracle at Delphi). He announced that the Atlantis point scores bore 'a very close resemblance to the Hay Control Points.' In this way Atlantis was given the go-ahead to proceed with the evaluation of non-benchmark jobs.

With this good news, the group flew back to Atlantis to relay the message to the other waiting deputies and to begin the evaluation of the 600 non-benchmark jobs (representing the jobs of 850 employees). The evaluation of these non-benchmark jobs proceeded, over the next several months, much as the previous evaluation had, but with committees of senior departmental staff rather than deputy ministers. These staff members did not mix with other departments, as did the deputy ministers. In the Department of Economic Development, for instance, the three senior directors (operations, planning, and strategy) graded the non-benchmark jobs in their own department. Members of the pay division led these committees (not the Hay consultant), armed with the scores awarded to the benchmark jobs by the deputy ministers.

A month after the first correlation session, another delegation (Burr, the consultant; MacRae, the director of pay; and Allen, the manager of pay) flew back to the Hay head office to watch, over a two-day period, another twenty jobs being evaluated.

Finally, Atlantis was given its own individual 'conversion' formula, since its evaluations had deviated by 0.02 per cent on the generous side. The two delegates and the Hay consultant assigned to the project were vigorously congratulated and told that this was an 'excellent score.' It was also mentioned, confidentially, that a large Canadian provincial government that had recently implemented the Hay plan had obtained 0.02 per cent on the conservative side. Apparently all was proceeding well. By May 1981, after a year and a half of evaluating, all the Atlantis supervisory, managerial, and professional jobs had been evaluated. Each one of the 1,200 jobs had been assigned a point score.

Conclusions

On the surface, the notion of evaluation committees made up of deputy ministers from each government department might have appeared to be the ideal medium through which the internal inequities identified by the efficiency consultants could be addressed. A few years later, MacRae told the researcher that the deputy ministers' wide span of knowledge and experience 'was exactly what we needed to correct all those anomalies that had crept in over the years.'

Three committees of deputy ministers had met over the period of a year and a half to measure the value of 230 'benchmark' jobs. This chapter described what went on in these committees. Those changes in relativity that were made appeared to stem from personal feelings of 'reward' or 'vendetta' as deputy ministers saw the opportunity to move a particular job upward or downward in the hierarchy.

This chapter also described how political process continued to operate under the veneer of the new system. Examples were given to depict the bias, the manipulation, the horse trading, and so on that occurred during these evaluation meetings. At the individual level, it was seen that evaluators used various strategies to influence other committee members and achieve certain desired outcomes. At the collective level, it was seen that tacit agreements were made to retain the basic structure of existing differentials.

What was also interesting was that the Hay correlator, or 'guru,' congratulated the delegates from Atlantis on their 'near perfect scoring.' Whether or not the 'hocus-pocus' of correlation is believed, one thing remains clear: The quirks of Atlantis and the many informal activities in which committee members engaged appear, in the long run, to have caused very little stir when matched against the rankings of a so-called perfect hierarchy (although rule bending might have served the purpose of making evaluators feel that they were exerting their own special influence on the eventual outcome of job rankings). It might be said that the 'ideal' hierarchy that is embedded in the weights and factors on the guide charts can withstand considerable interference.

The bias and manipulation witnessed in Atlantis need not, and should not, be seen as peculiar to Atlantis. Rather, it is possible to argue that bias and manipulation are central to job evaluation itself. The fact that 'political process' continued to exist despite the introduction of a formal job evaluation process should not, however, be all that surprising. While the evaluation process itself may have changed, the nature of the context and 'problem' had remained the same. A rational process had, in other words, simply been grafted onto an inherently political context, that is, a context defined by diverse goals and uncertain outcomes.

7 Pricing the Jobs:
The Objective of
External Competitiveness

Surveys reveal that job evaluation plans are usually introduced with
the intention of establishing a more equitable, manageable, and competitive pay structure (see chapter 3). Such objectives require the
conversion of job evaluation point scores to monetary values. One of
the more popular myths about job evaluation is that the technique
somehow determines absolute pay levels.

The Hay consultant who was employed by Atlantis asserted that
the introduction of the firm's job evaluation technique would enable
the organization to 'plug into the data bank' to obtain the 'correct'
rate of pay for any evaluated job in relation to a 'selected' labour
market. The notion that job evaluation determines pay was reinforced when the representatives of the pay division made their presentations throughout Atlantis. The three key stated objectives of
introducing job evaluation were internal equity, external competitiveness, and pay for performance. This chapter addresses the objective
of external competitiveness.

Here, it is maintained that there is considerable confusion about
the role played by job evaluation in the determination of pay rates.
This confusion stems from a variety of sources, not least of which is
the way in which job evaluation is packaged and sold to organizations
and, in turn, to employees.

By describing how the new Atlantis pay rates were derived. I hope
to demonstrate that 1 / there is a difference between the activity of
ranking jobs for the purpose of internal equity and that of pricing
jobs for the purpose of external competitiveness; these two discrete
activities are frequently confused in the minds of employers and
employees alike (it is maintained that consultants do not in fact do

anything to dispel such confusion and may even create it); 2 / the new Atlantis salary line (around which the minimum and the maximum of each pay grade was constructed) owed more to the government's concern over economic expedience than to any great desire to meet the objective of 'external competitiveness'; and 3 / the central pay division made use of the confusion that surrounds the powers of job evaluation to persuade employees that job evaluation had, in fact, 'scientifically' determined the absolute amount of their new pay rates. Later, in chapter 10, it will be seen that the obfuscation about both the grading and the pricing of jobs provided functional value for Atlantis management in the sense that a new 'rational' order could be evoked to defuse conflict over pay claims.

How Many Pay Grades?

A number of factors determine the particular money value that is allotted to each job or each group of jobs. One of these is the organization's decision regarding the number of pay grades. When the scores of 1,200 positions in Atlantis had been assigned points, it was found that there were 114 common point scores, ranging from 169 to 1,708 points (the highest and lowest scores). Many different jobs, therefore, shared the same total scores. The 114 different scores were meant to reflect the differing organizational value or worth of each job in relation to all the other jobs that were evaluated.

The first step towards attaching prices to these point scores lay in deciding whether to match each one of the 114 scores to an individual rate of pay, or to cluster the 114 different point scores into a lesser number of grades or levels for the purposes of easier pay administration.

The Hay consultant expressed his firm's preference for individual matching. A photocopied hand-out prepared by Hay Associates, entitled 'Guidelines for an Effective Salary Administration Plan,' recognizes the popularity of clustering point scores but also tries to discourage organizations from grouping the 'consensus' point scores that were decided upon in the evaluation committees: 'this shortcut eliminates the organizational analysis and job structure insights provided by analysis ... Problems can occur (at a later stage) when job content is added to two jobs in the same salary grade – one evaluated at the top of the grade and the other at the bottom. One job moves into the next grade while the second job may remain in its present grade. An event not likely to thrill the incumbent' (1980: 7–8). Nevertheless, the director and the manager of the pay division decided that it would be too cumbersome to administer 114 different grades and, therefore, selected clustering. This meant that jobs would be grouped into a lesser number of pay grades to create a simpler pay structure. The Hay consultant indicated that it was, indeed, far more common to cluster point scores than not. As the British Incomes Data Services (1979: 55) points out: 'Unless each job is to have its own rate of pay it must be included in a limited number of pay grades.'

MacRae informed the researcher that this decision had been taken, at the time, for the following reasons:

1 / Civil servants are used to thinking in terms of being in a system that says 'You are grade X.'

2 / From an administrative point of view, we thought that dealing with 20 or 30 grades would give us less problems than dealing with 114 different pay levels for 114 different point scores. It simplified the wage structure.

3 / We thought that we would avoid constant requests for regrading if the difference between jobs was firmly set into a limited number of grades. That way, if any point-score adjustments were made based upon some change in job content, the job would not automatically be moved into the next grade. Employees could be told that their new score still didn't cause the job to be pushed across the dividing line into the next higher (or lower) grade. (Interview)

Once it was decided to cluster the point scores into grades, the main problem lay in determining *how many* grades to have. The director of pay told the researcher that the challenge of this task lay in working out how many grades would prove administratively 'manageable' while still maintaining a 'noticeable' difference in responsibility levels between one cluster of point scores and the next. A pay grade would consist of jobs falling within a range of points. The more job grades an organization chooses to have the narrower the pay ranges attached to each grade will be, and the fewer the grades, the wider the pay ranges.

Attempts were made to divide the point spread of 169–1,708 in many different ways in order to reach some satisfactory number of grades. These points were broken up both geometrically (i.e., the point spread was divided into progressively larger fractions) and arithmetically (i.e., the point spread was divided into fractions of equal value). Breakpoints were attempted at gaps of approximately 5 per cent. This percentage spread produced more than 40 grades, which, according to MacRae, would have made the distinction between one grade and another 'too fine.' The pay division was worried that too large a number of grades would lead employees to believe that it was hardly worth the trouble to be promoted from one grade to the next.

However, when the members of the pay division managed to break the point spread to produce a total of fewer than 30 grades, they judged this level of distinctions too 'crude.' The director of pay feared that, with too few grades, jobs with many different levels of responsibility would be included in the same pay grade. In other words, it was feared that employees might look to the other positions in their job grade, sense that there were a lot of 'less important' jobs in the same grade as themselves, and flood the Civil Service Commission with requests for regrading.

Eventually, the pay division staff settled (arbitrarily, not statistically) for what it considered to be a 'manageable' number of grades, that is, 35. The point-score span of the eight lowest grades (under 300 points) was calculated using an arithmetic difference of 20 points between the highest and the lowest points of each grade (in other words, each grade from 1 to 8 included those jobs that fell between 150 and 169 points, 170 and 189 points, etc.), and that of the remaining grades by calculating a geometric (percentage) difference of 7 per cent between the highest and the lowest points of the same grade (that is, there was a proportional difference set between the top and bottom number of points in the same grade). Table 4 shows the point scores the pay division assigned to grades.

A certain amount of 'licence' had to be used in selecting the precise point score at which to set the borders of the grades. Although it had been intended that the cut-off points would occur at the 7 per cent mark, this was not always possible. In selecting these cut-off points, particular attention was paid to 'high population' scores, so as not to have, for example, 150 jobs carrying an evaluated point score of 677 located at the top end of a grade, with the cut-off for the next-higher grade beginning at 678. Without certain adjustments, it was believed that (should the point scores attached to each pay level ever leak out to employees) there would be large groups of employees discovering that they were only one or two points away from the jobs in the next-higher pay level. The director of pay told the researcher that this

TABLE 4
Point spreads assigned to grades

Grade	Point spread	Grade	Point spread
1	150–169	8	290–309
2	170–189	9	310–331
3	190–209	10	332–353
4	210–229	11	354–379
5	230–249	...	...
6	250–269	33	1,574–1,683
7	270–289	34	1,684–1,801
		35	1,802–1,927

SOURCE: Civil Service internal document

situation would inevitably have led to an 'impossible' number of requests for regrading. The decision to maintain a 7 per cent point spread in grades 9 to 35 was merely used as a guideline. Some manipulation was carried out by pay division staff to make certain that the largest population clusters of point scores fit 'well into' the new pay grades, not around the edges of the grade.

There was still no decision of what monetary values would be attached to these grades. The point score of each job was fitted into one of the 35 pay grades.

Single Rates or Pay Ranges?

Following the decision to adopt 35 grades, the pay division started working out what money values would be affixed to these grades for the purposes of pay. Just as there are no fixed rules in deciding upon how many grades an organization will create, there any no fixed rules about whether there should be a standard pay rate for all jobs in the same grade, or whether pay ranges should be set up with a minimum and a maximum dollar value.

In the case of Atlantis, the choice of pay ranges was based upon the government's earlier decision to introduce, via the Hay job evaluation plan, a system of performance appraisal. When performance appraisal was in place, it was intended that employees would eventually be moved, by their superior, upwards and downwards within the salary range according to how well they performed their job.

Drawing the Salary Line

The procedure most commonly used to assist organizations in making decisions about their salary structure is the 'scatter' diagram. A scatter diagram is a two-dimensional graph on which job evaluation points for benchmark (and sometimes non-benchmark) jobs are plotted against a pay rate (either actual or proposed).

To guide the pay division in choosing the pay rates that would be affixed to the 35 pay grades, a scatter diagram was prepared showing the job evaluation point scores along the horizontal, or 'X' axis, and the actual existing salaries, in dollars, on the vertical, or 'Y' axis. The existing salaries ranged from approximately $10,000 to $50,000. These were weighted according to the number of employees represented by each plotted point, and a 'line of central tendency' was drawn through the actual salaries to illustrate the average point–salary relationship. This line of central tendency, or trend line, graphically depicted the pay rates currently being paid for jobs in Atlantis relative to the points assigned to each job in the job evaluation exercise.

The line of central tendency basically provides the information around which a new pay structure can be built. Information on the way this salary line compares to others can be obtained through salary surveys. There are several ways to carry out these surveys, but the job evaluation plan purchased by Atlantis already included a 'data bank' of salary-survey information on other Hay clients. The Atlantis line of central tendency was therefore compared to the average salary lines of certain other Hay client organizations whose salary information was recorded in the 'data bank.'

The Hay consultant was asked by the director of pay to extract from the Hay 'data bank' salary information on the following three groups: Public Service – general, across Canada; selected government organizations; and regional private sector. The decision to compare Atlantis salaries of these three groups was made by MacRae with the input of politicians, some senior deputy ministers, and members of the pay division. Three salary lines were drawn up from the data bank, using the special Atlantis correlation formula of 2.42 to access the desired comparisons.

Following Hay 'analysis,' Atlantis was informed that its existing salary line was positioned considerably lower than that of their selected comparison groups. The Hay consultant recommended that Atlantis adopt the policy of having a salary line that would, in theory,

FIGURE 7
Relationship of Atlantis salary line to that of selected organizations

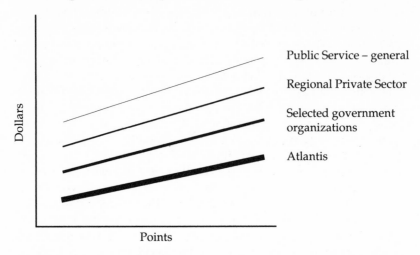

sit halfway between that of the 'Public Service – general' and the lower line of 'Selected government organizations.' This choice would result in an Atlantis salary line that would more or less coincide (the Atlantis line was not straight) with that of the third comparison group, that is, 'Regional private sector.' The director of pay was in agreement with the Hay consultant, and they both presented these findings to the Treasury Board. For the purposes of illustration only, a simplified chart of these relative positions is depicted in figure 7.

Treasury Board, which was made up of eight government ministers, agreed that this proposal would place Atlantis salaries in the ideal competitive position in relation to relevant organizations and gave approval 'in principle' (that is, pending information on cost) to the recommendation on the location of the Atlantis salary line. MacRae told the researcher that Treasury Board agreement with this particular salary line reflected a fundamental compensation decision in an important area of government policy – where Atlantis, as an employer, wanted the organization to be in terms of pay.

Economic Expedience Versus Bureaucratic Logic

To work out how much this 'ideal' competitive salary line would cost, the pay division measured the difference between the salaries represented on the scatter diagram against 35 breakpoints along the proposed salary line. Each of the 35 breakpoints would make up the 35 salary 'midpoints' of the new pay ranges. Most of the plotted jobs fell well under the new salary line, signalling that almost every newly graded job was now 'undergraded,' in other words, stood to gain a significant pay increase.

Complex mathematical machinations were carried out over the next few weeks to address a number of questions. How much width (dollar spread) should exist between pay grades? How much differential should exist between the midpoint of one grade and the next? Should there be overlap between the salary range of a grade and the grades above and below? If so, how much? The pay division moved closer to the development of a pay range. A dollar differential of 7 per cent was decided upon between salary midpoints. MacRae gave the researcher the following reasons for this decision: 'a 7 per cent differential happened to match the percentage spread of the point scores; we thought that 7 per cent would still reflect a "promotion" if an employee got a job that was one grade higher; and being limited at the top of the salary line by the deputy ministers' salaries, and at the bottom end by union salaries, this percentage spread seemed the most "realistic." Basically we just thought it would work.'

It was also decided to create some overlap between the pay range of one grade and that of another. This decision is not unusual in the design of pay structures, the rationale being that a person who has been on the job longer and is more experienced is of greater value to the organization than an entry-level person in the next-higher grade.

Although the limits of the pay ranges were to be adjusted later, they were initially devised by drawing two proportionally parallel lines, one 20 per cent above and one 20 per cent below the 35 breakpoints of the new salary line. In other words, the pay ranges started out at the following fairly standard (according to the Hay consultant) limits: minimum was equal to 80 per cent of midpoint; midpoint (i.e., the breakpoint plotted along the proposed salary line) was 100 percent; and maximum was equal to 120 per cent of midpoint.

The pay division could finally begin to compare existing salaries to the newly proposed 'midpoints.' According to MacRae, when this difference was calculated, the distance looked 'so wide' (i.e., costly to implement) that the Hay consultant was asked to devise a formula for gradual conversion from the old rates to the new. After members of the pay division had worked out the relationship between each existing salary as a percentage of its new midpoint, and after they had incorporated a conversion formula to reduce the immediate cost of the project, a formal presentation was made to the Treasury Board to present the results.

It soon became apparent, however, that these calculations presented more of an expense to Treasury Board than its members had anticipated when they agreed to the selected 'competitive' salary line. No financial limits had been set by the Treasury Board because, according to MacRae, 'they always thought that whatever came out of the Hay system was a cut-and-dried issue. They didn't realize how much of a role they had to play. It was basically up to them to decide how much they wanted to spend. We had to set the pay rates according to how much they gave us.'

Burr and MacRae returned from the meeting at Treasury Board visibly shaken. They declared that it was 'back to the drawing-board.' Apparently, the politicians (who were fast learning the ropes) had told them to 'get in touch with reality,' 'lower your sights,' and make the implementation a 'hell of a lot cheaper.'

MacRae and Burr, beginning now to fear for the 'success' of the project, attempted to lessen the cost of implementing the 'externally competitive' job evaluation plan by drawing a lower, but parallel, salary line. The concern of the consultant and of the members of the pay division, at this time, was to draw a salary line that would be as close as possible to that originally selected, but would prove 'affordable' to Treasury Board. As MacRae confided (to the analysts at the time): 'You know how it is, the higher the salary line, the less sore people we have out there!'

After another formal presentation to Treasury Board, the team was again turned away, with instructions to make the conversion even cheaper. According to the director of pay, the government did not appear to be 'so interested in external competitiveness after all.'

At this point, the pay division and the consultant attempted to deal with the challenge of designing a salary line that, by now, was beginning to show signs, at the bottom end, of being nipped at the heels by unionized civil-service pay scales and blocked, at the top end, by the pay of deputy ministers (whose pay was set annually by cabinet). In an effort to overcome those looming salary-compression problems, the pay division broke the slope of the relatively straight proposed salary line into three lines. This shape (which also mir-

FIGURE 8
Breaking the proposed 'straight' salary line into three

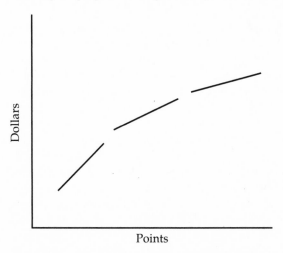

rored the existing line of central tendency is depicted roughly in figure 8.

As the proposed salary line was bent into this shape, changing the slope, it was no longer possible to maintain the earlier decision to use a 7 per cent pay differential between the 'midpoints' of the 35 pay grades. Through trial and error, once again, it was decided that the difference between the 'midpoint' monetary value of one grade and the next would be set at approximately 5.5 per cent at the low end of the scale, tapering to a 3.5 per cent difference at the higher end.

As well as lowering the salary line once again and bending it to prevent compression problems at the top and at the bottom of the pay scales, the pay division also made the 'gradual' conversion formula for transferring employees from the old to the new even more gradual. It was also discovered that, by shrinking the dollar spread of the pay ranges, specifically the maximum of the pay range, the project would, in both the short and the long run, keep costs down. By cutting the range 'maximum' from 120 per cent of midpoint down to 110 per cent, it was felt not only that conversion would be cheaper, but also that it would lower employee expectations about how much money they could get. The members of the pay division had long been aware of the way in which the top, or maximum step in a grade soon became the 'expected' rate.

Finally, a third proposal was presented to Treasury Board for approval. The job evaluation project was, by now, months behind schedule. To make matters worse, the pay division was operating under the additional burden of knowing that all Atlantis *unionized* employees had already received their annual increases. Time pressures were increasing as the supervisory, managerial, and professional levels remained frozen because of the 'job evaluation project.'

This time, the director of pay and the Hay consultant were successful in convincing the politicians that this new (lower) salary line, combined with a slow conversion to the new rates, would not cause too much financial hardship to the government. Treasury Board did insist, however, that the maximum of all pay ranges be reduced from a span of 110 per cent of midpoint to 104 per cent, with the option of providing a bonus for outstanding performance up to 110 per cent. In fact, Treasury Board requested that the maximum be clearly identified as 104 per cent of midpoint on all written materials.

Since the midpoint was no longer to be located in the *middle* of the pay range, the term 'midpoint' was dropped. The pay division selected the term 'policy' to represent the 35 dollar values plotted along the salary line.

By the time the salary line, or 'policy line' as it became known, had been approved, in August 1981, its relative positioning compared to that originally selected from the Hay 'data bank' had slipped considerably. The new salary line had now been lowered to somewhere between the old Atlantis salary line and the line representing the average salaries of 'selected government organizations.' Figure 9 shows this relationship in simplified form. Table 5 shows the newly derived pay plan for the supervisory, managerial, and professional employees of Atlantis, including money levels for the 35 pay grades.

Reinforcing the Image of External Competitiveness

Following the development of a 'workable' pay plan, all supervisory, managerial, and professional staff were called together, at various locations throughout Atlantis, to receive a presentation from pay-division representatives. The stated purpose of these presentations was to give employees an update on the progress of the job evaluation project. The derivation of the new pay plan was explained, and employees were told how their salaries would be converted from the old rates of pay to the new.

FIGURE 9
Competitive position of approved salary line

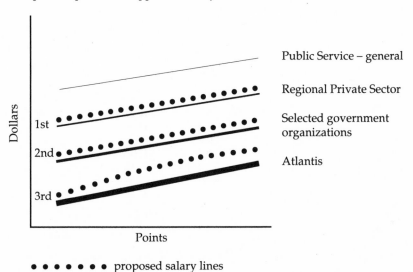

Public Service – general

Regional Private Sector

Selected government
organizations

Atlantis

• • • • • • • proposed salary lines

To government employees who had grown accustomed to belonging to one of many 'management' pay plans, e.g., education, technical, maintenance, and medical, it was a new experience to now be
grouped under the one single pay plan, entitled 'Management Compensation Plan' (MCP). Old pay plans had been made up of job
classes, each of which had a fixed number of 'increments' along which
employees would move, fairly automatically, on an annual basis,
until the top increment had been reached. This new pay plan spoke
of 'ranges,' with a minimum monetary value, a policy value, and a
maximum value attached to each grade.

At the presentations, employees were informed that the conversion of their individual jobs to the Hay plan was being worked out at
the central personnel agency and that they would each be informed,
by private letter, at some later date, of how their particular position
had 'come out of the job evaluation plan.' The format of these presentations was to show slides, read what was written on these while
adding a few explanatory sentences, and respond to any employee
questions before closing.

Although the original salary line that was recommended by Hay
and approved 'in principle' by the government had actually been
lowered twice and bent considerably out of shape, no mention was

TABLE 5
New Atlantis pay plan

Pay levels	Point spread	Minimum (80 per cent)	Salary policy (100 per cent)	Maximum (104 per cent)
PL 1	150 – 169	$12,408	$15,510	$16,130
PL 2	170 – 189	13,089	16,361	17,015
PL 3	190 – 209	13,770	17,212	17,900
PL 4	210 – 229	14,450	18,063	18,786
PL 5	230 – 249	15,131	18,914	19,671
PL 6	250 – 269	15,813	19,766	20,557
PL 7	270 – 289	16,494	20,617	21,442
PL 8	290 – 309	17,174	21,468	22,327
PL 9	310 – 331	17,890	22,362	23,256
PL 10	332 – 353	18,638	23,298	24,230
PL 11	354 – 379	19,456	24,320	25,293
PL 12	380 – 405	20,341	25,426	26,443
PL 13	406 – 435	21,294	26,618	27,683
PL 14	436 – 463	22,282	27,852	28,966
PL 15	464 – 499	23,371	29,214	30,383
PL 16	500 – 531	24,134	30,158	31,375
PL 17	532 – 571	24,914	31,143	32,389
PL 18	572 – 609	25,758	32,198	33,486
PL 19	610 – 653	26,546	33,308	34,640
PL 20	654 – 697	27,599	34,499	35,879
PL 21	698 – 747	28,618	35,772	37,203
PL 22	748 – 799	29,722	37,152	38,638
PL 23	800 – 855	30,891	38,614	40,159
PL 24	856 – 915	32,147	40,184	41,791
PL 25	916 – 979	33,490	41,862	43,536
PL 26	980 – 1,047	34,552	43,190	44,918
PL 27	1,048 – 1,121	35,526	44,408	46,184
PL 28	1,122 – 1,199	36,569	45,711	47,539
PL 29	1,200 – 1,283	37,680	47,100	48,984
PL 30	1,284 – 1,373	38,874	48,592	50,536
PL 31	1,374 – 1,469	40,150	50,187	52,194
PL 32	1,470 – 1,573	41,490	51,863	53,938
PL 33	1,574 – 1,683	42,843	53,554	55,696
PL 34	1,684 – 1,801	44,286	55,357	57,571
PL 35	1,802 – 1,927	45,829	57,286	59,577

SOURCE: Civil Service Commission internal document

made of any such activities. The pay plan that was being shown to employees was presented in such a manner as to suggest that the absolute values attached to each grade had somehow 'flowed' out of the Hay system. Amidst an otherwise mathematically complex presentation (e.g., line-slope calculations and correlation formula were mentioned) view-graphs were shown that listed the (well-known) names of organizations included in the selected comparison groups. The claims made earlier about the need for 'external competitiveness' with selected organizations were renewed.

The researcher, having been among those making presentations to employees, is well aware that employees were given the impression that it was by 'plugging Atlantis information into the Hay data bank' that the new Atlantis pay plan had been computed and churned out. Before setting out on these presentations, the director of pay warned the analysts to take care in spelling out the mechanics used to determine a salary line, including the statistical analysis and scatter diagram. No mention was made of the back-room attempts to make the new pay scale 'affordable.'

During these presentations a description was also given of the 'gradual' conversion formula that had been devised (and also much amended) by the pay division and finally approved by Treasury Board. The following information and table 6 were presented to employees in the form of view-graphs.

Conversion to New Compensation Plan

- Compa ratio $= \dfrac{\text{Actual base salary}}{\text{Policy}}$
- Normally, minimum compa ratio is 0.80 (80% of midpoint)
   - At this level, incumbent is usually in learning phase.
- Normally, when fully satisfactory performance is attained, compa ratio is 1.0 (rewarded at policy).
- In absence of performance evaluation appraisal system at conversion, it is proposed to increase base salaries inversely proportional to compa ratio; i.e., an incumbent with a low compa ratio will receive a higher % increase than an incumbent with a higher compa ratio.
- All incumbents should move to a compa ratio of at least 0.80.
- Incumbents presently with a compa ratio of 1.0 or more (above policy) could have an increase if considered outstanding performers (discretion of deputy minister).
- All adjustments should be considered maximum, subject to department approval (and modification, if necessary).

TABLE 6
Details of conversion plan: Proposed maximum salary adjustments

Present compa ratio (% rel. of existing salary to new grade 'policy')	Maximum increases in base salary (%)
0.71 & below	move to compa ratio of 0.80
0.72	11
0.73	10.5
0.74	10
0.75	9.5
0.76	9
0.77	8.5
0.78	8
0.79	7.5
0.80 – 0.85	7
0.86 – 0.90	6
0.91 – 0.95	5
0.96 – 1.00	4
1.01 – 1.04	3 (1% compa ratio point + 2% LSP)
1.05 – & above	3 LSP

LSP = Lump-sum payment

SOURCE: Civil Service Commission internal document

During this presentation, the term 'compa ratio' was introduced to employees. This ratio, which the Hay plan emphasizes as an important control device, is used in any number and variety of job evaluation plans.

It was explained to employees that the compa ratio is a calculation that depicts the degree to which a job within a paygrade is close to the 'policy' of the range. Since a figure of 100 was established as the policy value, a compa ratio of 1.04 would mean that the salary paid for a certain job is 4 per cent above the policy rate of the grade to which the job has been assigned. A compa ratio of 0.94 would mean that the job is now paid at 6 per cent below the policy rate of the grade to which the job has been assigned. Compa ratios are used not only to indicate the relationships of individual jobs to their policy but also to indicate the average relationships of groups of jobs, or even whole departments, to their respective policy rates.

At the end of each presentation, very few questions were usually asked. The bulk of these related to more specific details of what would happen to 'overgraded' jobs. Few questions were asked about the mechanics associated with setting the wage levels. Employees then returned to their offices to await a letter from the Civil Service Commission. In the mean time, those members of the pay division who were not at a presentation were feverishly converting salaries onto data sheets with the help of staff from the computer-services division.

The 'Results'

When the third salary line had been drawn up and costed for Treasury Board, it was possible to get a rough idea of how employees would fare. Calculations had been carried out on an estimate basis. However, now that the job evaluation point scores had been converted to the new pay rates, it was possible to see exactly how many employees stood to gain, lose, or stay much the same.

'Overpaid' employees were considered to be those whose existing rate of pay fell above the 'maximum' (i.e., 1.04) of their new range. 'Underpaid' employees were considered to be those whose existing pay rates fell below the 'minimum' (i.e., 0.80) of their new range. In summary, the relationship of Atlantis employees' existing salaries to their new policy was: 19 per cent, or 228 employees (no employee *after* conversion; all those whose salaries were below the minimum of the range were moved into the range upon conversion), were at salaries less than or equal to 0.79; 61 per cent, or 732 employees (71 per cent after conversion) were at salaries between 0.80 (minimum) and 1.00 (policy); 10 per cent, or 120 employees (19 per cent after conversion) were at salaries between 1.01 and 1.04 (maximum); and 10 per cent, or 120 employees (10 per cent after conversion) were at salaries greater than or equal to 1.05.

The 19 per cent of employees whose existing pay fell below the new minimum of their job grade (i.e., at below 79 percent of policy) stood to gain the most from the project, not only at the time of conversion, but also in future years as they moved closer to the policy of their grade, depending on their performance. Most of these jobs were female-predominant and in Health, the largest department of the government.

The majority of the 61 per cent of employees who were paid between the new minimum and policy of their grade (i.e., between 0.80 of policy and 1.00) also stood to gain financially from the installation of the Hay job evaluation plan. Those closer to 0.80 naturally stood to benefit more than those whose salary was already at 0.99 of the newly established policy.

The 10 per cent of employees whose existing salaries fell between the assigned policy (i.e., 1.00) of their new job grade and the grade maximum (i.e., 1.04) basically stood to gain little more than the promised minimum of 3 per cent, and that was allocated in a lump-sum payment. The salary was to be recorded at the same rate for the following year's calculations.

It had been decided earlier, as part of the 'red circle' policy, to give all employees affected by the job evaluation project, even the 'over-paid' ones, an increase of at least 3 per cent, partly to compensate for the (approximately) 4 per cent increase already granted to the unionized groups of civil servants. Under the old salary-administration scheme, all these newly evaluated employees would have received at least the percentage allocated to their pay-scale increase, and many would have also benefited from a 'step' or 'increment' jump on the anniversary date of their hire, at least until they reached the final step. The decision to grant everyone involved in the project at least 3 per cent was also partly made to pacify those employees who, in years to come, might suffer until their new pay range caught up to their existing pay (it was eventually decided not to 'freeze' overpaid salaries, but, rather, to permit the incumbents to receive a small per cent increase, at the discretion of the supervisor).

Finally, the 10 per cent of employees whose actual salaries were already higher than the maximum of their grade (i.e., at or above 1.05 of policy) stood to receive only the 3 per cent increase upon conversion.

The overall results, by government department, are shown in table 7. The figures listed represent the purest depiction of any relative changes that occurred in Atlantis because they do not incorporate the gradual conversion formula, as do, for instance, payroll sheets. It can be seen that the departments to fare the 'best' (apart from the Civil Service Commission, whose pay division staff, it could be said, had a certain 'influence') were divisions of the Department of Health (e.g., Atlantis General Hospital, 0.79; Atlantis Hospital, 0.83; and Atlantis Commission for Drug Dependency, 0.88). Each of these was

TABLE 7
Comparison by department of actual salary levels with proposed midpoints

Department	Actual dollars	Proposed dollars	Compa ratio
Agriculture & Marketing	1,404,421	1,499,878	0.94
Civil Service Commission	719,423	809,518	0.88
Consumer Affairs	201,503	253,124	0.81
Culture, Recreation & Fitness	79,386	83,526	0.95
Development	1,417,198	1,400,662	1.01
Education	3,182,061	3,228,253	0.99
Environment	560,053	540,714	1.04
Fisheries	258,731	273,019	0.95
Government Services	1,535,248	1,439,173	1.07
Health (selected positions)	1,777,374	1,840,913	0.97
Labour	432,696	510,310	0.85
Lands & Forests	2,819,772	3,031,234	0.93
Management & Policy Boards	363,923	435,721	0.84
Mines & Energy	590,711	690,888	0.86
Municipal Affairs	1,289,953	1,456,885	0.89
Atlantis Commission for Drug Dependency	359,808	409,706	0.88
Atlantis Hospital (Health)	1,115,491	1,351,283	0.83
Atlantis Housing Commission	687,028	714,556	0.96
Social Services	3,189,026	3,506,167	0.91
Transportation	4,550,107	4,866,736	0.93
Atlantis General Hospital (Health)	4,940,076	6,245,412	0.79
Overall total	31,473,989	33,587,678	0.94

Difference $2.1 million = 6.7%
NOTE: Departments not included in overall cost are Attorney General, Finance, and Tourism.

SOURCE: Civil Service Commission internal document

predominantly populated by female workers. Another department that had been 'undergraded' in the past was the Department of Consumer Affairs, the only department in the Government of Atlantis with a woman deputy minister. It should also be noted that the Civil Service Commission and Management (Treasury) and Policy Board also 'fared well.' Both of these departments were directly responsible for the Hay project. The overall Atlantis compa ratio was 0.94. This compa ratio indicates that the average of the 'old' salaries were considered to be approximately 6 per cent below the average of the newly calculated Atlantis midpoints.

The researcher was also given access to pay records that detailed the amount of change for each of the 1,200 positions within the government. Some jobs went up; some went down. The researcher could not, however, discern any particular pattern in change (with the exception, as mentioned above, of greater change within the female-dominated jobs). To give a general sense of the changes that occurred, I present specific data for four of the most 'undergraded' and four of the most 'overgraded' jobs – undergraded: Chief Cook (Social Services), 0.61; Chief Clerk (Provincial Magistrates), 0.63; Staffing Officer (CSC), 0.68; and Compensation Officer (CSC), 0.69; overgraded: Director Administration (CSC), 1.25 (Note: incumbent was ex-director of classification who had been removed from his duties during 'efficiency' reorganization); Director Project Implementation (Development), 1.25; Chief Clerk Payroll (Transportation), 1.19; and Assistant Director Testing (Education), 1.13. These changes to specific jobs, however, are not in themselves considered important for this research because the change that occurred is attributed here to socio-political motivations rather than to the technical dictates of job evaluation criteria.

The following information was shown to Treasury Board as a viewgraph to justify the costs of implementing the Hay plan:

Justification for the Conversion Cost of Proposed Compensation Plan

- Radically improving low compa ratios ensures that incumbents are rewarded more closely in line with the value of the position to the government.
- It minimizes possible human rights problems.
- Because of the recent level of settlement made for employees in the bargaining units, it would have been necessary to adjust salary levels of management and non-bargaining professionals by an estimated annual cost of $1.8 million (not to do so would cause severe compression and even inversion in the relationship between salaries paid to employees in the bargaining unit and those paid to excluded employees).

The introduction of a job evaluation plan would normally be attended with an increase in costs because, as the National Board for Prices and Incomes (1968: 42) report on job evaluation points out: 'those who have been downgraded will either receive personal allowances or have their pay unchanged, while those who are upgraded will have their pay increased.'

Conclusions

This chapter has attempted to reduce the confusion that exists between the activity of attaching points to jobs (i.e., the evaluation process), and the activity of attaching pay values to these points. By studying the steps taken by the Atlantis government in establishing a new pay structure, it was seen that new pay rates were derived arbitrarily and not scientifically, despite the scientific image that was attached to the setting of pay rates. In attempting to resolve such issues as how many grades to choose, how wide to make the span of these grades, what percentage differential to establish between grades, and even what money values should be attached to these grades, a series of efforts were made to suit the organization and its needs.

The sometimes confused pattern of activity followed by Atlantis in establishing the grades for the new pay structure is not considered to be particularly remarkable or different from that of any other organization in the process of implementing a formal job evaluation plan. The lack of standardized procedures in setting pay rates has also been noted in literature. Merrie (1968: 16–17), for instance, refers to the need for each organization to suit its own needs when faced with 'the conversion of marks to money': 'there is no one solution ... Some help in deciding the most practicable money/points scale can be obtained by "trial and error", with the aid of graphs where a variety of money scales are plotted against the assessed weighted marks. By this means, the most appropriate scale to meet the circumstances can be selected.' Despite the attempts of the consultant and of the pay division to keep the government to its selected 'competitive' salary line (seemingly in the interests of making employees happy and reducing potential employee opposition to the job evaluation plan), the line was dropped twice and had its shape changed at the extremities. Although it is believed that Treasury Board would not have wanted to pay 'below market' rates, the high cost of achieving the 'ideal' competitive position for Atlantis caused the objective of 'external competitiveness' to fall by the wayside.

This chapter has also demonstrated that the language and rhetoric of the job evaluation plan selected by Atlantis served to obfuscate the basis of pay determination so that it appeared that it was the science of job evaluation technique itself that dictated the absolute pay values. The new pay plan – and, indeed, the individual's new positioning within that pay plan – was presented to employees as a complex mathematical 'result' of the job evaluation process.

8 Organizational Reaction to a 'Rational' System

Very little, if any, research has been conducted on how organizations, at the time of implementing a job evaluation plan strive to balance the integrity (or, at least, the surface integrity) of a 'rational' technique against such pressures as internal traditional differentials and external market forces. This chapter illustrates the tremendous effort that went into projecting to the Atlantis organization that the 'rational' system was functioning smoothly and efficiently while, behind the scenes, the job evaluation rules came to be subjected to much the same political 'tug of war' as the system that preceded it.

It is argued that this 'political' process is integral and central to the job evaluation process itself. Even though there is a veneer of hard rationality and scientificity associated with the technique, the system functions through a series of subjective judgments. To the extent that we can understand organizations as political systems (Pettigrew 1973; Pfeffer 1981b; Bacharach and Lawler 1980), job evaluation needs to be seen as a series of subjective understandings arrived at through a continuous process of negotiation and compromise between various stakeholders and power groups. The subjective process within job evaluation represents the arena in which political activity takes place. The power of organizational groups to define 'value' is highlighted in this chapter through reference to the 're-evaluation' of job worth by staff engineers within the province of Atlantis.

In this chapter it is possible to see a panoply of political activities unfold. Here, I describe what happened in Atlantis when the results of job evaluation violated individual expectations, upset traditional relativities, or appeared to be uncompetitive in relation to the external labour market. The events are recounted with the help of responses to an employee survey conducted by the researcher, interview data, internal records and correspondence, and the researcher's personal experience of the project.

An attempt is made to reconstruct the reaction of various Atlantis individuals, groups, and coalitions to the new pay rates that were attached to jobs and to describe the way in which the pay division coped with any opposition. It will be seen that many of the problems that the efficiency consultants claimed would be eliminated by the introduction of a job evaluation plan began to re-emerge.

The Reaction of the Judges

When salaries were attached to jobs, certain unanticipated 'problems' appeared. Although the deputy ministers themselves had evaluated the jobs and subsequently approved the ranking of positions in their departments, this was the first time that they were confronted with the financial 'results' of the evaluations. Having been publicly drawn in as key actors in the evaluation process, these executives now expressed a certain anxiety over how their employees would receive the information relating to their pay.

The director of pay and a pay analyst visited each deputy minister's office with a list of the department's 'results.' The purpose of these meetings was to discuss the outcome of the of the job evaluations with the deputy ministers before their employees were informed of their new salaries. Prior to these meetings, the deputy ministers had been informed that jobs which were 'reasonably close together' in points had been placed in the same grade, with the same pay-range boundaries.

The result sheets were ceremoniously rolled out across the deputy's desk while polite banter was made about being 'the moment of truth.' Deputy ministers immediately examined the difference between their employees' actual salaries and their new salaries (both the absolute value and the dollar limits of their range). The reaction of the deputy ministers varied. Based upon the researcher's discussions with the director of pay, those reactions can be summarized as follows: 'some suggested that they felt no great surprise, others expressed disappointment, and one or two even claimed that the Hay system "betrayed" them.' At these early private meetings, the deputy ministers brought up certain anticipated problem cases and discussed what should be done about them.

In some ways, the earlier administrative decision to cluster 114 different point scores into 35 job grades was partly responsible for a certain amount of dissatisfaction over the pay outcome. The deputies generally indicated that grouping the points had wasted some of the time and effort that had been put into the evaluations. Grouping was seen to have eliminated the small, but fiercely-guarded differences in job content that had been deemed to exist at the time of the evaluation. Grouping was also seen to have exaggerated differences in job content where jobs had been deliberately scored very close together by the committee, only to be assigned to two separate grades at a later date.

Not all cases of deputy minister concern were, however, related to the 'grouping' issue. Sometimes, the deputy merely indicated a change of mind about relativities upon seeing the actual pay that had been attached to a job. Sometimes it was pointed out that the same job, or group of jobs, had not been given enough money; at other times, it was claimed that too much money had been given. The director of pay, who had a broad knowledge of job relativities across all government departments, also expressed his own reservations about certain jobs to the deputy minister.

These private meetings provided the director of pay and the deputy ministers with the opportunity to make certain 'adjustments' to the point scores that had been reached, by consensus, in the evaluation committees. Jobs were assigned new point scores that would place them in the grade above or below, depending on what the particular problem was seen to be.

The deputies were asked not to mention any 'adjustments' that were made to point scores so as to preserve the integrity of the system in the eyes of the other deputy ministers and of employees. It is therefore difficult to estimate the number of 'adjustments' that were made during these sessions. Changes were made in a secretive manner and were recorded by merely erasing the 'official' point score from the original master copy of the records and substituting the more recent score (interview with pay director). The researcher's own experience in attendance at one-quarter of these meetings and later discussions with the director of pay suggest that about 30 jobs (held by approximately 60 out of the 1,200 employees) were adjusted, that is, the point score of about 1 in 20 employees. None, however, was adjusted upwards or downwards by more than one grade.

Deputy ministers appeared to be primarily concerned over the way in which internal relativities and external competitiveness had been affected by the changes. All nineteen of the deputy ministers who were still working in Atlantis four years after the Hay 'results' had been shown to them were asked the following question by the researcher: 'When the pay ranges were affixed to the job grades by the CSC and you were given the opportunity to comment on the pay outcome, did you make any changes?' Fourteen of the nineteen admitted to having insisted on one or more score changes. Each of the deputies also pointed out that he did not bother to 'fix up' certain exceptionally high or low results if he felt that the individuals 'rightly deserved' this outcome. In other words, not all cases of 'disturbed' relativities were adjusted. Three of the nineteen deputies indicated that, although they knew there would be 'trouble' over one or two new salaries, they were still prepared to 'accept the ruling' of the Hay plan and leave the scores as they were. Only two deputies indicated that they had been 'fully satisfied' with the pay rates attached to their employees' jobs.

At this particular stage, recalculating point scores was not necessarily unproblematic. Deputy ministers and the director of pay were not always in agreement. Arguments arose over whether to make a point-score 'recalculation' and, if one were to be made, by precisely how much. Sometimes the director drew a deputy's attention to what he considered to be a serious problem and, to the director's amazement, the deputies sometimes indicated that they were prepared to live with the *committee's* decision on these 'problem' cases (interview with pay director) – even after the director had pointed out the potentially negative repercussions of *not* adjusting a score. Occasionally, a deputy would follow up such a statement with some indication of motive: I've been looking for a way to get rid of that guy for years; maybe this will do it!' It soon became apparent to the director of pay that the job evaluation project was being used in an opportunistic way, that is, as a vehicle for making certain, sometimes long-awaited, changes within a department (interview with pay director).

Just as the director of pay was occasionally unsuccessful in gaining a deputy minister's authorization to change certain troubling evaluations, a deputy was not always able to persuade the director of pay of the need for a particular adjustment. Although MacRae, the director of pay, admitted that he had been 'as flexible as possible with the deputy ministers so that the system would work,' a certain number (about one-half) of the deputies' requests for adjustment were refused (interview with pay director). The director of pay stated that there were any of a number of reasons for refusing a request at that particular stage of the project:

- Because the point score being proposed was just too mathematically 'unrealistic' or 'outrageous'; or
- because the deputy minister making the request was not powerful or strong enough to do anything about it if we didn't give in and we *were* trying to keep "these things" to a minimum; or
- because it was important to remind people, at times (i.e., to project the impression), that this was a 'system' and that it shouldn't be 'tampered' with; or
- because the evaluation of a particular job or group of jobs had caused such a controversy in the evaluation committee that its score would surely be remembered if it was quietly 'adjusted' to another grade; or, finally,
- because any point score adjustment to the job in question might precipitate a ripple or domino effect throughout the civil service. (ibid)

Two deputies who had been blocked over the scoring of a job were still complaining, four years later, about the inflexibility of the pay division. One drew, for the researcher, the following analogy between staff in the pay division and chimpanzees: 'You can teach a chimp to stop at red and go at green and he will do it beautifully, but if there is some reason that he should not go at green, he goes anyway – humans are supposed to be different in terms of understanding the need for deviation – the CSC just waves the 'rules' of job evaluation at you whether they fit the situation or not.' Another deputy made the following observation: 'Just because two different jobs in the government both scored 654 points, doesn't mean that they are necessarily worth the same in the job market!' Why, indeed, should the actual monetary value pinned to a job grade (derived, in this case, from the thrice-lowered salary line) necessarily coincide with the going rate for 'say' engineers, lawyers, accountants or agricultural representatives?

Where market problems were found to exist – that is, where it could be demonstrated that difficulties would occur in the recruitment or retention of staff as a result of any new pay rates – the pay division declared that a temporary 'market premium' would be attached to the job, in the shape of a percentage pay increase. This temporary market premium, 'for exceptions only,' was to be used only to raise temporarily the pay of a job when it could be demonstrated (by survey evidence collected by the pay division) that the job evaluation score obtained by the committee placed a job, or group of jobs, in a grade with an 'unrealistic' salary level, compared to that job's current labour-market value.

The director of pay often tried to get the deputy ministers to accept the notion of a temporary 'market premium.' Although the idea of using a market premium was recommended by Hay Associates, it is commonly used in salary administration as a means of compensation for when job evaluation does not have it 'quite right.' The problem encountered by the director of pay, however, was that the deputies didn't want it. In other words, instead of pinning some temporary sum of money to a job, deputy ministers preferred to adjust an individual's point score that the job would (permanently) belong to another grade. The point-'fiddling' method, they could understand. As one deputy put it, 'That so-called premium could have been removed from employees any time the Civil Service Commission felt like it. Who wants that?'

This market premium only applied upwards, that is, to jobs that were to be paid a rate that was lower than that the job would command in the labour market. Needless to say, there was no reverse provision for jobs that benefited from a new rate of pay that was considerably higher than what the market dictated. In these cases, however, the point scores of jobs were sometimes lowered by 'fiddling' the recorded evaluations.

It was rare, but not unheard of, for a deputy to insist that the new pay range attached to a particular job was 'way too high for that job.' The department in which this happened the most was Health. As table 7, in chapter 7, demonstrated, Health, the department with the highest numbers of women in supervisory, managerial, and professional jobs, was the department whose salary line was, on average, even *lower than the minimum* of their new pay ranges. The existing salaries in the Atlantis Regional Hospital (Department of Health) had worked out to a compa ratio of 0.79, that is, at an average of 21 per cent below the value of their 'policy.' Therefore, many positions stood to receive a considerable increase in pay.

Although it was suspected that the deputy minister requesting a number of point-score reductions was demonstrating sexual bias, the scores that certain jobs obtained in the evaluation committee were, nevertheless, brought down so that the jobs fitted into the next-lower grade. It was mostly in the Department of Health, one of the biggest departments of government, that any collusion between the deputy and the director of pay actually took place to *reduce* the point scores of jobs.

Thus, frequent exchanges took place between the deputy ministers and the pay division, and a great number of adjustments were made so that the new pay rates would 'look right' in each department. In some cases, disagreements had taken place over whether or not to change a point score. Before employees were informed of their new pay rate and range, MacRae observed to the analysts that he had done everything possible to gain the deputy ministers' support for the new pay rates. He also indicated, at the time, that there was still a good deal of apprehension on the part of deputy ministers before the pay notifications went out to individual employees. The implications of a 'participative' job evaluation system were being felt. There was not long to wait for the employees' reaction, some of which was anticipated by the pay division and some not.

The Reaction of Employees

By November 1981, all the presentations had been made to employees (explaining the operation of the new pay plan and the method of converting from old to new), each deputy minister had been visited by the director of pay to discuss the 'results,' and certain 'adjustments' had been made to point scores. It was then that each employee received a letter, in a sealed envelope, from the Civil Service Commission. This brief 'form' letter indicated the individual's existing salary, a new grade number, a salary within that grade, and the salary-range limits, i.e., the minimum, policy, and maximum values of the new pay range.

Employees were also informed that their mid-December paycheque would contain their pay increase. (Atlantis civil servants are paid twice a month via the costly means of a supervisor distributing the cheques by hand, and all Atlantis government employees being given twenty minutes of 'banking time' every second Thursday.) This increase was to be retroactive to the previous August, the month in which their old pay rates expired.

Staff from the pay division, computer services, and payroll had to work many hours of overtime to ensure that these increases were received by employees on time. It was considered an important part of the implementation strategy that employees receive these retroactive increases *before* Christmas (all employees were to receive at least 3 per cent increases). In the words of the director of pay, 'Even if the news doesn't meet their expectations, they'll be so happy to get the money when they need it most that they hopefully won't complain.'

How did employees react? It is hard to tell who would have been happy or unhappy about his or her new pay. It would be easy to suggest that those who benefited the most (financially) from the introduction of the job evaluation plan were the most satisfied. This was often, but not necessarily always the case. Each employee had his or her own reasons for being satisfied or dissatisfied over his or her new pay. Even some of the 19 per cent of employees who fell into the 'underpaid' category (those at or below 0.79 of their policy) and who stood to go up considerably in both ranking and pay resented the 'slowness' of their conversion (employee interviews).

Some of the 61 per cent who went up (i.e., those located between 0.80 and 1.00 of policy), although they went up to different pay levels, were dissatisfied because they did not go up as high as they would have liked, or because other jobs went up 'more' than did their own (employee interviews).

However, not all those 20 percent whose existing pay was already over the 'policy' value of their new grade were necessarily unhappy over the outcome. It is certain that some had expected that their jobs would have been lowered more than they had been.

Having been led to believe that the Hay plan would 'right the wrongs' that had long existed across government, some employees also believed the private pay grievances that they, personally, had been harbouring would be exposed and dutifully corrected. They were disappointed when this did not happen. As one employee wrote, 'I do all the work in this division and I should have been graded a lot higher than the two other guys I work with who do nothing!'

In the survey carried out by the researcher on 230 employees whose jobs had been selected as benchmarks, respondents were asked to place a check mark in a box indicating whether they had, at the time, been satisfied or dissatisfied by the absolute value of their new pay and the relative value of their new pay. If they indicated dissatisfaction in relation to either, they were asked to state what, if anything they did about it. Overall findings for the first part of the question were: 72 per cent were satisfied, and 28 per cent dissatisfied, with absolute pay; 51 per cent were satisfied, and 49 per cent dissatisfied, with relative pay; 43 per cent were satisfied, and 24 per cent dissatisfied, with both.

Thus, a greater number of respondents expressed dissatisfaction with their relative pay than did with the absolute value of their pay. Within Atlantis, employees did not apparently restrict their comparisons to those jobs that had been evaluated by Hay, but also compared themselves to unionized civil-service jobs, and particularly to those jobs that belonged to their previous counterparts in the unionized pay plan (employee interviews).

The second part of the survey question asked the newly evaluated employees to state what, if anything, they did if they were dissatisfied over either absolute pay, relative pay, or both. Of the employees who indicted dissatisfaction in either or both cases, 42 per cent stated that they did 'nothing,' with most of these indicating that there would have been little use in taking any action. One employee wrote: 'After 25 years with the government, I learned to accept the outcome – to do anything else is sheer frustration!' Others who did 'nothing' pointed out that the new pay rates had been presented as 'take it or leave it,' and, since there was no official appeal process to be instituted, 'what recourse did we have?'

All 'dissatisfied' employees were not passive, however. Of the employees who indicated some dissatisfaction over either absolute or relative pay, 58 per cent claimed to have taken some form of action to try to change their circumstances. This action ranged anywhere from a verbal complaint to the lodging of a formal protest. It is also known by the researcher that at least three individuals, in protest at the results of the job evaluation scheme, resigned from their positions and left the government. Also, although respondents did not mention this point in the survey, various employees did, over the years, let the pay division know informally that they no longer went 'above and beyond the call of duty' when it came to performing their jobs.

Those individuals who did remain with the government and responded that they had taken some form of action against their new pay can be divided into two categories. About one-half of them claimed to have expressed their opinion *verbally* about the failings of the Hay system to their deputy minister. The other half indicated that they had made a *written* representation to their deputy, spelling out the reasons for their dissatisfaction (examples are provided later in the chapter). Deputy ministers all reacted differently to their employees' appeals for a second evaluation. According to the employees, the extent to which they managed to achieve any change in their situation depended on whether or not they had their deputy minister's support.

The most common type of comments made about deputy ministers' attitudes are as follows: 'The deputy turns a blind eye to my problems'; 'My deputy says he fought hard for me but blames the other members of the evaluation committee for the points'; 'My deputy minister informed me that committee members felt that jobs like mine were a dime a dozen!'; 'My deputy told me that those were points that the committee got out of the job description – if I had written a better job description, I would have got more points!' This last answer is reminiscent of Goffman''s well-known paper 'On Calling the Mark Out - Some Adaptions to Failure' (1952). In it, he discusses the way in which the confidence trickster protects himself by either *directly involving* the victim in the crime or making the victim look ridiculous if he or she were to report the crime. In Atlantis, the fact that employees had written their own job descriptions was used by deputy ministers as a way of throwing back responsibility (or guilt) into the hands of the employee.

Many respondents seemed to suggest that deputies hid behind the 'abstract' and 'complex' language of the Hay system to 'bamboozle' them. One respondent, for instance, wrote that the deputy had responded to a complaint by saying, 'In your evaluation, the relationship between Problem-Solving and Accountability fits the profile of your type of job.' This type of language, used with employees who had only once been flashed the evaluation guide charts on a view-graph screen, appeared to intimidate some employees and prevent them from challenging the deputy's statements (survey evidence provided later, in chapter 10, seems to support this thesis). Despite the fact that deputy ministers knew what limited information employees had been given, fifteen of the nineteen deputy ministers interviewed admitted to having used 'Hay terminology' when employees confronted them with complaints. One deputy minister said, 'We're stuck with it, so why not use it?' Another stated that talking in Hay terms helped him to win over employees, that is, to 'close the sale.' Yet another deputy claimed to use the Hay language 'all the time,' chortling that 'Bullshit baffles brains!'

Deputy ministers sometimes called up MacRae to tell him that they had new information about a job, or a group of jobs, that necessitated a point-score change. Again, MacRae allowed some changes to be made (adjusting the computer printouts) and blocked others. The Hay consultant, who was, by this time, visiting Atlantis only occasionally, agreed with the need to change certain evaluations 'to make the system work' (see Stelling and Bucher [1973] for a discussion of 'Vocabularies of Realism'). But he also questioned some of MacRae's decisions. As MacRae announced to his staff at the time, 'Burr is now starting to interfere. I think we've learned all there is to know about the Hay system and it's about time that he moved on and let us run our own shop. He's become a nuisance.'

By and large, the deputies indicated that they were able to ward off 'the majority' of complaints. However, various individuals and groups successfully challenged their new pay range. Any changes that were made to point scores after the employees had been informed were treated as very 'hush-hush' by the pay department. In cases in which the information leaked, changes were referred to publicly as responses to 'errors' that had been discovered.

The most concerted employee attack on the new pay rates was launched by a group of engineers in the Department of Transportation. Their story makes an interesting statement about the importance of speaking the same language and the need for a deputy minister's support to effect change. A group of twenty-one engineers used their knowledge of the Hay technique itself to challenge the logic of the system and to restore what they considered to be the appropriate (i.e., customary) relationship between themselves (staff engineers) and field operating engineers.

When these engineering positions had been evaluated by the committee, the deputy of Transportation indicated that the low point scores allocated to the staff engineers would cause 'relativity' problems in his department. In this instance, however (perhaps feeling that this powerful deputy minister was too accustomed to getting his own way), the committee just would not give in to the deputy's request to raise the score of staff engineers so that it would be at least as high as that of the field operating engineer. The committee members claimed that, according to the 'rules' and the 'logic' of the job evaluation criteria, those engineers who were 'out there in the field, managing large construction budgets and large numbers of people,' were of greater value to the organization than those 'fat cats' in head office who 'shuffle paper.' The staff and the operating groups were independent, and one did not officially report to the other.

Before the job evaluation project, the staff engineers had been, for the most part, on a higher pay level than the operating engineer. Because the evaluators of Committee C unexpectedly 'insisted' (in this case) on the need for a change in relativities, this situation was reversed. On 2 November 1981, the day after the staff of the Department of Transportation received their official letters of announcement from the Civil Service Commission, a group of eleven service engineers forwarded a memorandum to the three senior engineering executives of their department. These three executives reported directly to the deputy minister. This memorandum from the staff engineers began as follows: 'The purpose of this memo is to protest the unfair treatment afforded the Staff Section of the Department of Transportation with respect to the Operations Section as a result of the introduction of the new Management Compensation Program. This new system has split the Department's engineers and has resulted in demoralization of the Managerial Staff of the Staff Section and can only lead to future deterioration of this section of this Department.' This memorandum went on to outline the 'immediate problems and inequalities the new system has created,' noting that individuals promoted to head-office jobs on the service side had, up until then, been drawn from the ranks of the operating side, and that it would no longer be possible to continue this practice. The employee memorandum also attempted to break the shroud of secrecy that had surrounded the details of job scoring under the three headings of Know-How, Problem Solving, and Accountability: 'We would also like to have the opportunity to see exactly how points were assigned to various positions throughout the Department that apparently forced the recent change in relative status in our organization.'

The three chief directors who received this memo showed it to their deputy minister, who forwarded it to the Civil Service Commission, requesting a 're-evaluation' of the staff engineers' position. By 26 November 1981, this group of engineers had received no response to their 2 November request for information. The group of protesters had now grown from a group of eleven to twenty-one staff engineers – the full complement. They forwarded another memo to the same senior-management group. This next memo opened with a reiteration of the dissatisfaction of the staff section of the department with 'the results of the new job evaluation program' and blamed 'the manner in which it was imposed' rather than the Hay plan itself:

We realize it would be foolhardy for us to attempt to discredit the Hay system per se. There are probably many systems of rating Management personnel and the Hay system is undoubtedly as good if not better than most. Unfortunately, because of the manner in which the system was introduced to us we were basically forced to "trust" Civil Service Commission to ensure that our positions were evaluated in a fair and equitable manner. Naturally, as a result of the outcome, we now have grave doubts that the best interests of the Department of Transportation ... were properly served.

The extent to which the group of staff engineers was determined to find out exactly how the Hay system worked and get to the bottom of their evaluations is exemplified in the following excerpt from the same memo: 'It has not been easy for us to obtain any literature on the Hay system, however we have gained access to a reprint from a book entitled "Handbook of Wage and Salary Administration" edited by M.L. Rock. In addition we have perused various other books dealing generally with the theory of the personnel management process. As a result of this search we have now become convinced that the Civil Service Commission did not properly introduce this new system to our Department.'

These engineers, having gained access to information on the operation of the Hay system and having acquired a certain proficiency in the language of this particular technique, tried to get their point scores raised so that their jobs would be in higher grades. Using the vocabulary and modes of expression used by those few who knew the 'inner workings' of the pay system, the engineers challenged their evaluation. Some of their newly acquired language can be seen in the following passage from their 26 November memo:

We have been told that the reason engineers on the Staff side of the Department did not fare as well as engineers on the Operation side of the Department was because we accumulated less points when our jobs were evaluated, based on these three aspects [Know-How, Problem Solving, and Accountability]. In particular, we understand that we fared poorly on Accountability. Therefore the definition of these three aspects becomes very important. We have to assume that because we are all engineers there should be little or no difference on the points assigned under the Know-How aspect. In our opinion the Staff side should score higher for the Problem Solving involved in planning and designing ...

The final crunch is probably Accountability and here the definition of Accountability is all important ... As a matter of fact in the section of the previously mentioned Handbook describing the Hay system under the heading 'Measuring People in Terms of Goals' it is stated that 'support' [staff] jobs will receive higher base salaries than operating jobs because Know-How and Problem-Solving (as compared to Accountability) form a relatively greater part of total job content.

The engineers also criticized the participative approach used by the government: 'it seems amazing to us that a committee of seven Deputy Ministers would be assigned the task of determining the relative value between various Directors or Managers in our Department. How could six Deputy Ministers who have nothing to do with our department be expected to have a "thorough understanding" of our jobs ... We feel that the Civil Service Commission was wrong to introduce a system which allowed "outsiders" to reorganize the relative status in the Department of Transportation.' This memo ended with an expression of concern for the morale of the department and another request to see exactly how points were assigned to these jobs by the evaluation committee.

The three senior executives who received this second memo from the service engineers showed it to the deputy minister of the department, who, on 1 December 1981, wrote the following in a letter to the Civil Service Commission: 'I feel that both the commission and the Hay Consultants should be made aware of views of the group concerned and I suggest that in this particular instance the Commission and Hay Consultants should seriously consider providing a specific response to this November 26 memo.' When the deputy minister telephoned the director of pay about his delay in responding to the 'engineers' situation,' the director of pay did indicate that the engineer problem was the subject of a great deal too much general interest to make any 'adjustments' at this late stage, and that engineering positions in other departments would also be affected if these particular jobs were to undergo any change in grade. MacRae indicated a number of times, to the analysts, that he felt that it would be 'risky' to respond 'in writing' to the specific requests of the engineers. Whenever the analyst visited the Department of Transportation, there was an atmosphere of hostility, even from the operating engineers (whose relative position had been raised in relation to the staff engineers). In the main reception area of the department (mounted and framed), and in a number of offices, the researcher found a caricature of 'Mr. Hay' (depicted as a monster) destroying the Department of Trans-

FIGURE 10
Caricature of Hay

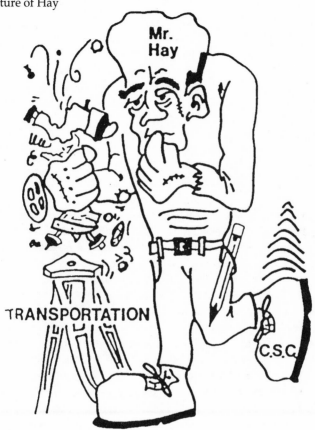

portation, with the help of the Civil Service Commission (see figure 10).

By 14 January, having waited six weeks for a formal response to be forwarded from the pay division to his engineers, the deputy minister of Transportation wrote to his counterpart, the deputy minister of the Civil Service Commission. This time the letter spelled out, in no uncertain terms, the *exact* grades requested for each of the twenty-one positions. Each of the twenty-one recommended changes would have involved an upward adjustment of only one grade. It was stated that if these changes could not be made on a permanent basis, then the department would settle for a 'temporary market premium' being affixed to these jobs. The deputy minister indicated his full support for the staff engineers, hinting at the possibility of 'political' intervention if satisfaction was not obtained.

One month later, on 15 February, the following rejection letter went out from the deputy minister of the Civil Service Commission (drafted by MacRae) to the deputy minister of Transportation. This letter stands as one of the very few examples of a *written* explanation of 'why' the evaluation committees' decisions must not be 'adjusted.'

Dear Mr. ——:

RE: *Management Compensation Plan*

As a result of your letters on this matter and the subsequent meeting at the Management Board office, the Commission has considered this matter at great length.

Although we appreciate the fact that internal relativities within the department have changed somewhat, it would be unacceptable for us to arbitrarily adjust the classifications of these twenty-one (21) positions.

At the time the evaluations were completed the relative ranking of positions within the department was considered appropriate by the Senior Management of the department. I realize that you did not know the actual salaries that would be applied but certainly everyone was aware of the fact that if one position received a higher evaluation than another position, there was a strong possibility that it would also receive a higher salary. Therefore, the fact that this has happened should not really be a surprise.

The idea of establishing a premium rate for one group of Civil Engineers within your department is also unacceptable to the Commission. We realize that it may be necessary from time to time to provide special consideration in relation to the market for certain occupational groups, however, we would expect that such a problem would manifest itself in a broader scope and require specific consideration across a wide span of engineering positions throughout the service. This particular request would suggest that we administer groups of engineering positions requiring similar training and experience at different levels and is impossible to justify.

Since the time of our discussion the Commission has developed a 'Red-Circle Policy' and employees will be informed of this policy at briefing sessions being held by the Civil Service Commission. We hope that these sessions will answer many of the questions which employees have and thus allow all concerned to get back to the task at hand and channel their energies toward the completion of assigned responsibilities to the best of their ability.

Yours very truly,

As reported in a number of accounts, the deputy minister of Transportation was outraged when he received this letter and immediately wrote back, saying that the minister would be informed (i.e., 'political' intervention was being sought) and that the Civil Service Commission had not heard 'the end of this.'

In the end, through the intervention of certain key politicians, the pay division was persuaded to have the twenty-one positions submitted for 'recalculation' to the newly created committee of deputy ministers – the 'Maintenance Committee' – set up to evaluate any new jobs whose content had changed over the years. Although the Maintenance Committee did not include in its mandate the revision of point scores allocated earlier by the job evaluation committees, the engineer issue (now well-known across all government departments) was addressed.

This newly created committee was made up of ten deputy ministers (most of whom had themselves, somehow or other, managed to secure an 'adjustment' or two following the 'results'). It was before these that the soon-to-retire deputy minister of Transportation pleaded his case. When the deputy saw that there was little sign of the committee's munificence, he pleaded for 'at least twelve of the more serious cases of injustice' to be upgraded, and produced already prepared calculations that the committee could use to fit the necessary Hay guide-chart boxes. The committee finally agreed that the deputy could have his way, but they pointed out to him, in a joking manner, that this was his retirement present. Even though almost all deputies knew, privately, that they had each, on the quiet, asked for similar (albeit lower-profile) favours of the pay division, there was still a general façade of uprightness and a reluctance to publicly admit any tomfoolery related to the earlier evaluation results.

The 'rationale' sheets that were meant to explain the scoring breakdown under each evaluation subheading were creatively composed by the pay analyst so that it would look like each point selection, under each category, had been given serious consideration by the committee (interview with pay director). Over the next two years, as the attention of civil servants shifted away from the engineers, the point scores of most of the remaining nine positions were quietly readjusted. As the newly appointed deputy of Transportation said to the researcher, 'We have been able to make other changes recently in the service side of the operation. We are almost back to normal.'

Back at the Civil Service Commission, the director of pay was trying to deal with a number of letters and phone calls from employees and other deputy ministers. Although the deputy ministers had tried to ward off any anticipated problems, a few relativity upsets had been left on the 'result' sheets either by oversight or by design. A series of problems had been encountered in the Department of the Attorney General (with evaluation of supervisory legal positions) and the Department of Education (with ex-teachers now in supervisory positions). Each of these groups's salaries had previously been carefully measured against that of professional organizations, and any slight disturbance of their relativity against these (provincial teacher or lawyer scales) caused an uproar. Requests were made for one-grade adjustments only, some of which were granted, some not.

Case-Study Epilogue

After the initial reaction to new pay rates, things quieted down in the supervisory, managerial, and professional ranks, although certain individual and collective demands for higher pay persisted here and there. Mostly, however, the employees who had had their jobs evaluated under the Hay plan turned their attention to implementing the new 'zero-base' budgeting system, another one of the efficiency consultants recommendations. The job evaluation project was generally considered to have been a success. While attitudes were not necessarily measured at the time, it is the researcher's experience that the atmosphere within the Civil Service Commission was congratulatory.

When the 'dust had settled,' so to speak, the Maintenance Committee, made up of ten deputy ministers (membership on an annual rotation), began its task of meeting to evaluate any new or changed jobs, using the Hay guide charts. Senior managers or deputy ministers from other departments were invited to attend these meetings to 'represent' a job in their department. The administration of the new job evaluation plan followed much the same procedure as that used in installation. An employee's superior was responsible for reporting changes in job content, by means of submitting a revised job description, through the appropriate channels, to the pay division for the consideration of the Maintenance Committee.

Upon returning to the Civil Service Commission some three years after implementation, I discovered that less attention was given to the maintenance of job evaluation than to its inauguration. In other words, certain administrative arrangements had fallen down. To 'speed things up,' jobs were being evaluated by the pay division *before* they were presented to the committee and a 'tentative evaluation' (or suggested evaluation?) was handed to evaluators at the same time as the new or revised job description. The deputy ministers on the Maintenance Committee indicated, in their interviews with the researcher, that they found it extremely difficult to define 'significant change' in the job descriptions and that they were, as one deputy put it, 'prepared to go along with the Civil Service's evaluation – unless, of course, it's a job in my own department.'

It was interesting for me to listen to the frustration of deputies who had somehow been roped into a familiar game of semantics that has long been wearily watched (and played) by salary administrators the world over. In this case, job-description writers were pitted against an evaluation committee that had to discern, through much obfuscation, the extent to which a job had become 'enriched,' more 'complex,' and so on. To the researcher, it was not surprising that the pay division staff intercepted the evaluations, lest bureaucratic logic win out over efficiency, or procedure over price.

Right after the employees received their new pay rates, the director of pay viewed the Hay consultant's job as complete. Graciously, the Hay consultant admitted that he had equipped the pay division staff with all that he knew and agreed to 'fade' from the scene. His visits became less frequent and soon ceased. On the strength of the Atlantis contract and a potential list of new clients in the area, a new Hay branch office was opened in the Atlantis region of Canada, headed by a different Hay consultant. Mr. Burr was promoted from the position of senior consultant to manager of a large Hay office, and, more recently, has been made a vice-president.

After Burr's departure, the pay division set about devising the performance-appraisal scheme that made up the third of the three stated objectives of the job evaluation project: internal equity, external competitiveness and, pay for performance. A grid was established, limits were set on how much or how little employees could be moved up or down , and those with staff to review were given brief training sessions by the training division of the Civil Service Commission. The first attempt at consistent performance appraisal in Atlantis was made in the spring of 1982, a few months after the pay announcement. Prior to this exercise, performance appraisal was a decentralized activity. Some departments had developed or selected their own schemes, but the majority ignored the idea. Many claimed that it was difficult to comment on performance when no sanctions or rewards could be applied to the (basically) automatic step-, or increment-related pay plan.

In the year following the introduction of performance appraisal, while the pay division was 'brushing up' the performance categories defined in the grid (over which there had been a variety of complaints relating to ambiguity), the Canadian economy was experiencing the effects of an economic recession. Treasury Board announced a freeze on performance-related increases (the salary-range movements were still approved, although the percentage increase was more conservative than in previous years). The following year, Treasury Board allowed departments to grant some merit increases, as long as costs did not exceed 1 per cent of payroll.

Such was the state of pay-related activity during my stay in Atlantis in 1985. Since then, by all accounts, it would appear that the Hay plan continues to 'satisfy the needs' of the organization. When the economy picked up, employees received more generous performance-related pay increases.

Conclusions

This chapter has described how various individuals and groups in Atlantis reacted to the new pay rates that had been assigned to jobs following the introduction of formal job evaluation. Upon seeing the financial 'results' of their evaluations, deputy ministers were eager to make some last-minute adjustments, before the pay information was communicated to their employees. This adjustment process involved gaining the support of the director of pay to rearrange or undo certain decisions that had been made in the evaluation committees. Based on his knowledge of cross-departmental relativities and the personalities involved in the request, the director of pay sometimes allowed an 'under the table' adjustment to be made, and sometimes he did not.

When employees were informed of the new annual salaries affixed to their jobs, they were, for the most part, pleased with the results. After all, as MacRae pointed out, 'about 80 per cent gained more from the introduction of Hay than they would have if we hadn't introduced it.' Of those who were dissatisfied, some managed to persuade their deputy minister to make a case for 'recalculation,' and some did not. In later interviews conducted by the researcher, deputy ministers claim to have warded off, or at least tried to ward off, employee complaints by using the complex language of the Hay guide charts to confuse employees and make them think that their jobs had been given a lot of thought in the evaluation committee. Of those that the deputy ministers brought to the attention of the Civil Service Commission, not all were seen to be legitimate problems. As a result, some bitterness still exists in Atlantis to this day.

The Hay consultant had recommended, and the pay division indeed bought, the notion of 'secrecy.' The notion of secrecy is generally considered to make the system more 'impregnable' to employee objection. In Atlantis, although the guide charts and their operation had been briefly shown to employees, the development of secrecy can be seen to have acted as a potent source of defence against employee challenge.

Fourteen of the nineteen deputy ministers interviewed admitted to having had 'one or two adjustments' made to evaluations, either before or after the new pay rates had been announced to employees. It was observed that sometimes a deputy's decision *not to request adjustment* (or temporary market premium) could also be seen as an attempt to legitimize, through the so-called job evaluation exercise, either a favour to some valued employee or a personal vendetta against a long-disliked employee. The pay division could do nothing more than point out a 'glaring anomaly' to the deputies, if they had not already spotted it themselves, but the director of pay could not change a score without the deputy's approval.

It was also seen that the director of pay and the Hay consultant were willing to compromise or risk the apparent integrity of the job evaluation plan in order to make the system work. Although they tried the device of a temporary market premium, departments showed a marked preference for the more permanent solution of 'fiddling' the point scores instead. Some form of market premium is, however, common where the right 'fit' does not occur between bureaucratic logic and competitive logic (Lupton and Gowler 1969; NBPI 1968). As the British National Board for Prices and Incomes report (1968: 39) indicates: 'The final results of the job evaluation process will not always correspond with what is paid outside ... Companies introducing job evaluation can often meet this problem by paying individual "job allowances."' Although the use of deputy ministers as evaluators was meant to remove the adversarial, or 'confrontation,' relationship that had previously existed between the department and the Civil Service Commission, it was seen that the requests for secret 'adjustments' to the point scores were still being demanded of (or forced upon) the pay division and the deputy minister of the Civil Service Commission.

It could also be said that the 'culture' of the organization not the set of 'rational' criteria that was superimposed upon the existing Atlantis hierarchy, graded the jobs in Atlantis. This phenomenon resembles that described by Metcalfe and Richards (1984: 442) as 'cultural lag' in a study of change in the British government: 'As so often happens, cultural lag means that the ruling ideas appropriate to an earlier age persist and continue to exert an influence on administrative behavior and organizational structure long after the conditions in which they developed have disappeared.'

The 'weight of the past' was evidenced in this chapter, with the re-evaluation of the staff engineer's position. Job worth was defined, in this case, by the power of individuals and groups to impose their own value definition on a job – above and beyond the so-called rational powers of formal job evaluation. As Routh (1965: 49) observes, 'there is something elemental in this attachment of a person to his level of income, measured in terms of its purchasing power (the maintenance of a standard of living) and in terms of the earnings of other occupations, that is not unlike the attachment of an animal to its young.'

This chapter also demonstrated the way in which job evaluation, by incorporating into its weights and factors the notion of a perfect or 'ideal' hierarchy, still allows considerable scope for decision making. The fact that all 'fiddles' in Atlantis occurred over a mere one-grade difference in relativity reveals the irony of job evaluation. The chapter has shown, further, how requests for 'adjustments' were treated on an ad hoc basis that appeared to depend as much on personalities, power, and politics as had the previous salary-administration practices of Atlantis that had been so forcefully discredited by the 'efficiency' consultants. In other words, where the logic of the 'rational' job evaluation plan could not be reconciled with individual expectations, pressure was applied on the pay division to 'fiddle' the official point scores obtained in the evaluation committees.

The apparent 'rationality' of the formal job evaluation plan was to be undermined by the deeply felt notions of fairness in pay and the strong political and cultural currents of the organization. The hierarchy that existed in Atlantis had evolved over a period of years. As is the case in many organizations, a number of exceptions and allowances made their way into the process. Individuals usually have a strong interest in seeing that the status quo is maintained.

This case-study should not be interpreted, however, as that of a 'failed' job evaluation plan. Rather, the case of Atlantis demonstrates that job evaluation cannot operate at a 'rational' level, as the number of 'exceptions' will attest. Changes did, indeed, occur in the relativities and in actual pay levels. In Atlantis, it could be said that the Hay plan achieved 'results.' Through this case-study, it is argued, however, that job evaluation provided the change vehicle for making desired adjustments according to the existing political and social environment.

PART III

Job Evaluation Reconsidered

9 The Failure of Job Evaluation: *A Triumph of Political Action over Bureaucratic Logic*

It was seen in chapter 3 that writers from the personnel-management and the industrial-relations schools make various claims about what job evaluation does and the way in which the technique helps management to exert control over employees. The claims made about job evaluation seem to imply that a set of objective criteria exists that can ①
provide the required rationale for ranking one job higher or lower than another. Job evaluation, as put forward by the personnel-man- ②
agement school, is based upon the assumption that all jobs have a number of common factors that can be measured to determine their relative value. While some subjective factors are seen to be drawn into the evaluation process, 'political' forces are considered to play a disrupting or disturbing role in relation to the effective operation of a scheme.

Moreover, the personnel-management school attributes certain technical powers to job evaluation, such as establishing the organizational hierarchy, determining the extent of differentials between jobs, and even determining the pay rate or range of a job. Taking the assumptions of the personnel-management school for granted, industrial-relations researchers focus upon the (supposed) power of job evaluation to reduce conflict, restrict collective bargaining, and bureaucratize unions and shop stewards. The pay-equity movement also takes the personnel assumptions for granted, holding up job evaluation as the key to eliminating gender-based pay discrimination.

In this chapter, the case-study material is evaluated primarily against the personnel-management claims, demonstrating that commonly held beliefs about the properties of job evaluation have been based upon unexamined assumptions that, upon closer inspection, are found to be simply not true. By debunking the popular myths about job evaluation, this chapter takes us a step closer to understanding that there are other, hidden, meanings, associated with the use of job evaluation. In this way, it is hoped to understand what job evaluation really does and what it is about job evaluation that makes this costly and time-consuming technique increasingly so attractive to organizations.

Both the personnel-management and the industrial-relations perspectives impute a certain 'rationality' to the job evaluation process; that is, both assume that, by introducing job evaluation, the stated goals of the technique will be achieved. It is the purpose of this chapter to expose these claims as either exaggerated or entirely erroneous. In doing so, the chapter forces me, again, to pose my original question in a somewhat more penetrating way: *What does job evaluation really do?*

Reconsidering Personnel-Management Claims about Job Evaluation

The case-study revealed that, after a new Conservative government came to power in Atlantis, an 'efficiency team' was established to investigate management systems across government, to make recommendations for increased efficiency, and to report its findings to a cabinet committee. The existing method of assigning pay grades to jobs was portrayed as chaotic and characterized by haggling and horse trading. In other words, the consultants laid stress on the ad hoc nature of classification practices, the lack of a systematic approach, and the 'personality' basis of decision making. The efficiency consultants claimed not only that introducing job evaluation would facilitate a departure from chaos to a new systematic and rational method of determining pay, but that other areas of personnel, such as recruitment, training, and manpower planning, would be enhanced by the introduction of a job evaluation technique that provided new 'results-oriented' job descriptions. The description of the 'old' system by the efficiency consultants resembled all other reports and evidence provided to the researcher about the operation of job classification at that time.

The case-study has shown that there was a complex set of motivations at play in the decision to introduce a formal job evaluation plan to Atlantis. On the one hand, it appeared that various motives existed (e.g., projecting the image of efficiency, professionalizing jobs in the central personnel agency) that had little to do with the 'rational' justifications of job evaluation as laid out in standard personnel text-books. On the other hand, it appeared that some motives did have a direct relationship to the claims of personnel management. For example, the Hay consultants who were later to introduce the new job evaluation system claimed that this system would replace the personality-based method for determining pay by a 'rational' method. Indeed, the claims made by the Hay consultant (and written in the 'letter of interest') were much the same as the claims about job evaluation that abound in the personnel-management literature. Thus, the Atlantis case-study stands as a good example to be used to test potential powers of job evaluation as a rational technique. According to Hay, a formal job evaluation scheme would:

1 / create new job descriptions to be used as a basis of evaluation
2 / establish an internally equitable organizational hierarchy
3 / provide 'rational' criteria for the evaluation of jobs
4 / ensure external competitiveness by determining actual pay rates achieved through 'plugging' into the data bank
5 / facilitate the day-to-day operation of the salary system.

Let us now re-evaluate each of these claims in relation to the Atlantis case-study.

THE REAL VALUE OF JOB DESCRIPTIONS

The job description was portrayed by the consultants as the rational basis for the entire job evaluation system as it was to stand as the only reference point to be used by the evaluation committees in evaluating the jobs. The faceless job description was supposed to distance the evaluation process from political factors. The iron law of the evaluation process is that it 'evaluates jobs and not individuals' (International Labour Office 1960). The Atlantis case-study data demonstrate a rather dramatic departure from popular 'theories' about the value of the job description. Reality stood firmly at odds with theory.

First, certain extraneous factors appeared to impinge on the writing of the job descriptions and produced variations in 'quality'. Some employees, for instance, became (to varying degrees) adept at the use of the Hay language to present their jobs in the best possible light; moreover, employee grapevines or networks operated to gather and disseminate key expressions to be used in, and 'tips' for writing the job description. Furthermore, the competence of the Civil Service Commission pay analysts was seen by the civil servants to be critical to the quality of the job descriptions, and employees sometimes connived to have more than one analyst revise their job descriptions.

It also needs to be pointed out that, after all the effort put into writing the job descriptions, more often than not they were used only selectively by the job evaluation committees. Evaluators continued to discuss 'individuals' and existing (or desired) relativities to evaluate jobs. As one deputy minister put it, 'I know my people and I know my jobs ... I can't simply give up my departmental knowledge for some trumped-up matrix in front of me.' Another deputy minister expressed himself more directly: 'Let's face it, job descriptions are a blend of fact and creative writing. You have to learn to read in between the lines. You get to read between the lines by knowing your department. This takes time and experience. I'd rather rely on my experience than on a job description.'

The rhetoric of job description 'parlance' seemed to be accepted only when it fitted in with existing notions about what the job did and how the job rated to other jobs. Interviews with Civil Service Commission staff confirmed that there was a considerable lapse back to the 'old ways,' both during the meetings of evaluation committees and after these committees had been disbanded. While the job descriptions would accompany analysts in day-to-day reviews of departmental jobs, 'informal discussions' still dominated the grading process. This was also found to be the case in the job evaluation Maintenance Committee.

Moreover, the selective use of the job descriptions cannot simply be interpreted as a political process of 'mobilization of bias.' It is possible to suggest that the 'selective' use of job descriptions also reflects the evaluators' own understanding of the limitations of the job description itself as a device that can perfectly 'freeze' a job in time. While rational theorists suggest that job descriptions are essential documents without which no proper evaluation can take place, the fact remains that such descriptions are only 'limited' projections of the nature and content of jobs. As Turner (1971: 72) has suggested,

even when these job descriptions are very lengthy, they cannot specify everything about a job, and the individual still has to decide where the limits of his job lie, often by means of a process of interaction and negotiation with other members of the organization. Only in situations of extreme constraint – for example in solitary confinement or some other prison-like situation – is it possible that the limited role required may be fully outlined by something akin to a job description, and even then the fit would only occur because the person was 'institutionalized' and prepared to limit himself to the prescribed role.

It is simply not possible to 'adequately describe the fullest implications of job responsibility, introspection, intuition, behavioural psy-
chology and demonstrated technical competence demanded by most positions in a one or two page written document' (Britton 1983: 832). The job-description process is also based upon the assumption that jobs are relatively static and do not change appreciably over time. Jobs, however, are rarely frozen and fixed in time; rather, they are created and re-created over time by the jobholder or incumbent. What is relevant and important today may be totally redundant the next day. The variability of job content in response to environmental disturbance means that it is impossible to define or describe a job once and for all. Environmental disturbance makes a job description relevant for only a particular time. Provincial government employees were themselves more than aware of this reality, and tried to define the content of their jobs selectively, highlighting those parts of their jobs that would 'score' the most Hay points (even though those parts might no longer be 'relevant' to the job), while trying to downplay other parts of their jobs (which were relevant but which they thought would not score as high).

The reliability and validity of job descriptions are also confounded by the ability (or inability) to separate out the 'job' from the 'indi-vidual.' Much of the discipline of job-description writing is based on the need to achieve adequately this separation. At least to some extent, the act of separating the job from the individual needs to be seen as a bureaucratic illusion, and nearly always open to some interpretation.

It is precisely these kinds of limitations that make a 'selective' use of job descriptions a 'necessity' rather than just a politically motivated act. The evaluators cannot simply be seen to have 'selected' informa-tion in order to 'mobilize bias'; the evaluators also need to be seen as rational actors who understood the limitations of the job description and accordingly 'worked in and around them.'

While the evaluators tended to eschew and ignore the job description as the supposed pillar of the job evaluation process, the job description did appear to have meaning and significance for those whose jobs were being evaluated. It was seen that the job-description-writing exercise did serve as a 'socialization' process for government employees. The logic and rationale of the job evaluation project was basically explained to employees during the job-description-writing training sessions and, later on a one-to-one basis with the pay analyst. Emphasis was placed on the strong link between the language of the guide charts (Know-How, Problem Solving, and Accountability) and the individual's job description. It could be said that the endless rewrites and recycling of job descriptions served to indoctrinate employees ideologically, to the logic of the new job evaluation system. The full implications of this 'socialization' will be explored in the next chapter.

THE CREATION OF AN INTERNALLY EQUITABLE JOB HIERARCHY

The elegance of job evaluation theory suggests that the process has the power to restructure and reorder the job hierarchy in relation to scientific criteria. The end-result is the supposed 'correction' of pay anomalies of unjust pay differentials, i.e., 'internal equity.' However, as the case study has revealed, such is far from the truth.

While the introduction of job evaluation did result in the shifting of job relativities at Atlantis, the hierarchy fundamentally remained intact. The deputy ministers' remarks were particularly graphic about the impact of the Hay job evaluation system on the hierarchy and relative worth of jobs within it. As one deputy minister put it when asked what was achieved, 'the hierarchy looks much the same as it was before. The only area where we had some change was with some female jobs.' Another deputy minister stated: 'My department looks the same as it always has.' This view was consistent among the nineteen deputy ministers interviewed by the researcher some three years after the Hay plan was implemented. In response to the question 'How would your department hierarchy look without the Hay formal job evaluation plan?,' not one of the deputies claimed that it would be much different.

This is not to suggest that there were no changes to relativities, but rather that they were not significant or dramatic; the hierarchy was much the same as it was before the job evaluation exercise. Typical of what changed is expressed in the following quote from a deputy minister: 'We shifted a few positions down. But we had been after those people anyways.' Another deputy minister noted (and this opinion appeared to be consistent among the deputies) that the power of informal lobby groups – in particular, women – influenced some of the changes. As one deputy minister noted, 'it gave me an opportunity to raise some women's salaries. We were getting some pressure in this area. The job evaluation exercise helped me make these changes. It was convenient. Some changes, of course, turned out to be a little higher than I meant them to be, but I can live with it.'

The survey of 230 benchmark jobholders also indicated little if any change to hierarchy. In response to the question 'In your division, did the basic hierarchy of reporting relationships remain the same following the implementation of the MCP job evaluation project?,' 92 per cent of the respondents indicated that it had remained the same. Moreover, 76 per cent of the respondents said that they did not know of 'any position or group of positions that changed dramatically in their relative position to other groups as a result of the job evaluation project.' Changes considered by the Civil Service Commission to be dramatic involved Health Services (mentioned three times in statements). This group was female-dominated. The survey also revealed that 68 per cent of the respondents felt that their relative position had been maintained compared to other jobs considered (by them) to be of the same weight or value to the organization.

The Atlantis hierarchy remained, therefore, relatively stable in spite of the job evaluation process. Where there was change, it reflected more the belief systems of the actors involved than the powers of the job evaluation process to sort out 'objectively' and 'rationally' the relative worth of jobs (in this regard it could be suggested that a relative shift for female workers is more reflective of existing organizational biases rather than the discriminating powers of the job evaluation process. In other words, some changes are intended *before* the beginning of the job evaluation process.)

Few studies have actually documented the extent of change to an organizational hierarchy as the result of the introduction of a formal job evaluation scheme. However, Industrial Relations Review and Report (1987: 12) have presented the results of a local-authority job evaluation exercise, claiming that it has 'almost certainly been the largest and costliest of its kind. It has cost about one half million pounds to carry out.' The degree of change, interestingly is not far from my own case: 'As expected a number of jobs currently carried out predominantly by women, such as home help, have moved up. However, there has been no wholesale realignment and the changes are ones of degree' (12). This result and the results of my own study of Atlantis pose the question 'Why was there no fundamental change to the hierarchy?' McNally and Shimmin (1984: 29–30) provide one reason why organizational hierarchies will remain fundamentally the same. Reporting on various cases, they note:

It appeared that the selection of benchmark jobs is, if not the principal mechanism by which a pre-existing grade/wage structure is reproduced, at least one of its earliest indicators. A benchmark job was described in one organization as a job which is 'known to be correctly graded' – i.e. *prior* to the job evaluation exercise; while another company, making the same point in a slightly different way, suggested that a sound way to establish a set of benchmark jobs is to select those jobs which are *representative of various levels* in the salary structure. In other words, the original rank order of jobs is reproduced by the reaffirmation of the status of these key posts. The remaining jobs are then grouped around the benchmark jobs and, with the exception of a small number which are regraded the 'new' job hierarchy takes on an appearance which, to all intents and purposes, is identical to the old. Confirming this a trade union official commented: What we did, we introduced a job evaluation and we tried to use that to determine the grades in accordance with the existing grading scheme, although we did make one or two alterations.

While this is an important point, it is suggested here that 'little change' may be the result of something even more fundamental: the fact that the job evaluation criteria (the 'weights and factors') already fit with preconceived notions of value and the relative worth of jobs. It should not, therefore, be surprising that there was little deviation from the existing hierarchy of jobs.

What organizations purchase when they introduce a formal job evaluation system like that of Hay Associates is a formal stamp of approval for an already existing set of informal 'weights and factors' that justify structured hierarchies. The weights and factors accepted in job evaluation plans – created by academics (Jacques, Paterson), consulting firms (Hay, MSL, Akin), or practitioners, for the purposes of determining job worth – already mirror the occupational-status hierarchy of positions in society. Wooton (1962: 146–7) has pointed to the arbitrary nature of both the initial selection of particular factors from the multiplicity of characteristics that might, in principle, be evaluated and the assignment of weights to the various factors. The logic of job evaluation is seen to contain biased value judgments about which aspects are more valuable to society. Similarly, Offe (1976: 120) has noted, 'job evaluation has no option but to create indices which include cultural definitions of the prestige of the different types of requirements. As a result, despite the impressive use of apparently objective measurement procedures, analytic job evaluation has to fall back on the normative substructure – the institutionalized value hierarchies which these very procedures disguise.

Seen in this way, job evaluation is a simple 'mirror' of the value systems or custom and practice traditions of the society involved. If, in certain cases, there is a position characterized by temporary or undersupply of available manpower, or if history and tradition have bequeathed a certain status on a position incumbent that conflicts with the job evaluation plan, there is a need either to 'fiddle' the result or to conveniently label it as an 'exception.'

Job evaluation works backwards from an existing hierarchy, not in accordance with a neutral or value-free set of criteria but simply by tapping into the existing value systems that are already deemed to be acceptable in society. Because the operation of weights and factors produces an outcome more or less in line with prevailing beliefs and values, it stands to reason that the 'results' of job evaluation will not cause a major disturbance to the hierarchy and will largely be 'acceptable.' Job evaluation, in other words, can be seen as a process of reflecting (and, at the same time, legitimating) entrenched social values, rather than making an objective statement about absolute values.

Barkin has himself noted this 'mirroring' process:

These formal systems of job evaluation are anything but objective. They merely reflect in an orderly, rigid manner the preconceptions of the men who prepare the scales. Every plan to be worthwhile is tailor-made for a specific plant and is premised on specific objectives.

Many installers frankly consult management on its objectives; while others hide the preconceptions even from management in their hope to find a greater air of objectivity. Unfortunately, the original purposes can only be discerned by close study and often from the actual application to a specific plant. (1946, quoted in Gomberg 1948: 77–78)

Once again, Offe offers important insights here, in relation to a broader social context:

... neither input nor output categories can be used to create a valid way of relating the jobs in industrial organizations to each other in terms of their value. Instead, the existing system of wage relationships is based on a hierarchy of position-specific claims, sanctioned by a relatively stable consensus amongst the participants. This consensus itself is stabilized by the fiction that the hierarchy of wages and authority can be technically justified. In reality, however, this hierarchy tends to be based exclusively on cultural definitions stating which claims to status can be legitimately linked to other work functions ... The cultural conditions which define status thus have a 'technical' pseudo-justification, and this is obviously functional in maintaining the legitimacy of an overall social system which is characterized by massive inequalities of power and income ... In contradiction to its own self-understanding, job evaluation does *not* have the function of explaining or even correcting this system, but instead its function is merely to confirm the status quo by means of 'objective' measurement procedures. (1976: 123)

We need only refer to other societies and other economic structures to appreciate the power of this point. In the former Soviet Union, for instance, the prevailing social values dictate that certain 'weights and factors' are assigned greater importance than in Western capitalist societies (hard physical labour is assigned the highest point ratings). What I am suggesting here is that the weights and factors employed within job evaluation are not objective, are not based on some 'higher order' logic, but simply reflect the value systems of the society in question. Within capitalist systems, job evaluation tends (almost without question) to simply reflect the structured inequalities of the system. As Lockwood (1958: 209) has noted, 'A dominant class has never existed which did not seek to make its position legitimate by placing the highest value on those qualities and activities which come closest to its own.' It is possible to summarize my last point by suggesting that, despite its objectivist and rational appearance, the relative job worth determined by job evaluation is nothing more than the expression of culturally sanctioned status claims.

There is, therefore, minimum change to the existing hierarchy simply because the system itself 'endorses' the hierarchy. Pressure to maintain the status quo can, however, also seen to be built into the *process* itself. The use of 'committees' and the built-in value of consensus lead to disturbance minimization. As Frank (1982: 242) points out, 'the quantitative systems also rely heavily on pooled judgment. Such judgment is the *sine qua non* of these systems. It is necessary to use pooled judgment in order to determine key job factors, benchmark jobs, guide charts, and point assignments. It should be noted that pooled judgment has been criticized on the ground that it tends to ratify the status quo through the influences of the labour market and job evaluation technique prevailing at the time of the plan development.'

It is also possible to argue that job evaluation as a device or tool has gone through a process of 'reification' in which it has been assigned 'independent' powers to alter hierarchies and pay structures. Job evaluation is frequently abstracted from the individuals or actors who manage it. This separation of the 'individual' from the 'act' has led to belief that job evaluation is an independent and objective tool that somehow magically rearranges the hierarchy, creating order where there was once chaos and redressing pay anomalies. Job evaluation, however, cannot be properly seen as separate from the individuals who run it. Job evaluation is a system *created* by individuals, implemented by individuals, and *managed* by individuals on a day-to-day basis. Once we see job evaluation in this way it is easy to understand why there will be pressure in the system for the maintenance of the status quo. The people who create, implement, and manage the system do so within the context of their own values. This is the point that Woods has indirectly made: 'through this process [job evaluation] the perceptions and values of people can be changed in a gradual, evolutionary way without upsetting stability. Relativities between jobs are likely to be changed in the direction that reason demands but *only so far as the people concerned can stomach*' (1976: 27; emphasis added). This point is also implicit in Brown's definition of job evaluation: 'Job evaluation is the term applied to a variety of ways in which, through more or less systematic analysis, the relative pay of different jobs within an organization comes to be established *in a way broadly acceptable to the workers concerned*' (1979: 120; emphasis added).

Baker and True (1947), early researchers into the job evaluation process, put this need to 'respond' to organizational value systems in more direct terms: 'Wise managements do not ignore "illogical" reactions of their employees in the company's effort to maintain a "logical" rate structure' (1947: 90).

In the case of the job evaluation plan adopted by Atlantis, the need for the organization to operate its own value systems within the dictates of the guide charts is made clear. In an article entitled 'The

Hay Guide Chart-Profile Method,' Bellak, a general partner of the group claims: 'While in house compensation experts would be the most technically proficient group to use for installing a job evaluation program, it has proved to be more beneficial to use a group of non-experts for the benchmark effort. Since the benchmark committee is building the foundation and framework for all subsequent evaluations, it is important that it be built to reflect the values of the total organization' (1984: 15/8).

Thus, there is an expectation built into the job evaluation process itself that the organizational relativities will reflect the beliefs and values of evaluation committee members, thereby legitimating the desired hierarchy through the use of 'rational' job evaluation. The ranking of jobs according to 'relative worth' can be seen in this way to be no more than the objectification of belief systems held by various actors within the organization. As Klatt, Murdick, and Schuster (1979: 232) note, 'the objective of job evaluation is to ensure that internal relationships among the pay of various jobs are appropriate in light of the factors which are considered important by the members of the given organization.' There is, in other words, some form of expectation built into the job evaluation process that certain considerations outside the limits of direct 'job content' will enter the process to reflect the beliefs and value of committee members. As Phelps Brown (1962: 129) has noted, 'job evaluation is only a painstaking application of the way in which people do continually think and argue about relative pay.'

To expect job evaluation to subdue the vexed problem of sorting out relativities is too much, for, as Lupton (1972: 10) notes, however much one tries to establish a rational scheme of relating effort to reward, or a just system of pay relativities, one is likely to be defeated by either the intervention of product and labour-market forces or the working groups, or the changing shape of power relationships in the organizations.

While the bulk of managerial texts have emphasized the 'rational' and 'objective' features of the job evaluation process, some have pointed to the dependence of job evaluation upon human judgment. Lupton and Bowey (1974: 26), for instance, have pointed out that job evaluation is not an 'objective' procedure but rather an attempt to make explicit and to accommodate some beliefs about what is fair and what should be highly rewarded in an organization. Armstrong and Murlis (1980: 42), moreover, indicate that the exercise of judgment in job evaluation is 'subject to different interpretations and varying standards among assessors and their preconceived notions will ensure that subjectivity creeps in.' This point has also not been totally lost by workers and the labour movement itself. The Institute for Workers Control explains that workers should not be taken in by job evaluation: 'workers must not allow themselves to be impressed by jargon or even by the less exalted claims for "objectivity." In the field of relative pay for jobs there is no "objective" ideal truth' (quoted in Collins 1969: 12). There is nothing to say, therefore, that those evaluating jobs can reproduce the same consistent assessments over time, or that their judgment is necessarily correct. As Livy (1975: 120) notes, the mental processes of judgment are extremely variable. Judgment will be based on different standards that, in turn, have been derived from the individual backgrounds, training, and experience of the evaluators. The extraordinary persistence of the belief in the objectivity of job evaluation has also been observed by Klatt, Murdick, and Schuster (1978: 233), who suggest that 'the objective of job evaluation is to ensure internal equity in the eyes of the members of the organization not to ensure equity in terms of some "objective" standard external to the organization. Although such a task is impossible as a practical reality, managers have sometimes thought and textbooks have implied that an objective standard of equity was the goal of job evaluation. Job evaluation is still very much an art and by no means a science. Managers lose sight of this fact at their peril.'

The use of senior management personnel in the initial evaluations can itself be seen as a reason why such little change occurs. Senior personnel are perhaps the most likely to endorse the status hierarchy and the key values of the organization (simply because they have the most to lose in a fundamental change to the structure).

Finally, the force of intra-organizational politics can be seen as another principal reason for minimal change to the existing job hierarchy. The case of personnel officers and accounting officers being divided into three different pay grades to match their existing pay levels is a prime example of retaining a tradition of different pay grades for employees performing the same job.

THE 'RATIONAL' CRITERIA: POLITICAL ACTION VERSUS BUREAUCRATIC LOGIC

While the hierarchy at Atlantis did not change in any fundamental way, change nevertheless did occur. Regardless of the extent to which job evaluation criteria depict an 'ideal' organizational hierarchy, there is bound to be, within this broad framework of inequality, some distance between 'ideal' evaluations and the evaluations based on the particular values and beliefs of each organization. Although Western capitalist notions of occupational inequality are embedded in job evaluation criteria, certain flexibility is also 'permitted' in order to allow the organization to retain or create particular hierarchical twists.

Just as there was built-in structural pressure for system stability, so too was there pressure for some (limited) change. It could be said, in the first case, that the consulting firm and the consultant himself have their own reasons or motives for making at least some adjustment to the hierarchy. Had there been no change whatsoever to the relative structuring of jobs within Atlantis, then it might have been easy for the 'client' to assert that the new system was a 'waste of money' or that no magic wand was waved over the organization after all. At least some change can serve to signal or symbolize that the system 'does work,' that it does systematically restructure relativities with-in the workplace. The consultant's occasional interventions or attempts to 'override' the committee's assessment of certain jobs might have helped to ensure that the new evaluations would not perfectly match the old structure – an unlikely goal for an expensive consulting house.

The consultant, therefore, can be seen to have his own set of political motivations and to possess a felt need to make some marginal change in the existing hierarchy in order to justify the use of the Hay system in the first place. It appeared from the case-study data that the 'weak' deputy ministers were the particular victims in those rare cases where the consultant would supposedly 'stick to his guns.'

It could also be suggested that the client has a direct incentive to see at least some minimum change to the hierarchy. 'No change' reflects as poorly on the client as it does on the consultant. The client has a vested interest in realizing at least some change, otherwise the client is made to look ridiculous for purchasing a service that yields very little, if anything at all.

To be sure, some changes were made to the existing hierarchy. What the case has demonstrated, however, is that changes that were made were 'political.' The process associated with the determination of the internal-equity objective was seen to be motivated by political forces rather than by 'rational' standards set out by job evaluation technique. Job evaluation was seen to be 'political' and 'subjective' rather than 'rational' and 'objective' and was defined ultimately in 'political' terms as a process of negotiation and compromise against a set of constructed criteria. Case-study evidence revealed considerable fiddling activity by the evaluation committee. There was only token resistance on the part of the consultant when committee members tried to override the Hay job evaluation 'criteria.' Allegiances between deputy ministers were found to be rife, and there was much evidence of reciprocal activity, or 'you scratch my back and I'll scratch yours.' The job evaluation system, in other words, yielded to what was considered to be important by important people.

The job evaluation process also came to be used as a means of 'rewarding or punishing' employees. It provided a smokescreen for political and personal acts to rectify situations which senior managers, at that time, took the opportunity to fix. Moreover, the individuals, groups, and coalitions that were likely to benefit from the job evaluation exercise tended to be those who were powerful enough to put forward and make acceptable their own particular beliefs. In the case of Atlantis, the most significant change occurred around female-predominated jobs – a segment of the labour-market that represented an informal, yet powerful lobby. As one deputy minister put it, 'these days, you've got to be doubly careful, you know. You just have to read the newspapers. Job evaluation gave us the chance to respond to pressure from women in jobs that they felt were undergraded.' In this way, job evaluation can be seen to permit prevailing belief systems to be enacted in organizations. It is as Lupton (1972: 7) says: 'No matter how elaborate the procedure for ranking, the scope for experience and judgment is wide ... the rankings and groupings will, to some extent reflect the power of the parties to the procedure, and will shift as that shifts.'

The 'system' always seems to be at the mercy of the powerful. As one deputy minister put it, 'while the consultant knew how the system worked, and even knew the numbers in the boxes by heart, there was no way he could tell a group of deputy ministers what to do.' According to another deputy minister, the consultant himself recognized this political reality and used it to his own advantage and ends: 'he made friends with some deputy ministers and not others. He saw who was important and who wasn't. You could say that he used some of us. He cajoled some of us to get the evaluations he thought were right. He was a good guy.'

Bringing deputy ministers together, on a regular basis, for the first time, the evaluation process served to increase the deputies' awareness about which of their colleagues were in the 'business of fiercely protecting their own patch.' Deputy ministers no longer saw the 'political game' as just internal to their own department. The job evaluation exercise broadened the arena. There was now an external political dimension to the process, i.e., horse trading across government departments. As one deputy minister put it, 'each deputy felt that his department was more important than anyone else's. We ended up fighting for our evaluations and our departments.' Another deputy minister put it more bluntly: although we entered into the process with openness and honesty, much of what happened depended on the strength of the deputy.'

It is argued here that bringing the deputy ministers into the evaluation process served to shift the terrain of political activity. As one deputy minister said (in reference to the evaluation process), 'I found new allies. I found people you could trust. I found assholes. I appraised people and people appraised me.' This language is far removed from the neutral language of traditional managerialist texts on job evaluation.

The political process did not, however, begin and end with the 'tug of war' of the initial committee evaluations. It was also seen in the 'sorethumb' meetings. Even if a particular deputy minister was unable to mobilize his power to 'win' a particular 'appropriate' evaluation in either the evaluation or the sore-thumb process, further political manipulations were made possible in the 'performance appraisal' process. Evaluations not deemed acceptable by a deputy minister (or by employees) could be combatted within the departments themselves through what is known as 'range control.' By granting an individual a high or low performance appraisal – by apparent reference to individual performance criteria – a deputy minister could further manipulate the location of an employee within his or her salary range. One of the deputy ministers openly admitted using this 'range control' device in this way and even suggested he was given tacit approval to do so: 'the [Hay] consultant told me that other factors would come into play later on. It was his way of telling me to lay off my push for a rating in the committee.'

The evaluation process at Atlantis, further, was never clear-cut. The 'neat' categories of 'Know-How,' 'Problem Solving,' and 'Accountability' became reduced to messy and unorganized categories.

As one deputy minister suggested, 'Accountability was always a little tricky. We had long debates about the distinction between direct and indirect accountability and what was meant by degree of freedom. The same thing happened with the know-how. There is know-how on the technical side and know-how on the managerial side. What you need to know to do a job was never clear. On the know-how dimension we often jumped on one aspect of a job and got stuck there. Because of these debates we often ended up going with what we felt was right.' This quote was not untypical and highlights the problems associated with systematically breaking down a job into its component parts. This breakdown was, in the end, often resolved by a feel for 'what was right.'

The deputy ministers themselves acknowledged obliquely the political and subjective aspects of job evaluation. One suggested, in the form of a homily, that 'the system is only as good as the people on the committee and their knowledge of their jobs.' This quote is telling simply because it puts 'people' and all their biases back into the 'system.' Other quotes suggested considerable freedom of manoeuvre in and around the system. One deputy minister suggested, for instance, that 'the new system provides the track you want to run on, if you want to run on the track!' Another suggested that 'the trouble with any system is that you can be a slave to it ... you have to make sure it has the flexibility to take common sense into account.'

In one way, job evaluation can be said to 'conceal.' The political forces associated with the determination of relative worth do not go away; rather, they are concealed or hidden away under the cloak of rationality and scientificity. All other reasons for getting formal job evaluation in Atlantis in the first place flooded back in, both during and after implementation. The new job evaluation plan 'smuggled' back in all the practices, all the non-rational elements, that it was supposed to remove. For instance, the new plan actively promoted 'fiddling' of the system. 'Fiddling' was seen as an informal process of adjusting originally established evaluations without basing the judgment on either evaluation criteria (during the meetings) or 'significant change' in the job (in the Maintenance Committee), as per the 'rules' of job evaluation. Informal activities such as 'fiddling,' while seen as an accepted part of the evaluation process, caused little threat to the overall 'plan of things,' while reinforcing the success of job evaluation technique in organizations. For some, like McNally and Shimmin, 'fiddling' in job evaluation takes on even greater importance: 'In the practice of job evaluation "fiddling" the outcome of a scheme is an accepted feature of the exercise and constitutes an acknowledgment of the legitimacy of the claims of groups who hold power in an organization' (1984: 30).

Many of the deputy ministers had a somewhat resigned attitude to political process within job evaluation. One stated that 'sure there's fiddling, but you can't get rid of it, can you?' Other deputy ministers expressed this sentiment in terms of comparisons of the old system with the new; for example, one said, 'The old system was based on "the squeaky wheel gets the oil." People could be manipulated. Personal aims were easy to achieve. With the new system the silver tongued devil still talks, but he talks in a different way.'

What I have argued thus far is that in Atlantis, the 'silver-tongued devil' does not go away, but is simply disguised in a cloak of rationality. The disguising of the political under the rational has been noted more generally by Pfeffer (1981b: 194), who has suggested that 'the use of rational analysis and planning in formal organizations can, in many instances, be viewed as the development and use of political language to accomplish the justification of decision outcomes, while at the same time making the politics producing the decision less salient. Indeed it might be suggested that beliefs in the value and efficiency of analysis and planning constitute ideologies, which are like religions in formal organizations.'

THE ACHIEVEMENT OF EXTERNAL COMPETITIVENESS: PRICE VERSUS PROCEDURE

Much confusion appears to exist about the power of job evaluation to determine actual pay levels. It is commonly suggested (and seemingly believed) that job evaluation actually determines the pay rate or range of the job, i.e., the actual monetary values, and the actual differentials between one job grade and the next. These can be seen as two of the more powerful fallacies about the job evaluation process.

The Atlantis case-study has shown that the process of attaching pay ranges to point scores was a 'hit or miss' proposition. Actual monetary values were fixed, first, by external market reference and, then, by the crucial 'ability to pay' factors. It was seen that the pay-policy line was dropped twice below the consultants 'ideal' location. Moreover, there was nothing scientific about the process of setting differentials. The percentage differential between the midpoint of one job grade and the midpoint of the next was determined by the Civil Service Commission's own 'internal' calculations of the desired number of pay grades, the highest and the lowest salaries, and a 'perception' of appropriate motivational differences between pay grades.

There appears to be a belief, among practitioners, that internal evaluations will link neatly to the external market. Internal 'evaluations' do not necessarily correspond, however, to the nature of the external market. As Klatt, Murdick, and Schuster (1978: 233) note,

Implicit in the process of compensation determination ... is the assumption that internal job evaluation will create the same relationship among benchmark jobs that are found in the outside firms participating in the survey. Obviously this may or may not be the case. If we are lucky, our internal relationships will turn out to be rather close to the relationships determined by the survey. However, it is certainly possible that due to unique internal circumstances or traditions some of our benchmark jobs are felt to be worth relatively more than our external surveys say that they are worth in other organizations.

This is the point that Sibson (1967: 32) makes, when he suggests that 'market worth, social worth, importance, and difficulty are not identical and may not always correlate properly. This can be one of the inherent limitations of job evaluation.' Baker and True's (1947: 60) survey data reveal this basic reality: 'faced with the necessity of reconciling the external pressure in wage determination with the sometimes conflicting standards of job evaluation, many of the reporting companies recognized that it was not always practical to follow the results of job evaluation.' Furthermore, Brown (1973) has documented a variety of examples where, on grounds of custom alone, gross anomalies in relative earnings are accepted as legitimate. It is possible to suggest, in this respect, that one of the limitations of job evaluation is attested to by the ever-mounting number of exceptions that must be made to original findings to adjust them to actual market conditions (Barkin 1946: 78) and to the force of custom and practice (Brown 1973).

The Atlantis case also demonstrates how the 'evaluation' process and the actual 'pricing' of the jobs were conveniently 'merged' so that it appeared that the evaluation of jobs also somehow included the 'pricing of the jobs.' Little was done or said by the Hay consultant or by pay division members to make this separation clearer in the minds of employees. The 'ability to pay' factor and the repeated negotiations over the positioning of the salary line were given short shrift and low profile. What I am suggesting here is that there exists a rather 'convenient' association of the 'evaluation' of jobs (seen to be done in an objective/neutral fashion) with the 'pricing' of jobs (which, by association with 'evaluation,' is also seen to be objective and neutral).

THE DAY-TO-DAY OPERATION OF THE SYSTEM

The Hay consultants claimed that a 'political model of salary deter- mination would be replaced by a "rational model."' Jobs would be regraded only in accordance with 'changes to job content.'

The case-study data reveal that a complex fiddling process took place at three levels of the organization after pay was attached to points. First, the deputy ministers, themselves were seen to collude in regrading of employee 'requests for review' in order to 'take the heat off' themselves and shift the pressure to the Civil Service Com- mission. For the first time, deputy ministers were blamed directly for pay inequities instead of the full blame lying with the 'impersonal bureaucracy of the Civil Service Commission.' Deputy ministers con- tinued, therefore, to rely on political processes to resolve issues of staff discontent over the grading of jobs.

At another level of the organization, some employees took action to change their evaluations when they found that their jobs were graded infavourably. This action resulted in employee fiddling of the system. Employees were seen to rewrite and recycle their job de- scriptions, incorporating the language of job evaluation into their arguments for higher point scores to move into the next pay grade. The re-evaluation of the Atlantis staff engineers' position demon- strated the point that the 'value' of any job is ultimately defined in terms of the ability of powerful individuals and groups to impose their own value definition on jobs – regardless of the bureaucratic logic of the 'rational' evaluation criteria.

Finally, the Civil Service Commission entered the collusion process in the manipulation of the so-called results, in order to minimize the resistance to the job evaluation plan. As the implementers of the (high-profile) job evaluation plan, department members could be seen to have made their individual careers contingent on the acceptance of the plan by the employees themselves.

Over time, job evaluation tends, gradually and imperceptibly, to lose the purpose for which it was designed. Job evaluation has to cope, as do other control systems, with constant situational changes and pressures emanating from both internal and external sources. The way in which management reacts to these inevitable pressures has much bearing on the life span of job evaluation itself. Lupton and Bowey (1974: 23) have pointed out, for instance, that the most likely management reactions to this type of situation is either to fiddle the job ratings or to ignore pressures and persist with a rigid structure. Similarly, Lupton and Gowler (1972: 28) have pointed out that, if management ignores pressure for change from various individuals or work groups and persists with a rigid structure, 'one might reasonably predict changes in the social composition of the workplace as people transfer, leave or are replaced.

The story of formal job evaluation in Atlantis might be seen as the story of a political process masquerading as a cold, impersonal, and rational job evaluation system.

Industrial-relations commentators on job evaluation have suggested that the technique serves, among other things, to reduce conflict (expressed principally in the reduction of pay grievances), reduce the number of pay grades, and restrict collective bargaining (e.g., by freezing pay grades)

Atlantis experienced a definite increase in conflict (mostly over allegations of new inequity between jobs), expressed as an increase in the number of formal gradings in the first year following the introduction of the system (interview with the director of pay). However, after the second year, the number of formal requests for regrading was, according to the director of pay, 'much the same as before the introduction of the system.' In the short term, it would appear that the Atlantis experience supports Daniel's (1976) and White's (1981b) position that job evaluation tends to increase the number of grievances over comparability. In the longer term (two years plus after implementation), however, there appears to have been no effect, as shown by neither more nor less regrading.

The job evaluation process did, in fact, reduce the number of job families (e.g., Education, Technical, Professional), forming one group called 'Management,' although the actual number of grades (now 1 to 35) increased. It could be said that job evaluation lends itself to a proliferation of grades through its underlying logic that a sound basis exists by which to distinguish one job from another.

The case-study data also reveals that the pay differentials were not themselves frozen. Some of the shifted differentials drifted back, gradually, to the old structure. Basically, the variety of industrial-relations claims do not hold because they are based upon the 'rational' assumptions of personnel management, which, as we have seen, are questionable at best.

Conclusions

This chapter has assessed the Atlantis job evaluation experience in terms of the personnel-management and industrial-relations schools' claims about the technique. job evaluation was not seen to possess the powers that these schools have assigned to it.

While, at the surface, it could be posited that job evaluation failed in Atlantis because the 'tenets of good practice' were not kept (for example, the abandonment of the job descriptions), it is suggested here that there was good cause for the events to unfold as they did. The 'tenets of good practice' had to be 'managed' simply because the bureaucratic logic was not, in itself, sufficient to meet the demands placed upon it. What does job evaluation do that makes this costly and time-consuming technique so attractive to organizations? Chapter 10 seeks to explore some of the hidden meanings of job evaluation.

10 The Success of Job Evaluation: *The Creation of an 'Institutional Myth'*

This chapter changes the perspective from which job evaluation is commonly perceived. It is argued that the overwhelming commitment of personnel-management and industrial-relations researchers to the 'rational' view of organizations has led to their failure to grasp the organizational and societal implications of the technique. By viewing job evaluation as an eminently 'rational' process, with rational people setting rational standards and ending up with rational outcomes, researchers have allowed their attention to be deflected from other possible ways of perceiving or interpreting the functions of job evaluation.

The theoretical perspective from which job evaluation is viewed here is that of 'social constructionism' (Berger and Luckmann 1966). This perspective is based on the assertion that we can know reality only as a complex set of symbols or mental images. Attention is directed to this perspective because the case-analysis suggests that job evaluation does not realize the rational claims held up in the conventional personnel-management literature. It is suggested that the key reason for the proliferation of job evaluation techniques lies not so much in the attributed technical capabilities of the process (which we have seen are few) but rather in the more diffuse arena of 'meaning management' and social construction and reconstruction of reality.

From the social-constructionist perspective, job evaluation is defined here as an 'institutional, rationalized myth'. Job evaluation is *institutional* because actions are repeated and given similar meanings by the custodians of the system and those who fall under its administration. The set of meanings that evolve from job evaluation is expressed in belief (ideology), activity (norms and rituals), language, and other symbolic forms through which the members of an organization both create and sustain views and images of job worth and value. Job evaluation is *rationalized* because it takes the form of rules, specifying the procedures necessary to accomplish the end goal of determining an internally equitable and externally competitive pay structure. Job evaluation is a *myth* because it is a process based on widely held beliefs that cannot be objectively tested; the technique is accepted as 'true' because it is believed (for an earlier development of this theme, see Quaid [1993]).

In short, what this chapter attempts to do is to take another look at job evaluation from a different perspective. Here the level of analysis is shifted from the surface level (rules) to a deeper level (codes). This focus necessitates a change in method and language. Rather than relying upon more conventional notions of 'classification,' 'standardization,' and 'hierarchy,' our method and language turn to 'myths,' 'rituals,' and 'symbols' of equity, utility, performance, and legitimacy. From this perspective, job evaluation gains significance through the social construction and reconstruction of reality and the management of meaning.

To examine these assertions, this chapter begins with a brief review of the social-constructionist perspective, then discusses the importance of this approach to the analysis of job evaluation. It is this approach that will be used to reinterpret case-study findings. Job evaluation is seen to act as a myth that appears to mediate between the desired objectives of internal equity and external competitiveness.

The process of job evaluation is analysed in terms of Berger and Luckmann's (1966: 76-9) three 'moments' in the reconstruction of reality: 'externalization,' 'objectification,' and 'internalization'. In addition, job evaluation is interpreted within the context of 'institutional isomorphism' (Meyer and Rowan 1977). From within this perspective, the various functions that job evaluation performs are explored. Finally, I comment (speculatively) on the various organizational and social-control functions of job evaluation.

The Social Construction of Reality: Three Moments

The origins of the social-constructionist perspective can be found in the work of such German idealists and phenomenologists as Dilthey and Husserl and shaped by the work of Alfred Schutz (1962), while more current work is based on the ideas of Berger and Luckmann

(Scott 1987: 113–14). Berger and Luckmann have influenced much of contemporary social-constructionist analysis, which is based on the simple proposition that social reality is a human construction and that social reality is created in social interaction.

At its most basic level, the social-constructionist perspective is all about the way in which social reality is created. Reality is seen to be nothing more than a set of socially constructed images. The social construction of reality is a process of creating rationales which give order to a chaotic array of actions arising out of the pragmatic problems facing society (Richardson 1987).

Berger and Luckmann (1966: 76–9) suggest that social reality is constructed through three different phases or 'moments': externalization, objectification, and internalization. In the first phase, our conception of social reality is given tangible form, or externalized, in our performances, rituals, myths, symbols, and artefacts. The second phase, objectification, refers to the process in which these conceptions of reality are given an objective status in our lives; that is, when we begin to accept the things that we have constructed as immutable parts of reality. The final phase, internalization, occurs when the objectivated constructions of past action are internalized through socialization processes (training and development activities, education, etc.) and become even further divorced from the processes which created them. This last phase or moment corresponds with that stage in which reality is 'taken for granted.'

Importantly, the social-constructionist perspective does not see socially constructed images as either unique or neutral. Berger and Luckmann suggest, in fact, that the production of social reality is typically the domain of particular dominant occupational groups who not only maintain and expand social images, but also, often at the same time, engage in activities that ensure that individuals conform to the 'official' version of reality. In this sense, social images are legitimating symbols that may support an existing authority structure in society. It is interesting to note that a reviewer recently commented on the compactness and force of conviction of Berger and Luckmann, 'whose work, even today, has lost nothing of its appeal' (Hofstede 1988: 124).

Research within this perspective is directed at uncovering the means by which people participating in any situation make sense of and sustain it through their actions. Such discovery involves examining conceptions of reality in their tangible form (rituals, symbols, and artefacts) in order to understand how apparently 'rational' processes, programs, and initiatives have influenced our world-view. Hopwood

(1984), for instance, has analysed accounting systems within this perspective and suggest that accounting has been used in the public sector to symbolize the new emphasis on efficiency by the state and, simultaneously, to provide a rhetoric that can be used to bring about a change in operating procedures. Accounting provides selective visibility to particular issues, which result in the 'creation of the significant' within the bureaucracy (Richardson 1987: 348). By providing a vocabulary of motives for action and a system of evaluative criteria, accounting is used to change the set of legitimate actions within the public sector (ibid).

While Berger and Luckmann pioneered the sociological foundations for this approach, Meyer and Rowan (1977) provide the most influential application of social-constructionist analysis to the study of organizations, and developed this into what is now known as 'institutional' theory. Meyer and Rowan (1977) suggest that modern societies contain many complexes of institutionalized rules and patterns – products of professional groups, the state, and public opinion. These social realities are seen to provide a basis for the creation and elaboration of formal organizations. According to Meyer and Rowan, these 'complexes of institutionalized rules,' more often than not, take the form of rationalized myths. The process by which actions are repeated and given similar meaning by self and others is defined as institutionalization. According to Meyer and Rowan, (1977: 343–4) the myths generating formal organizations have two key properties: 'First, they are rationalized and impersonal prescriptions that identify various social purposes as technical ones and specify in a rule-like way the appropriate means to pursue these technical purposes rationally (Ellul 1964). Second, they are highly institutionalized and thus in some measure beyond the discretion of any individual participant or organization.' In this way, Meyer and Rowan suggest that institutionalization is the means by which social processes, obligations, or actualities come to take on a rule-like status in social thought and action. For Meyer and Rowan, these institutionalized rules 'define new organizing situations, redefine existing ones, and specify the means for coping rationally with each' (ibid: 344). These myths are important to the actors involved because they help make sense of ambiguous and uncertain phenomena. They make the subjective objective and the non-rational rational. Myths enable, and often require, participants to organize along prescribed lines.

From the institutional perspective, a central focus of analysis is organizational language:

The labels of the organization chart as well as the vocabulary used to delineate organizational goals, procedures and policies are analogous to the vocabularies of motive used to account for the activities of individuals (Blum and McHugh 1971; Mills 1940). Just as jealousy, anger, altruism, and love are myths that interpret and explain the actions of individuals, the myths of doctors, of accountants, or of the assembly line explain organizational activities. Thus, some can say that the engineers will solve a specific problem or that the secretaries will perform certain tasks, without knowing who these engineers or secretaries will be or exactly what they will do. Both the speaker and the listeners understand such statements to describe how certain responsibilities will be carried out. (Meyer and Rowan 1977: 349)

Meyer and Rowan point, for instance, to the myths of personnel service, which 'not only account for the rationality of employment practices but also indicate that personnel services are valuable to an organization. Employees, applicants, managers, trustees, and government agencies are predisposed to trust the hiring practices of organizations that follow legitimated procedures – such as equal opportunity programs, or personality testing – and they are more willing to participate in or to fund such organizations,' (ibid). They suggest that modern societies are filled with institutional rules that function as myths, depicting various formal structures as rational means to the attainment of desired ends.

Furthermore, the myths generated by certain organizational practices are seen to have legitimacy based on the supposition that they are rationally effective. Meyer and Rowan (1977: 347) note, however, that many myths also have legitimacy based on legal mandates. They suggest that societies frequently give collective authority to institutions that legitimate particular organizational structures. We will see below that this is precisely the case with job evaluation as it has been used in association with the 'pay equity' movement.

The final thread of institutional analysis developed here relates to Meyer and Rowan's notion of 'institutional isomorphism.' They argue that 'organizations are driven to incorporate the practices and procedures defined by prevailing rationalized concepts of organizational work and institutionalized in society' (1977: 340). They go so far as to suggest that 'organizations that do so increase their legitimacy and their survival prospects, independent of the *immediate efficacy* of the acquired practices and procedures' (ibid; emphasis added).

Meyer and Rowan argue that, because institutional structures and rules are considered to be proper, adequate, rational, and necessary, organizations must incorporate them to avoid illegitimacy: 'Thus, the myths built into rationalized institutional elements create the necessity, the opportunity, and the impulse to organize rationally' (1977: 345). Therefore, to command legitimacy, organizations expand their formal structures so as to become isomorphic with the dominant and newly evolving myths. Organizations that incorporate socially legitimated rationalized elements in their formal structures maximize and increase their resources and survival capabilities.

Institutional isomorphism has, according to Meyer and Rowan (1977: 348-9), some crucial consequences for organizations: '(a) they incorporate elements which are legitimated externally, rather than in terms of efficiency; (b) they employ external or ceremonial assessment criteria to define the value of structural elements; and (c) dependence on externally fixed institutions reduces turbulence and maintains stability.' At the same time, they argue, organizations that 'omit environmentally legitimated elements of structure or create unique structures lack acceptable legitimated accounts of their activity. Such organizations are more vulnerable to claims that they are negligent, irrational, or unnecessary' (ibid: 349–50).

Shifting from 'Rational' to Social-Constructionist Theory

The rational-systems approach (see Scott 1987: 32–48) is perhaps the oldest approach to organizational analysis and, some might say, remains the orthodox perspective. The rational perspective views organizations as oriented to achieving specific goals through formalized structures: 'Rational system theorists stress goal specificity and formalization because each of these elements makes an important contribution to the rationality of organizational action' (Scott 1987: 32).

Job evaluation has, for the most part, been seen by researchers as a rational tool, which, perhaps, should not be all that surprising since job evaluation is a derivative of the classical school of management and embodies the rhetoric of bureaucratic organizational structuration. While job evaluation is often associated with 'state of the art' organizational principles, it is rooted within a rational-bureaucratic logic.

Traditional bureaucratic management depends, for instance, on a steep, well-reinforced hierarchy for effectiveness. The claim that the point-system type of job evaluation measures differences in terms of 'hierarchical' relationships can be said to fit the bureaucratic mode. The concept of hierarchy represents a structured, well-defined system that decreases uncertainty, clearly defines relationships, and is consistent with the rational approach to organizational studies.

Job evaluation also fits the rational-bureaucratic logic to the extent that the 'job' itself becomes the property of organizations (replacing individual rights and the notion of tenured incumbency). In traditional and charismatic forms of organization, the rewards of the job are appropriated by the incumbent; that is, the rewards for performing the job are the personal property of the individual. In a bureaucratic organization, the incumbent cannot claim proprietary rights to the job: the job 'belongs' to the organization. This itself represents a method of formalizing the organizational structure, which is consistent with the rational approach. Scott (1987: 33) states that 'a structure is formalized to the extent that the rules governing behavior are precisely and explicitly formulated and to the extent that roles and role relations are prescribed independently of the personal attributes of individuals occupying positions in the structure.' According to this definition, the actions of the government of Atlantis (i.e., slotting jobs into grades based on a structured system) resulted in increased formalization of structure. As Scott (ibid: 34) notes, 'formalization also serves to make the definition of roles and relationships appear both objective and external to the participating actors.' Because it is asserted that job evaluation is 'scientific' and uses 'statistical' charts, the process implies that the evaluation is done objectively and externally to the participating actors.

The associations of job evaluation with the rational-bureaucratic logic are, therefore, wide-ranging. However, the associations do not begin and end here, but receive full force in the proposition that job evaluation can apply scientific-rational precision to the murky concept of job worth and relative value. The underlying intellectual assumption is that there exists an objective, scientifically valid method for determining the relative value of an organization's jobs. Within the rational perspective, job evaluation is seen as a logical choice of a legal rational organization precisely because it removes 'particularism' and substitutes 'universal criteria.' The method is based on the underlying assumption that it is possible to split up a job into its

FIGURE 11
Job evaluation as mediator

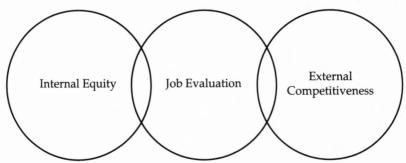

parts, assess the parts in an objective-rational manner, and ascertain the 'value' of a job through the summation of the value of the parts.

Job evaluation, from within this rational perspective, is seen, in fact, to be able to resolve the vexing problem of how to mediate organizational objectives of 'internal equity' and 'external competitiveness.' As seen in chapter 2, McCormick (who writes within this rational mould), claims: 'Job evaluation should be a basis for, on the one hand, setting salary scales for the jobs *within* an organization, which are felt to be acceptable, relative to each other, by the employees. On the other hand, the resulting salary structure ought to be properly related to the going rates in the labour market in general' (1976: 365). This rational claim is depicted schematically in figure 11.

The Atlantis case-study has revealed, however, that rational attributions to the job evaluation process have been far from valid. In reality, job evaluation was seen to be far from an exact and rational science. More than anything, job evaluation was seen to provide a rational framework within which to make highly subjective value judgments to reduce uncertainty. The only thing that was eminently rational was the language itself.

Given its failure to attain its stated objectives, we must ask why job evaluation techniques continue to be endorsed in organizations (certainly in Atlantis, the Hay plan was widely praised and the project considered a success). It is suggested here that to answer this puzzling question we need to shift our mode of analysis to a social-constructionist/institutional perspective. This perspective (and the aligned symbolic frame) is most applicable in organizations with unclear goals and uncertain technologies (Meyer and Rowan 1977; Pondy et al 1983;

Bolman and Deal 1984: 150). Myths and cultural symbols have been found, in fact, to be more important for those organizations where the 'output' is ambiguous and difficult to measure. It is possible to argue that the establishment of the income hierarchy is fundamentally indeterminable and therefore open to symbolic manipulations. As Bolman and Deal (1984: 150) point out, 'when faced with uncertainty and ambiguity, humans create *symbols* to reduce the ambiguity, resolve confusion, increase predictability, and provide direction. Events themselves may remain illogical, random, fluid and meaningless, but human symbols make them seem otherwise.' What this frame of analysis suggests is that, while specific organizational activities may not produce concrete results, the organizational structures and activities may serve other functions and purposes. This is precisely what Morgan, Frost, and Pondy (1983: 20) say: 'It is often not sufficient for activities to be performed, so that given ends are fulfilled; it is the nature of the way in which they are performed that is sometimes all important, for the manner of performance reinforces or contravenes a whole range of symbolic meaning associated with the event in question.'

Symbols are subjective means and, as such, they complement the rational means on which theorists have generally focused (Dandridge 1983: 72). What I propose to do now is to leave the perspective of the rational and turn to the perspective of social constructionism - which takes us inevitably into the world of symbols, myth, rhetoric, and legitimacy.

Job Evaluation and the Social Construction of Reality

It is possible to interpret job evaluation precisely as a complex set of images or symbols that serves to help define a social reality. In this sense job evaluation is *the activity of creating a rationale for payment issues that provides order and logic to an otherwise indeterminable process.* The collective rationale is itself presented as an institutional, rationalized myth. It is possible to suggest that claims about job evaluation mediating the twin objectives of internal equity and external competitiveness can be reinterpreted so that what mediates these two objectives is not 'job evaluation' but rather a 'myth' – or, in its full sense, an institutional, rationalized myth. A myth is defined here as a 'sacred narrative explaining how the world and man came to be in their present form' (Dundes 1984: 1). Job evaluation as *myth* is presented in figure 12.

FIGURE 12
Job evaluation as myth

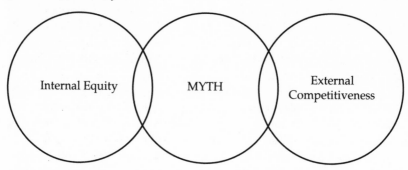

Job evaluation is a myth because it is not possible, scientifically or objectively, to determine the relative value or worth of jobs. Job evaluation provides organizations with a set of language, rituals, and rhetoric that has transported an otherwise impossible and indeterminable process to the realm of the possible and the determinable. In this way, what job evaluation serves to do is to code and recode existing biases and value systems to re-present them as objectifiable data. In one sense it reconverts what is ostensibly a subjective and political process into an objective and apparently neutral (e.g., pay equity) process.

Frequently organizations and societies have been found to invent myths when confronted with ambiguity and intangible outputs. When there is no apparent logic or rationale to an activity, organizations and societies need to invent one, if only to cope with the management of this uncertainty. Job evaluation, itself, can be seen as expressing and enhancing beliefs and, thus, as a vital ingredient in the production of organizational reality. Job evaluation 'codifies' issues and feelings, which otherwise could not be handled, or might be handled in a much more primitive and possibly detrimental way.

Job evaluation itself fits the definitional requirements of myth to the extent that it is a process in which people 'believe.' The idea that job evaluation can measure the relative value of jobs is 'believed,' by workers, practitioners, consultants, and academics alike, to the extent that it has become 'taken for granted' as a reality. It is true because it is believed.

Job evaluation is something more than a myth; it is, a 'rationalized' myth. It is rationalized because it takes the form of rules and procedures that are seen to be necessary to accomplish a given end. It is possible to argue that job evaluation gains its power as a myth *because of its rational basis*. The elaborate rational basis of job evaluation, with its detailed statistical charts, complex scoring devices, 'systematic' job descriptions, and 'definitive' job evaluation criteria (skills and knowledge, problem-solving capabilities, responsibility, working conditions, and so on), lends credence to the idea that it is possible to place the 'correct' value on jobs. The rational framework helps to ensure that job evaluation (or the myth that the worth of jobs can be measured) is seen as a valid process that can do the things that it purports to be able to do.

The rationalized rules and procedures associated with most modern job evaluation techniques provide the concrete substance for the myth. These rules and procedures can be viewed as an elaborate story or narrative that serves to help managers explain to workers why jobs are valued as they are. As is true of any system of beliefs, the job evaluation process provides a framework for 'interpreting' events. Without such a narrative or story, managers would be at a loss to make sense of the existing hierarchy and to defend it. These narratives or stories are not unique but can vary from culture to culture and from nation-state to nation-state. The kind of narrative or story told by job evaluation will likely be based in the wider cultural belief about what constitutes 'fairness' in the evaluation of jobs.

In the former Soviet Union, for instance, job evaluation systems place more weight and importance on working conditions. Their narrative or story is, therefore, different from that used in Western capitalist societies. While the narrative may be changed to fit particular value systems, job evaluation nevertheless is still interpreted as myth. Just as Western societies need myth to sort out the problems of the valuation of jobs, so, too, do other cultures. Job evaluation provides a firm logic with which to buttress societal views about job worth. Viewed in this way, job evaluation is not a universal scientific device but simply a reflection of society's beliefs at specific times. Pfeffer (1981a: 1) has interpreted 'administrative interventions' within this light:

Organizations are viewed as systems of shared meanings and beliefs, in which a critical administrative activity involves the construction and maintenance of belief systems which assume continued compliance, commitment, and positive affect on the part of participants regardless of how they fare in the contest for resources ...

Administrative interventions are successful in enhancing positive senti-ments and compliance to the extent that they build shared beliefs using political language and symbolic acts to cause action to be interpreted in a way compatible with the emergent norms and values.

Smircish (1983: 55) refers to the critical importance of 'shared un-derstandings' for organizational functioning: 'The stability, or orga-nization, of any group activity depends upon the existence of common modes of interpretation and shared understanding of experience. These shared understandings allow day to day activities to become routinized and taken for granted. Through the development of shared meanings for events, objects, words, and people, organizational members achieve a sense of commonality of experience that facilitates their co-ordinated action.'

The idea that job evaluation simply reflects society's beliefs at spe-cific times is evidenced by the recent pay equity movement where the technique is being used as the tool or device in which to pursue pay claims on behalf of women. It is interesting to note that organi-zations that used systematic job evaluation techniques prior to the pay equity movement did not recognize (within the narrative at that time) the importance of certain female-based jobs. Only with a shift in values did job evaluation reinterpret its own narrative to allow for pay adjustments for these 'ghettoed' positions.

Job evaluation is, however, more than just a rationalized myth. It is also an *institutional* rationalized myth. It is institutional because, during the job evaluation process, actions are repeated and given similar meanings by participants and onlookers. This institutional-ization takes two forms. First, it is institutionalized to the extent that it is pervasive and now covers the majority of large companies in North America and in other countries, such as Great Britain (see Treiman 1979; Industrial Relations Review and Report 1983). Second, it is institutionalized to the extent that the process is acted and re-enacted in a continuous manner within organizations that use it. Job evaluation is an ongoing process, with organizations typically having permanent job evaluation committees. Jobs are evaluated on a continu-ing basis so that the process becomes a permanent fixture of the organi-zational culture. This repetition of actions itself serves to reaffirm the ritualistic/mythical process. Job evaluation is more than just rationalized; it has established itself as an institutional myth. In this way, it is suggested that, within the social-constructionist/institutional perspective, job evaluation becomes defined as an *institutional, rationalized myth*.

The actual 'social construction of reality' can be seen, as was suggested above, typically to follow three different phases, or 'moments': externalization, objectification, and internalization. These phases can be seen vividly in the Atlantis case itself.

THE FIRST 'MOMENT': THE EXTERNALIZATION OF JOB
EVALUATION

As was suggested above, in the externalization phase, conceptions of social reality are given tangible form in rituals, myths, language, symbols, and artefacts.

Rituals can been seen to serve a number of functions: 'to socialize, to stabilize, to reduce anxieties and ambiguities, and to convey messages to external constituencies' (Bolman and Deal 1984: 159). A ritual can be defined as 'a standardized, detailed set of techniques and behaviours that manages anxieties but seldom produces intended, practical consequences of any importance' (Beyer and Trice 1987: 6). Turner (1971: 18) has noted, further, that, 'in many cultures, the ritual use of symbolic objects, the repetition of ritual verbal formulae, and the experiencing of certain types of behaviour in a ritual setting play a major part in transmitting configurations of meaning which are of central importance in the culture.' Because job evaluation is typically assumed to be rational and instrumental, it is rarely viewed as an important organizational ritual. It was seen, however, in the case of Atlantis, that job evaluation is rich in ritualistic behaviour.

The ritualistic nature of the job evaluation process was evidenced, first of all, in the Hay consultant's 'sales pitch' and involvement in the introduction of the process. In the selling process, Hay placed stress on the idea that what was being sold was a 'coordinated system' that works in accordance with a series of 'systematic steps.' Atlantis was reminded, time and time again, that what was being bought was a 'participative process' that would involve a number of different groups in a variety of specific activities.

Atlantis, the potential client organization, was briefed on each of the discrete steps in the process. These steps were contrasted to the apparently non-systematic process Atlantis was using. For example, in selling the Hay system to the province of Atlantis, the Hay consultant built upon the 'efficiency' consultants' findings that Atlantis's existing system was 'haphazard, chaotic, and non-rigorous' (Hay presentation). The old way of doing things was criticized for not having 'systematic progressive procedures' (Hay presentation). This kind of attack on the 'old' should not be seen as unusual but as an important ritual in itself. As Pfeffer (1981b: 216) suggests, 'consultants' status as outsiders and whatever credentials they possess symbolize their supposed objectivity; their activities actually are rituals designed to produce a needed artifact – a report that "demonstrates to all concerned the error of the decisions that were made."' It is possible to suggest that the attack on the old is, itself, a necessary 'rite,' one of degradation (see Berger and Trice 1987). An important part of this initial stage is the language used, which Gephart (1978: 575) calls 'degradation talk' and Moch (1980: 14) calls 'chewing ass out.' The 'old' needs to be discredited before the 'new' can be ushered in.

In the language of social reconstructionism, it might be said that the old classification system no longer functioned as myth. Its status as myth had broken down, and, as a result, an important aspect of social reality (pay determination) began dangerously to unravel. The old system was discredited in the minds of employees and managers alike; what was needed was a new myth, a new set of rituals to better manage the salary system. Many aspects of the 'new' formal job evaluation plan indicated the emergence of a new ritual-myth.

The importance of the systematic steps (or rituals) were continually affirmed by the Hay consultant who was put in charge of introducing the system. The Hay consultant saw his job in Atlantis as 'maintaining the integrity of the system and ensuring that the system was being introduced in accordance with the Hay steps' (interview).

This attempt to ensure the integrity of the system was to take place at each of the discrete steps of the process. During the job-description-writing phase, for instance, a number of newly written job descriptions were rejected by the consultant as not meeting the 'format and rigour' required by Hay system. Similarly, in the 'evaluation committees,' the consultant frequently reminded the deputy ministers that they were falling back into the logic of the old system and were not 'doing it the Hay way' (for instance, the consultant frequently reminded the deputy ministers that they had a tendency to evaluate the incumbent and not the job). This verbal stress on integrity can be interpreted as an attempt by the Hay consultant to import new 'rituals' to a culture where they did not exist before. It can be seen as an attempt to replace one set of rituals (one version of social reality) with another set of rituals (a new social reality).

Myths and rituals are the glue that binds culture together. As a result, they tend to be stable, and fixed over time. It is possible to argue that Hay recognizes this tact implicitly and, therefore during the introduction of this particular system (or view of social reality), places considerable emphasis on contrasting the old with the new in order to break down the 'old' and usher in the 'new.'

Each of the so-called systematic steps of the job evaluation process can be seen as rituals in the process. The ritualistic nature of each of these steps – job-description writing, approvals of job descriptions, the actual evaluation of jobs in committees, and the process of converting 'points to dollars' – is now reviewed.

The job-description-writing procedure is a key ritual in the job evaluation process simply because it is the step in which employees are directly involved (under some plans, the job description is written by the supervisor or an analyst, and approved by the jobholder). The job-description-writing process can be seen to have a critical information-disseminating function.

In Atlantis, each employee was asked to write up a job description (in accordance with the strict rules of the Hay format). A counselling session was also provided whereby each employee met with one of the compensation analysts. It is in this phase that the employee is first exposed to the new language of the Hay format and is informed about how the new job evaluation process will be used.

The case-study demonstrated that this step proved to be a 'painful process' for employees, necessitating numerous hours of writing and rewriting (most of the job descriptions submitted to the analysts required rewrites because they did not meet the Hay standards). Employees exchanged stories during the writing process about their analysts' 'fearsome demands.' In turn, analysts fostered the myth that writing a job description in a 'certain way' was essential to the employee's obtaining a 'good' evaluation. This process of endlessly 'rewriting' one's job description can be seen to have functional value for the integrity of the system itself (and, therefore, for the reconstruction of a new social reality). The demand for countless rewrites of job descriptions left the idea in the minds of the employees that a rigorous system was in place, a system that operated from a higher level of rationality than did the old system. The countless rejections of the job descriptions accorded the new system a certain 'respect' in the minds of the employees.

The researcher's survey of 230 benchmark jobholders revealed that the job-description process was seen to be painful. Eighty-five per cent of the respondents claimed that the job-description-writing was 'difficult' (15 per cent claiming it was 'simple'). Some of the comments made by the benchmark jobholders about this process and the difficulties it created include: 'great care was taken,' 'I had personal inexperience in writing a job description,' 'it was frustrating,' 'it required serious thought over relatively short period of time' (note: employees were given, at the very least, one month to write their job descriptions), 'it's always hard to put down on paper what you do,' 'it required proper terminology,' and 'it was both time-consuming and thought-provoking.'

Not only can the job-description-writing phase be seen as an important 'rite of passage' (facilitating the transition of persons into new social roles and statuses), but it can also be seen as an important *rite of humiliation and degradation* designed to dissolve the organizational identities of the persons subjected to the job evaluation exercise. The function of these rites is to instil respect for the 'new.'

This writing ritual also served to invest the custodians of the system (the Civil Service Commission) with a new status as 'experts' in the management of salary administration. Salary administration was not merely a matter of 'common sense' but required professionals, with specific 'technical' expertise, to manage and run the system. The delegation of the pay division as experts was important because it implied that the system was sophisticated. The reorganization of the classification division signalled that experts and expertise were required because of the complexity of the new system. This kind of expertise or attribution of expertise can also be seen to contribute to the integrity of the system.

It is perhaps not surprising that the Hay consultant insisted that the compensation analysts demand high standards from employees in the writing of their job descriptions. The Hay consultant went as far as to suggest to the analysts that the 'rejection of a submitted job description should be commonplace' and that 'more are usually rejected than accepted.'

The job-description-writing process did more than 'introduce' the employees to the system. It also served as a powerful 'socialization' device for the compensation analysts (the future custodians of the system). The job-description-writing process, as was suggested, bestowed on the analysts a certain expertise, and therefore a power base that had not existed previously. This increase in power and status can be seen to have had an effect on the commitment of the analysts to the system itself. The new respect accorded to the system by the employees was, at the same time, accorded to the analysts themselves. As Weber (1946: 235) stated, 'More and more the specialized knowledge of the expert became the foundation for the power position of the officeholder.'

The job-description-writing exercise was not the only ritualistic aspect of the job evaluation process. Many of the committee meetings, for instance, and other forms of meetings connected with the job evaluation project had a number of ritualistic aspects. Committees have long been seen as an important ritualistic activity. Turner (1971: 28) suggests that meetings 'are formalized gatherings with a prescribed set of participants, and prescribed procedures for opening and closing, and in some cases the prolonged and repetitive nature of the proceedings very strongly suggests parallels with ritual forms.' The 'evaluation committees' stood as powerful rituals. The composition, organization, and structuring of the committees were critical to the ritual. It is standard procedure for the Hay consulting company to have the most senior personnel in the client organization evaluate the first round or set of evaluations. In the case of the province of Atlantis, the deputy ministers were that personnel. The full evaluation committee consisted of the deputy ministers, the chief Hay consultant, the director of pay, and the compensation analysts (the last-named being ostensibly recorder/observers). The idea is to have the most senior personnel perform the initial round of evaluations and to have the groups of departmental staff take over the evaluation process thereafter, using the evaluated 'benchmarks' as a guideline.

The fact that the deputy ministers would be in charge of the first round of evaluations has obvious symbolic significance for the future integrity of the system. It is clearly more difficult for employees to challenge the evaluations if the most 'powerful' of the managers have given their formal stamp of approval to each of the evaluations. While it is the case that others (e.g., the pay analysts) could have evaluated the jobs, to have these people do the evaluations and not the deputy ministers would remove the symbolic significance of having a 'powerful' group conduct the evaluations. What better people to do the initial evaluations than those who normally are charged with setting the direction and philosophy of their departments?

In summary, because the 'evaluation committees' were associated with the deputy ministers, the job evaluation process was assigned instant credibility, status, and integrity. Myths are often associated with the actions of strong leaders, and are the products of 'big men' in 'big positions.' By associating the job evaluation process with the deputy ministers, it is possible to argue that Hay (consciously or unconsciously) was aiding and abetting in the creation of a new myth.

For a myth to function it must be 'believed.' It is also possible to argue that the evaluation committees served an important socialization function for their participants, in particular, the deputy ministers. As a result of the evaluation committee process, the deputy ministers came to 'believe' in the process (although, as we saw, this belief was far from complete and often 'instrumental'). It is possible, however, to suggest that, to some extent, belief in the system was fostered through the deputy ministers' participation in the evaluation process. It is one of the few truths of organization theory that the more an individual is involved in a change activity and directly participates in it, the more committed he or she will be to the project (see, e.g., Bennis, Benne, and Chin 1975).

It could even be argued that the deputy ministers came to believe in the system through the consultant's 'rejection' of their evaluation judgments in the committee. In each of these rejections, the consultant stressed the need to do 'the evaluations strictly within the structure of the system.' Such rejections served to signal to the deputy ministers that there was, indeed, a 'rational' system, a systematic way of evaluating jobs, and that, once they had learned or mastered the system, they, like the consultant, would be able to evaluate 'definitively' the worth of a job. The problem, therefore, in evaluating jobs (in the minds of the deputy ministers) came to be a purely 'technical' issue, one of learning the method and gaining familiarity with the guide charts.

Myths are often seen to be associated with 'critical incidents.' These incidents become future stories, and folklore. The evaluation committees were not without their own critical incidents. One of the committees had reached an impasse in the evaluation of a position, and could not agree on its value. The debate ensued over a period of three hours, with no resolution. The consultant reacted to this impasse by suddenly departing the room, claiming the need for 'a walk in the park.' Before leaving the room, however, he asserted in a forceful manner that the reason agreement could not be reached was that the committee was not 'adhering to the logic and rationale of the system.' He said that he would 'return in an hour' with the hope that the committee 'would have worked it out by then.' The consultant returned, the job was promptly evaluated in accordance with the 'rules' of the process, and the committee was praised by the consultant for having gained 'mastery of the system.' The story of 'Burr going for a walk' was told many times over. The myth had, in other words, been born in the minds of the deputy ministers.

The assignment of 'pay to points' can be seen as another critical ritual associated with job evaluation. This process is usually shrouded in mystery and secrecy. The first step in pricing the jobs took place at the Hay office, where 'a careful computer analysis is done of the evaluations' and 'through the use of our [Hay] data bank pay levels are associated with evaluation points' (Hay letter of interest, June 1979). What is important here, from a symbolic perspective, is that the initial analysis is done 'scientifically' at the Hay office. In a symbolic sense, 'Hay' is the custodian of the magic formula that has the power to manage the conversion from pay to points. Hay, in this sense, acts as the witch doctor who has the extraordinary ability to conjure up the correct dollar-value for each position. Any debate about the correctness of a pay level is dismissed because a body of 'experts,' armed with sophisticated computer equipment and a vast data bank, has managed the process. The complex statistical charts themselves lend credence to the idea that job evaluation somehow has the ability to determine the actual pay levels, that is, to manage the external-competitiveness dimension of the salary-administration process. Unfortunately for Hay, however, the scientifically determined 'competitive' pay levels were, as we have seen, rejected by the Atlantis government for cost reasons.

The complex statistical charts and language used in the conversion of pay points lead us to consider a second dimension of myth making, that is, the use of rhetoric and language. Language and rhetoric have long been seen as central to the management of meaning: 'Socially built and maintained, language embodies explicit exhortations and social evaluations. By acquiring the categories of language we acquire the structured "ways" of a group, and along with the language, the value implications of those ways ... The study of organizational vocabularies is long overdue' (Mills 1963: 433).

Pfeffer (1981b: 193) has suggested that language is a catalyst for focusing and developing interests and points of view: 'If politics involves the rationalization and justification of those courses of action desired by the power holders, then language is the vehicle through which this justification occurs. Language can mobilize support by convincing others of a commonality of interests, thus enhancing the coalition building process. Language provides the justification for action necessary for the legitimation of political choices.'

Rhetoric can be seen to perform a similar function. For instance, in a discussion of the rhetoric of bureaucratic control, Gowler and Legge (1983: 206) identify the following features of written rhetoric:

1. tend to pose and then answer their own questions
2. frequently couched in 'high flown language'
3. directed at a given audience or community, with
4. the express intention of influencing thoughts, feelings and actions.'

It is suggested here that job evaluation is a kind of rhetoric. Job evaluation is rhetoric, first, because it tends to 'pose and then answer its own question.' Job evaluation, as we have suggested, works backwards from an already established hierarchy. The weights and factors selected in point job evaluation schemes, for instance, simply mirror the criteria already valued or used in society. What job evaluation does is simply to codify the 'societal values' of occupational worth in complex language and to regurgitate these codified values, supposedly to tell workers what constitutes the value of their jobs. In other words, the language of the guide charts simply embodies explicit social evaluations mirroring the views of society.

Job evaluation is also rhetoric because it is 'frequently couched in high flown language.' Those engaged in the business of job evaluation seem to encourage mysteriousness, mysticism, and complexity by talking in terms of factor comparisons, point values, benchmark jobs, and the like – terms that are not part of people's ordinary vocabulary. If there is an organizational change that necessitates a 'language change,' it is certainly job evaluation.

With respect to various statistical, quantitative techniques (such as the ones used in conjunction the point system), Devons (1961) has suggested that their utilization in formal organizations has much in common with the practice of primitive magic in decision making. Both quantitative and statistical techniques are said to be used in such a way as to lend decision making a semblance of rationality and substance. While the use of such techniques does not actually reduce risks, it does function to increase the credibility of action in situations that might otherwise have been guesswork. It can be said that an exaggerated faith is placed in such techniques, while a corresponding lack of reflection and critical awareness accompany their use.

What is suggested here is that employees, like those of Atlantis, who use the point system of job evaluation could easily conclude that just because numbers are used in the system, the results are 'accurate' and that jobs which score the same points are, in fact, equal. Devons (1961) has suggested that quantitative and statistical methods can and are often used as a means to preserve credibility in the system, as modern organizations are sustained by a belief system that stresses the importance of rationality (noted in Morgan 1986: 134). This legitimating effect of quantification has been noted by Trice, Belasco, and Alutto (1969: 49) who have suggested that 'the main organizational value of job evaluation lies not in its ability to precisely weigh jobs, but rather in its "scientific sounding" approach to this problem.' To maintain legitimacy in the workers' eyes, the custodians of the system must be able to demonstrate objectivity in action.

It should not be surprising that practitioners frequently claim that complex plans are more accurate than simple plans. Lutz (1969: 610), for instance, asserts that 'administrations in which the job analysts enjoy the respect and confidence of both employees and management can make their final evaluations on any sound reasoning basis, or with any combination of methods; but where only a small measure of such respect is accorded, a more *formal quantitative system* will help assure maintenance of the classifications plan's integrity, (emphasis added). Lutz's statement can be seen as an attempt to create a kind of ideological obfuscation. Following Gowler and Legge's (1983: 210) rhetoric of bureaucratic control, it is possible to suggest that the complex rhetoric and language of job evaluation serve to present a 'rational,' goal-orientated image of managerial action that symbolizes not only managerial competence but also moral superiority.

THE 'SECOND' MOMENT: THE OBJECTIFICATION OF JOB EVALUATION

It was argued that the description of the rituals, language, and rhetoric of job evaluation correspond to Berger and Luckmann's (1966) first phase, 'externalization.' It is in that phase that conceptions of social reality are given tangible form. The 'objectification' phase refers to the moment at which we begin to accept things that we have constructed as immutable parts of reality. In the case of Atlantis, it is possible to suggest that this moment existed when the politicians decided to accept the 'efficiency' consultants recommendation to introduce a formal job evaluation scheme, since the scheme was blindly accepted. There was no attention paid whatsoever to the origins of the selected factors and assigned weights. There was, in other words, no debate about the validity or reliability of the plan.

One of the reasons for this lack of debate relates, presumably, to the fact that this type of job evaluation plan had been 'successfully used' elsewhere. The 'socially approved' factors and weights merely formed part of yet another language of categorization to an already acronym-oriented organization.

Findings from the researcher's survey of benchmark jobholders suggest that the Hay job evaluation system had taken on the status of 'myth'; that is, the system had moved into the objectification phase (this survey was conducted two and a half years after the implementation of the system). For example, 87 per cent of the respondents, when asked whether they 'understood the purpose, goals and basic outlines of the project, after the briefing session,' said yes. As well, 76 per cent reported an understanding of the relationship between the job-description-writing process and points used in evaluation.

Responses to other survey questions indicate an 'understanding' and 'belief' of the new system. Seventy-eight per cent of respondents claimed that they were aware of the 'three key dimensions upon which the evaluation of their job was based'; 60 per cent claimed that they were aware of the 'breakdown or subcategories of these three dimensions.' While the respondents indicated a good understanding of the 'general' features of the plan, its finer details did not appear to be as well-developed in the minds of the benchmark jobholders: 52 per cent of respondents claimed that they were familiar with the operation of the 'guide charts,' 43 per cent claimed to understand the Hay Guide Chart Profile method'; and 65 per cent claimed to understand why their jobs were evaluated as they were.

It is interesting to note that the 'finer details' of job evaluation plans are rarely fully communicated to workers. It could be argued that only so many of the 'technical' aspects of the system are served up by the management so that, while the complexity of the system is 'revealed,' ultimate control remains in the hands of management.

The language and logic of the new job evaluation system were communicated and transmitted through more than just formal channels. They also appeared to be an important part of the 'informal terrain' of the organization. Survey results revealed, for instance, that 51 per cent of respondents claimed the Hay job evaluation project was a 'major source of informal discussion' with other Management Compensation Plan members of their department, while 25 per cent said that the Hay project was 'occasionally mentioned' in informal discussion (only 14 per cent said that the project was 'rarely brought up').

In response to the question 'Do you have greater faith in the new formal system of job evaluation than the old system?,' 71 per cent of respondents said that they did. This survey question also asked respondents why they felt the way they did. The language used by those who claimed that they had a greater faith in the system is particularly revealing and more often than not refers to a 'higher rationality of the system.' Samples of these employee responses to the questionnaire, presented as artefacts, include: 'it's a system'; 'there's a potential to be more objective'; 'the system has some tangibles, like charts, guidelines, better job descriptions'; it's more factually based than the old system, which was prone to pressure tactics'; 'seems more objective'; 'more regimented approach, criteria clearer'; 'more formal, reviews more thorough'; 'greater potential exists for more responsible evaluations'; 'more objective and fair, the old system was badly abused in my perception and lacked objectivity'; and 'I know more about the new system.'

While the results and language suggest a greater belief in the job evaluation process, this belief was by no means complete. Those who did not have greater faith in the system provided their own insightful reasons (and, to some extent, were able to see through the myth): 'the committee basically brought their previous ways of doing things to a more formal level, but there was no fundamental change'; 'not a lot more faith because the same misconceptions are held by those who can influence'; and 'because the rules are confusing, the evaluation is inappropriate and ill-informed ... the pay raise is arbitrary.'

Other survey data appear to affirm the idea of an emerging myth. Benchmark jobholders were also asked the open-ended question 'What do you see as the main difference between the old methods of determining job grades and the new MCP system?' The answers to this question fell into three response types: positive reference to the new system, little difference, negative reaction to new system. Seventy-two per cent of respondents to this question made a positive reference to the system. As they did in the question discussed above, respondents made reference to the more 'rational' and 'systematic' nature of the process. A representative sample of these 'responses' as artefacts includes: 'new system is more mathematical ... better potential for fairness'; '[new system has] better job descriptions and scientific measurement of know-how, problem solving and accountability'; '[new system has] broader range of criteria ... this can reduce chance of subjectivity and personal bias'; 'use of weighted factors now better [in new system]'; '[in new system] relative comparisons now organized instead of depending on [Civil Service Commission] to choose'; 'numerical reasoning ... [in new system] to some extent removes personal bias, reduces the role of lower paid [Civil Service Commission] people in judging higher paid positions'; 'old system based too much on historical precedent and we therefore got inequities out of this. The new system should overcome this'; 'better able [under new system] to give concrete reasons for ratings and more reasons for not changing whatever has been decided'; 'the old ways were in place too many years. The old system was based on solving the problems of individuals rather than comparisons'; '[in the new system] formality is required. The old system wasn't structured as well. The old system did not even appear to be a system'; '[in the new system] there is greater potential for fairness. There is an attempt to have a real evaluation process'; 'really systematic and not judgmental'; and 'comparisons are rated against common factors.'

The language used by respondents in making the distinction between the old and the new systems is telling. The overwhelming belief in the new system over the old is based in the respondents' belief in the greater power and validity of the 'quantitative' (over the qualitative), of the 'formal' (over the informal), and of the objective (over the subjective). These values and beliefs tend to be (deliberately) built into the fabric of formal job evaluation and tend, as my survey results reveal, to be endorsed and believed by employees covered by such schemes.

The belief in the new system (or myth) is also indicated by the belief in the process used to grade jobs. Sixty-eight per cent of respondents considered that the 'combination of job description, CSC information and deputy minister representation was sufficient to fully grade' their jobs. Some individuals who responded in the negative appear to have based their answers on their own particular evaluations. The majority of negative responses focused upon the inability of the deputy minister (not familiar enough with the department, too new, biased, and so on) to fairly represent a cross-section of jobs within his department. Interestingly, the survey results indicated a less than a complete desire for direct employee participation in the evaluation process: 54 per cent did not believe that there should have been 'participation from lower levels in the organization' in the benchmark evaluation process, citing 'confusion' and 'delay' as the most frequent reasons. Some of the comments reflected a deep faith in the system: 'I must point out that I am very interested in my salary rating, but I have no particular desire to learn about the rating system. In my opinion, some input from individuals is very important, but only the basic outline. The remainder should be done either by or with continuing assistance from a trained person in this type of assessment.'

In response to the question, 'In your opinion, would it now be more difficult to obtain a position review or classification?,' 63 per cent of respondents said that it would, in fact, be more difficult to get a reclassification through the new system (6 per cent said that it was more difficult only for a 'short while'). The reasons given are revealing and support the idea that it's more difficult to 'beat a rational system': 'now written in stone'; 'I tried it and failed'; 'the evaluation is expertly set and is more difficult to challenge'; 'there is a clear message through the channels that nothing can be done'; and 'tighter controls ... not as easy to fabricate a justification for review.'

Of those 31 per cent who responded that it would not be more difficult to obtain a position review, the reasons given related to the greater 'fairness' and 'rationality' of the system: 'I believe if justification exists a job can be reviewed'; 'any additional duties will be readily apparent to the system'; 'changes in jobs are more identifiable now and we can get a change quicker'; and 'because what you need to do is spelled out.'

Perhaps more telling was the response to the question "Do you believe that it would be more difficult, under the new system, to challenge a request for reclassification that had been turned down by the MCP evaluation committee?' Seventy-one per cent of respondents claimed it would, indeed, be more difficult to 'challenge' a request for classification. It is within the terms of this question that the new 'myth' can be seen to have positive functional consequences for Atlantis management. Once again, the reasons for such a belief lay in a perception about the greater 'rationality of the new system' (employee comments from survey): 'the [new] process is clearly established. Standards are in place'; 'the decision making process is at a higher level ... makes it difficult for us to challenge'; 'the new system is thorough ... no bias'; 'now there is a basis or foundation on which to base a decision'; 'we will be told we wrote our own job descriptions ... it's our fault'; 'the broader base of evaluation adds credibility'; 'there is better documentation and more rules to follow'; it's more complicated'; 'evaluation is on paper'; 'expertly set ... more difficult to challenge'; and 'the complexity of the system.'

Interestingly, a somewhat smaller percentage (70 per cent) of employees said that they 'would have more faith in a turned-down request for reclassification under the new system than the old.' Respondents were not asked why they felt this way.

Survey data further revealed that 71 per cent of respondents who were supervisors use the 'language' of the Hay system when explaining salary issues to employees, whereas 63 per cent of respondents claimed that their supervisors use the language of Hay in explaining salary issues to them. Finally, 67 per cent of respondents felt that the new MCP system provided a better understanding of why certain jobs are paid higher than others. The answer to the open-ended survey question 'What was achieved by introducing a formal job evaluation plan to the provincial government?' also indicated a belief in the system: 72 per cent of respondents provided a favourable response, with the dominant response type being a reference to the 'rational' or 'objective' features of the system.

Importantly, survey findings also revealed that 69 per cent of respondents believed that the system was 'objective,' and 65 per cent of the respondents claimed that, when their jobs were being evaluated, they felt that the Hay system had a 'rational basis'; only 27 per cent felt that the system had 'some rationality but was much like the old system' (8 per cent said that the system made no sense at all). From the survey results and language used (heavy emphasis on such words as 'objective' and 'system'), it is possible to argue that we have witnessed the evolution of a new 'belief' system within the provincial government of Atlantis. Here, it is interesting to note, that 'rational' theorists themselves stress the importance of creating 'belief': 'One of the most important elements in developing and applying a job evaluation system in any organization is the indoctrination and information programme of managers and employee. No attempt should ever be made to develop and install an evaluation plan from textbook material alone' (Lutz 1969: 619).

The final phase of the social construction of reality, according to Berger and Luckmann (1966), is the 'internalization' phase. Here, constructions of reality become even further divorced from the processes that created them. It is possible to suggest that job evaluation has moved, or is moving, to this moment. With the onslaught of the pay equity movement, job evaluation technique has been hailed as the device for removing inequality in pay. The rather uncritical acceptance of the technique by the movement suggests that the effectiveness of job evaluation has become 'taken for granted' as a reality. This reality is, I believe, captured in the language of the following, from an article, reporting on an equal pay program in the province of Manitoba: 'How does one determine the value of a nurse and compare it to the value of an electrician? it took a *complicated point system with thousands of permutations and combinations*, but Manitoba has finally become the first Canadian province to *make a scientific comparison of the value of the work* performed by its men and women employees. The government spent 16 months evaluating its workers and slotting them *into a series of detailed statistical charts*' (*Globe and Mail*, 1 January 1988; emphasis added). The 'internalization' of the job evaluation myth is also happening outside of North America. In Britain, for instance, a pay researcher has stated that 'job evaluation is unique in that it is the only management technique that has been given the stamp of respectability by an Act of Parliament' (Armstrong 1974: 73).

Job Evaluation: Institutional Isomorphism and Membership

The institutional-isomorphism thesis states that successful organizations incorporate already legitimated formal structures and activities. It has been put forward, moreover, that institutional isomorphism promotes the survival of organizations. Meyer and Rowan (1977: 310) have suggested, in this way, that 'moving toward the status of a subunit rather than an independent system ... can enable an organization to remain successful by social definition, buffering it from failure.' It is possible to suggest that the adoption of a formal job evaluation plan in Atlantis (and, indeed, in other organizations) can be seen as an aspect of institutional isomorphism. It could be argued that Atlantis was attracted to the job evaluation plan partly because the process had a wider organizational and societal legitimation. Not only would the technique provide an image of scientificity and objectivity, but it would serve to bring the province 'in line' with other organizations. The adoption of the job evaluation system signalled Atlantis's entry into an 'élite' club.

The consequences normally associated with institutional isomorphism (Meyer and Rowan 1977: 348–9) fit neatly with the job evaluation process. First, it is suggested that organizations incorporate elements that are legitimated externally, rather than in terms of efficiency. In the case of Atlantis, it was seen that the new job evaluation scheme was no more technically superior to the old salary-administration scheme. The new system may be a more efficient 'myth,' but it is not impossible to argue that it is technically superior to the old system. Its superiority can be found solely in its organizational legitimacy. Second, institutional theory suggests that external criteria tend to be used to define the value of the structure. In other words, it is good because other organizations have said it is. In the case of Atlantis, the entire process, as we suggested, was taken for granted as a valid system.

The reason for organizations to pattern themselves on each other is likely closely related to the idea of 'impression management.' Public support and widespread acceptance of the Hay job evaluation plan by many large and influential corporations appears to have provided the Government of Atlantis with an opportunity to improve its 'backwater' image. In this way, job evaluation can be seen to be conveying the impression that the province of Atlantis was forward thinking, progressive, and modern. Bolman and Deal (1984: 171) point out that 'image' can be an important influence in deciding whether or not to adopt change in organizations: 'Another purpose of organizational structure is to convey a "modern" appearance – to communicate to external audiences that this is not a horse and buggy operation but is fully up to date.' In Atlantis, this appeared to be very much the case. Much of the 'sales pitch' of the Hay consultant focused on this motive. According to the Hay consultant assigned to the project, his sale was based on the fact that 'Atlantis was one of the few

Canadian provinces that operated without a formalized job evaluation plan.'

The Province of Atlantis, already considered a 'poor cousin' province in purely economic terms, also had to suffer the indignity of operating with outdated and unsophisticated management practices. The efficiency consultants, brought in by a newly elected Conservative government, themselves defined the Hay scheme as 'sophisticated and modern' while defining existing Atlantis practices as 'backward and outdated.' Hay attempts to affirm the sophistication and modernity of their scheme by asserting that their clients 'are the leading corporations throughout the world.' Much fuss is made over the client list in their 'sales pitch,' providing each potential client with a listing of all the 'top' companies currently operating with a Hay job evaluation system. The idea here is perhaps to have the clients begin to question why they have not fallen in line with other high-performance companies with respect to salary administration.

Job evaluation, in this sense, provided a 'membership' function. The introduction of the technique can be seen as an affirmation that Atlantis used the same modern business methods as other large, 'high-performance' organizations. It is even possible to suggest that formalized job evaluation schemes have become part of the specific language of 'primary sector' labour firms, and that this language has contributed to the symbolic divisions that exist between those progressive and moneyed primary-sector firms and those considered to belong to the more 'primitive' secondary-labour-market firms.

The impressive list of Hay clients shown to all new customers indicates that, by far, most of these organizations fall into the category of primary-sector employer. The division between primary- and the less-advantaged secondary-labour-market organizations is thus reinforced, and those secondary-sector firms 'who don't talk the same language' are farther left out of the 'club.'

Moreover, the costs associated with the technical introduction of a job evaluation plan as well as the usual initial pay increases associated with selling the plan are more likely to be incurred by organizations that can afford it, i.e., large, complex organizations in the primary sector of the labour market (see Batstone [1984] for characteristics of users). I would also suggest that the complex language of some of the more sophisticated plans, such as that of Hay Associates, may be used in discussion with senior-level counterparts in other organizations to intimidate or 'show off' the advanced techniques of one's organization. 'Membership' in the primary-sector job evaluation 'club' was not just symbolic but extended concretely into the Hay salary-administration club in which pay comparisons were ritually made between all participating Hay clients. This ritualistic salary-survey process served to bind the 'club' members together and to reaffirm the 'élite' nature of these firms. Pay comparisons between those clients whose salary information was recorded in the 'data bank' would likely lead to a degree of standardization at the top end of the labour market.

Those individuals and organizations unfamiliar with the language of Hay and other complex job evaluation schemes can be disadvantaged and 'shut out.' An example of the power of 'membership' in this sense is highlighted in the following advertisement for a compensation manager in New York City (*Wall Street Journal*, 5 January 1985):

Manager of Compensation

F113	460
F4(50)	230
E4C	200
	890

Box CCC-576, The Wall Street Journal
An Equal Opportunity Employer

This advertisement, coded in Hay factors and weights, provides but one example of how the specific Hay language can include 'members' while excluding 'non-members.' What I am suggesting here is that job evaluation can be seen to reinforce a culture and language for the primary sector of the labour market. It is possible to suggest, furthermore, that job evaluation may actually serve to reinforce 'dual labour market' tendencies in our society. The ability to pay, coupled with the love of the new and the fear of 'falling behind' in the use of modern business methods, may provide some explanation of the attraction of so many primary-sector firms to sophisticated job evaluation techniques.

Job evaluation can also be seen to segment groups *within* organizations, providing membership for some and not others. It serves to widen the trenches between white-collar and blue-collar workers and, by doing so, reinforces the notion of a managerial élite. It is commonplace to assert that white-collar and blue-collar workers require different types of job evaluation schemes (because of differences in the nature of their work). In the case of the Province of Atlantis, only the non-unionized, supervisory, managerial, and professional group was covered by this new job evaluation scheme (although such exclusivity was not a deliberate management strategy). The effect was that those groups remaining under the old scheme had become increasingly conscious of themselves as a separate group from those who had transferred to the new plan (interview with union representative).

The idea of a separate scheme for different categories of worker could possibly be seen as yet another means of legitimizing the structure of inequality in society (to the extent that the need for separate schemes represents an ideology rather than a reality). Different job evaluation plans to tend to be used for different categories of workers. With respect to job evaluation coverage in the United States, Treiman (1979: 5) has noted that 'relatively few organizations have "top-to-bottom" coverage by a single job evaluation plan. Far more typical is the use of several systems to cover different categories of jobs, e.g., a shop plan, an office plan for non-exempt clerical and technical positions, and a plan for exempt professional and administrative positions.' Similarly, the British Pay Board (1974: 19) claims that, in Britain, 'separate schemes for manual, white collar and managerial groups appear to rule.'

My employee questionnaire appeared to support the idea that a divide was growing between the Atlantis Management Compensation Plan (MCP) group and the counterpart group in the bargaining unit. In response to the question 'Do you believe that the job evaluation project for the MCP group drew a stronger dividing line between this group and its counterpart group in the bargaining unit?', 67 per cent of respondents felt that the dividing line had grown. The growing divide was explained in the following types of language: 'not particularly rigid, but stronger by degree'; 'Two systems of salvation will naturally draw a dividing line. Those not included in Hay will think that the other gained an advantage'; 'to a small degree it unites all management personnel with lip service to differential treatment'; and 'other groups used to push management up, now management is in a push process'.

Evered (1983: 125–43) has noted the importance of language in making distinctions within and between organizations: 'The language used by the members of a particular organization characterizes that organization in terms of a) its similarities to and differences from other organizations, b) its societal role, and c) the world view and "reality" definition of its members. Language variations occur both *between* and *within* organizations, partly from task/activity reasons and partly from social/behavioural reasons.'

Conclusions

This chapter has identified job evaluation as an institutional, rationalized myth. It has interpreted job evaluation within the context of Berger and Luckmann's (1966) 'three moments' in the construction of reality: 'externalization,' 'objectification,' and 'internalization.' In the externalization phase, it was seen that job evaluation takes on tangible form in rituals, language, and symbols. In the second moment, objectification, it was seen that job evaluation has led people to believe that relative job worth can be objectively determined. In the third moment, internalization, this belief becomes so institutionalized that it becomes taken-for-granted as part of reality.

Most of the functions that have been attributed to myths, narratives, and stories have to do with the maintenance of social order. Such narratives have been associated with shared values, which are used to legitimate such social arrangements as economic systems or status hierarchies or to present and resolve inherent contradictions in society (Levi-Strauss 1965, cited in Wilkins 1983: 83). It is possible to suggest that job evaluation, with its various forms of ritual and language (which create certain forms of meaning), facilitates the maintenance of socially desirable inequality.

Job evaluation can be interpreted, therefore, as a concrete materialization of implicit assumptions and traditional values hidden amidst a set of charts and graphs. In this sense, job evaluation removes the pay-determination process from everyday economic discourse and places it on the realm of the scientific or the mystical. It provides a verbal explanation and justification for an organizational hierarchy that might otherwise have been difficult to explain. Job evaluation beams back to employees and workers the notion that the current structure of inequality is right and just.

Appendices

APPENDIX A

Guide Chart for Measuring
WORKING CONDITIONS

GENERAL: Working conditions includes two dimensions: physical and mental, each consisting of two elements, as defined below.

•• PHYSICAL ENVIRONMENT The combination of intensity, duration and frequency of exposure to physical and environmental factors is such that it results in: • PHYSICAL EFFORT The combination of intensity, duration, and frequency of physical activity is such that it results in:	a. Minimal discomfort or risk of accident or ill-health.	b. Considerable discomfort or moderate risk of accident or ill-health.	c. Great discomfort or substantial risk of accident or ill-health.	d. Extreme risk of accident or ill-health.
A. Mild fatigue or physical stress.				
B. Moderate fatigue or physical stress.				
C. Considerable fatigue or physical stress.				
D. Severe fatigue or physical stress.				

• **PHYSICAL EFFORT:** Jobs require levels of physical activity that vary in *intensity, duration* and *frequency*, or any *combination* of these factors, to produce physical stress and fatigue.

Some *examples* of these activities include: lifting, handling of materials or objects, stretching, pulling, pushing, climbing, walking, carrying, sitting, standing, and/or working in awkward positions, or other unusual circumstances.

•• **PHYSICAL ENVIRONMENT:** Jobs may include progressive degrees of exposure of varying intensities to unavoidable physical and environmental factors which result in discomfort or increase the risk of accident or ill-health.

Some *examples* of these include: fumes, temperature, noise, vibration, dirt, dust, and unavoidable exposure to hazardous substances, equipment, and/or situations.

•••• MENTAL STRESS The combination of intensity, duration, and frequency of exposure to factors in the environment is such that it results in: ••• SENSORY ATTENTION The job demands:	1 Minimal mental stress.	2 Moderate mental stress.	3 Considerable mental stress.	4 Severe mental stress.
I Limited sensory attention.				
II Moderate sensory attention.				
III Considerable sensory attention.				
IV Intense sensory attention with little or no interruption.				

••• SENSORY ATTENTION : Jobs may require levels of sensory attention (i.e., seeing, hearing, smelling, tasting, touching) during the work process that vary in intensity, duration and frequency.

Some *examples* include: auditing, inspecting, operating mechanical equipment, tabulating data, monitoring video display terminals, proofreading, or technical troubles-shooting.

•••• MENTAL STRESS: Mental stress refers to progressive degrees of exposure of varying intensities to factors inherent in the work process or environment which increase the risk of tension or anxiety. (These are different from the factors considered in the *"Physical Environment"* element. See definition at left).

Some *examples* of such factors include: disruptions in life-style caused by travel requirements; work repetition; lack of control over work pace because it is irregular or machine controlled; emotional deprivation resulting from isolation or lack of privacy; exposure to emotionally disturbing experiences.

Correlation

One of the outstanding characteristics of the Guide Chart-Profile Method is the ease with which company salary structures developed as described here can be compared with external pay practices. A key to this comparison is called 'correlation.' It is not to be confused with the term *correlation* used in statistics.

The correlation process is simply the extension of the measurement process described previously to the measurement of job content in one company's job family (where numerical, or point, values are already established in that company) on the evaluation structure of another company. Thus, for example, a 1,000-point job in Company A might be equivalent to one of 500 points in Company B.

The result is an index, or ratio, which permits the translation of the numerical measurement of job content for a given job in one company to a numerical measurement of that same content in another company or to a numerical value on a common scale. It is not unlike physical conversions in science – pounds to kilograms, for example. One company, in this analogy, might measure job content in pounds, another in kilograms, and a third company in stones. Appropriate conversion factors (like 1 kg=2,205 pounds) permit a given content to be stated in either pounds, kilograms, or stones.

Correlation, as the term is used in Hay Associates' compensation studies and programs, develops a *conversion* factor for a given company. Thus, when salary levels between companies are compared, the comparison is based upon salary levels for *like* job content in both or all companies.

In the beginning there were eight companies involved, seven of which were compared with the eighth, whose scale represented the common yardstick. As our experience and data increased, there developed a standard or common scale to which all companies' points for a given job were reduced. The standard scale represents the collective judgments of seasoned consultants as well as of many executive in all fields of endeavor and is based on experience with a great variety of enterprises of all sizes – basic industries, scientific-oriented, marketing, service, nonprofit, governmental, etc. The standard scale always reflects real situations and not a sterile, mechanistic model.

The correlation ratio or conversion factor is a number statement of the relationship between the evaluation structure in one company and the standard evaluation structure. With the common structure as a link, it is easy to relate one company's evaluation structure to that of another company or group of companies. The ratio has no interpretive significance such as correlation has in statistical analysis.

Source: Van Horn 1972: 12/10–12/11

Employee Questionnaire

In order to keep your responses confidential please do not affix your name or department

In March 1980, Management Board approved the introduction of the Hay method of job evaluation for all government managerial and professional employees (non-bargaining).

The following survey questionnaire explores certain aspects of this major change project. If your current (or previous) position was not evaluated under the Hay system during this period, please mark an X below and return the questionnaire to:

Maeve Quaid-Ahlstrand
Civil Service Commission
[Address]

Please indicate years of service   −5   5–10   +10

PART I
1 Do you believe that the relative importance of positions (point score) is primarily determined by: (Affix numbers 1, 2, 3, ... below, 1 being primary influence.)
   a job description breakdown/use of guide charts
   b Hay consultant's perceptions of job importance
   c CSC's perception of job importance
   d Deputy Minister's perception of job importance
   e already established traditional/historical pay differentials
   f labour-market value
   g other (explain)

2 Did the new job evaluation system have an effect on your old 'salary range,' resulting in:
   a an upward movement
   b a downward movement (position was red-circled)
   c stayed much the same
3 To your knowledge, how did your new MCP 'grade' relate to the jobs with which your job had been previously comparable?
   a higher than
   b lower than
   c stayed much the same
4 In your *division*, did the basic hierarchy or reporting relationships remain the same following the implementation of the MCP job evaluation project?
   YES   NO
5 Do you know of any position or group of positions that changed dramatically in their relative position to other groups as a result of the job evaluation project?
   YES   NO   IF YES, can you explain?
6 Why do you think you are paid at your current rate of pay?

PART II
7 Do you consider that the combination of job descriptions, CSC information, and Deputy Minister representation was sufficient to fully grade your job?
   YES   NO   If NOT, explain.
8 Do you believe that there should have been participation in the benchmark evaluation process from lower levels in the MCP group?
   YES   NO   WHY
9 Do you believe that the fact that the Deputy Minister, in person, participated in the evaluation of benchmark jobs has any effect on the system?
   YES   NO   If YES, in what way?
10 Were you satisfied with the results of your job evaluation in terms of:
   PAY: YES   NO
   RELATIVITY COMPARED TO OTHER POSITIONS: YES   NO
   If not what did you do about it, directly or indirectly, and what was the final outcome?
11 Do you have greater faith in the new formal job evaluation system than the old system?
   YES   NO   WHY
12 What do you see as the main difference between the old method of determining job grades and the new MCP system?

13 In your opinion, would it now be more difficult to obtain a position
review or reclassification?
a YES   WHY
b YES, but only for a short while
c NO   WHY

14 Do you believe that it would be more difficult, under the new system, to
challenge a request for reclassification that had been turned down by
the MCP evaluation committee?
YES NO WHY

15 Would you have more faith in a turned down request for a reclassification under the new system than under the old?

PART IIIA

16 Are the responsibilities and the results expected from your job more
clearly outlined in the Hay job description format than in the previous
format?
YES NO

17 Did you benefit from the experience of writing your job description in
the prescribed Hay format?
YES NO WHY

18 Do you believe that your superior(s) have a better understanding of
your job based on this exercise?
YES NO IF NO, WHY NOT?

19 Was there any overlap in responsibility between your job and that of
your superior or subordinate?
YES NO IF SO, HOW WAS THIS RESOLVED?

PART IIIB

20 Has the information in your job description (eg, specific accountabilities)
been used as a basis for your performance appraisal?
YES NO IF NO, how has your performance been evaluated?

21 Do you fully understand the performance appraisal system?
YES NO IF NO, which aspect?

22 Is there a more significant link between performance and pay
(discounting current economic restraint) under the new performance
appraisal system?
YES NO EXPLAIN

23 Do you work harder than before in order to achieve or maintain a
certain performance standard?
YES NO IF NO, EXPLAIN

24 Could the current performance evaluation system have been possible without the introduction of the Hay format of job evaluation?
YES   NO   IF NO, EXPLAIN

25 Does the performance appraisal system make you feel that there is a greater interest in the notion of 'promotion from within'?
YES   NO

PART IIIC

26 Why do you believe that the management, professional, and excluded jobs were the ones chosen to be evaluated under the Hay System?

27 Do you believe that the job evaluation project for the MCP group drew a stronger dividing line between this group and its counterpart group in the bargaining unit (eg PRM-PR, TM-TE, etc)?
YES   NO   EXPLAIN

28 In informal discussions with other MCP members of *your* department, was the Hay job evaluation project: (please tick)
a a major source of discussion   positive   negative
b occasionally mentionned   positive   negative
c rarely brought up   positive   negative

29 In informal discussions (bus, ferry, lunch, etc) with MCP members of *other* departments was the Hay job evaluation project: (please tick)
a a major source of discussion   positive   negative
b ocassionally brought up   positive   negative
c rarely brought up   positive   negative

30 Do you think that the job evaluation project served to unify or to divide the MCP group?
UNIFY   DIVIDE   EXPLAIN

PART IV

31 Following the initial information/briefing session on the Hay project, did you feel that you understood the purpose, goals, and basic outline of the project?
YES   NO   IF NO, WHY?

32 Following the general update and job description writing session did you feel that you understood the purpose, goals, and basic outline of the project?
YES   NO   IF NO, WHY?

33 Briefly describe how you found the job description writing exercise:
DIFFICULT   SIMPLE   EXPLAIN

34 Did you understand how the job description related to the points used in evaluation?
YES NO

35 The Hay format uses three key dimensions upon which the evaluation of your job is based. Are you at this moment aware of what these three factors are?
YES NO

36 Were you aware of these at the time of evaluation?
YES NO

37 Are you aware of the breakdown or sub-categories of these three dimensions?
YES NO

38 Do you believe that the system is objective?
YES NO

39 Are you familiar with the operation of the guide charts?
YES NO

40 Do you understand the Hay guide chart 'profile' method?
YES NO

41 When your job was evaluated did you understand why it received the results that it did?
YES NO

42 Are you aware of:
a your point score   YES NO
b your point cluster   YES NO
c your salary range   YES NO

43 What did you consider the most difficult aspect to grasp in the MCP job evaluation project (prior to the performance appraisal stage)?

44 To what extend do you think you should be trained in the operation of the job evaluation system:
a) generally familiar   b) knowledgeable on a detailed basis

45 If we had ongoing training on the job evaluation process, who do you think should provide this training:
a) Department   b) Civil Service Commission

46 Does MCP staff report to your position:
YES NO
If yes, do you now use the 'language' of the Hay system (eg, account-ability) when explaining salary issues to your employees?
YES NO SOMETIMES

47 When your job was evaluated did you think that the Hay system of job evaluation:
   a had a rational basis
   b had some rationality but was much like the old system
   c made no sense at all – Why?
48 Does the new MCP system provide you with a better understanding or rationale as to why certain jobs are paid higher than others?
   YES NO
49 What do you think is the *best* feature of the MCP job evaluation system? The *worst*?
50 What do you believe could have been done differently to improve the process?
51 What was achieved by introducing a formal job evaluation to the provincial government?

+ ADDITIONAL COMMENTS SHEET

Thank you for your assistance. Please return to Maeve Quaid-Ahlstrand, Civil Service Commission.

References

Acker, J. 1989. *Doing Comparable Worth: Gender, Class and Pay Equity.*
Philadelphia: Temple University Press

Ahlstrand, B. 1990. *The Quest for Productivity: A Case Study of Fawley After Flanders.* Cambridge: Cambridge University Press

Akalin, M. 1970. *Office Job Evaluation.* Des Plaines, IL: Industrial Management Society

Ahlstrand, B., and M. Quaid. 1992. 'Can Job Evaluation Survive the Transformation of Work?' *Association of Management Proceedings* 10/2

Armstrong, M. 1974. *Principles and Practice of Salary Administration.* London: Kogan Page

Armstrong, M., and H. Murlis, 1980. *A Handbook of Salary Administration.* London: Kogan Page

Arvey, R.D. 1986. 'Sex Bias in Job Evaluation Procedures,' *Personnel Psychology* 39/2: 315–35

Austin, W.C. 1977. 'The Federal Government's Compensation Structure.' In H. Suskin, ed., *Job Evaluation and Pay Administration in the Public Sector,* 442–8. Chicago: International Personnel Management Association

Bacharach, S.B., and E.J. Lawler. 1980. *Power and Politics in Organizations.* San Francisco: Jossey-Bass

Baker, H., and J. True. 1947. *The Operation of Job Evaluation Plans.* Princeton, NJ: Princeton University Press

Baldamus, W. 1961. *Efficiency and Effort.* London: Tavistock

Barkin, S. 1946. 'Wage Determination: Trick or Technique?' In W. Gomberg, ed., *A Labor Union Manual on Job Evaluation,* 2d ed. 1948, 63–70. Chicago: Labor Education Division, Roosevelt College

Bartley, D.L. 1981. *Job Evaluation.* Reading, MA: Addison-Wesley

Batstone, E.V.B. 1984. *Working Order.* Oxford: Basil Blackwell

Beatty, R.W., and J.R. Beatty. 1984. 'Some Problems with Contemporary Job

Evaluation Systems.' In H. Remick, ed., *Comparable Work and Wage Discrimination*, 59–78. Philadelphia: Temple University Press

Belcher, D.W. 1974. *Compensation Administration*. Englewood Cliffs, NJ: Prentice-Hall

Bellak, A.O. 1984. 'Specific Job Evaluation Systems: The Hay Guide Chart-Profile Method.' In M. Rock, ed., *Handbook of Wage and Salary Administration*, 15/1–15/15. New York: McGraw-Hill

Benge, E. 1984. 'Specific Job Evaluation Systems: The Factor Method.' In M. Rock, ed., *Handbook of Wage and Salary Administration*, 12/1–12/15. New York: McGraw-Hill

Bennis, W.G., K.D. Benne, and R. Chin. 1975. *The Planning of Change*. New York: Holt, Rinehart and Winston

Berger, P., and T. Luckmann. 1966. *The Social Construction of Reality*. New York: Penguin

Beyer, J., and H. Trice. 1987. 'How an Organization's Rites Reveal Its Culture,' *Organizational Dynamics* 15/4: 5–23

Blum, A., and P. McHugh. 1971. 'The Social Ascriptions of Motives,' *American Sociological Review* 36 (December): 98–109

Bolman, L.G., and T.E. Deal. 1984. *Modern Approaches to Understanding and Managing Organizations*. San Francisco: Jossey-Bass

Bradley, K. 1979. *Job Evaluation – Theory and Practice*, Report no. 46. Ashford: British Institute of Management Foundation

Brandt, A.R. 1984. 'Describing Hourly Jobs.' In M. Rock, ed., *Handbook of Wage and Salary Administration*, 2d ed., 2/1–2/15. New York: McGraw-Hill

Braverman, H. 1974. *Labour and Monopoly Capital: The Degradation of Work in the Twentieth Century*. London: Monthly Review Press

British Institute of Management. 1952. *Job Evaluation: A Practical Guide*. London

Britton, D.E. 1983. 'Rational Salary Management,' *Personnel Journal* 62/10: 832–5

Brown, W. 1979. 'Social Determinants of Pay.' In G. Stephenson and C. Brotherington, eds., *Industrial Relations: A Social Psychological Approach*, 115–30. Chichester: John Wiley and Sons

Brown, W.A. 1973. *Piecework Bargaining*. London: Heinemann Educational Books

– ed., with contributions by E. Batstone, D. Deaton, P. Edwards, M. Hart, K. Sisson, and B. Weekes. 1981. *The Changing Contours of British Industrial Relations: A Survey of the Manufacturing Industry*. Oxford: Basil Blackwell

Burns, M. 1978. *Understanding Job Evaluation*. London: Institute of Personnel Management

Burton, C. 1987. *Women's Worth: Pay Equity and Job Evaluation in Australia.* Canberra: AGPS

Canadian Human Rights Commission. 1978. *Equal Pay for Work of Equal Value: Interpretation Guide for Section 11 of the Canadian Human Rights Act.* Ottawa

Cliff, T. 1970. *The Employer's Offensive: Productivity Deals and How to Fight Them.* London: Pluto Press

Cobb, A.T., and N. Margulies. 1981. 'Organizational Development: A Political Perspective,' *Academy of Management* 6/1: 49–59

Collins, R. 1969. *Job Evaluation and Workers' Control,* Pamphlet series 16. London: Institute of Workers' Control

Craver, G. 1977. 'Job Evaluation Practices in State and County Governments.' In H. Suskin, ed., *Job Evaluation and Pay Administration in the Public Sector,* 427–41. Chicago: International Management Association

Crouch, C. 1977. *Class Conflict and the Industrial Relations Crisis.* London: Heinemann

Cuneo, C. 1990. *Pay Equity: The Labour-Feminist Challenge.* Toronto: Oxford University Press

Curston, L.C. 1976. 'Take the Fat Out of Job Evaluation,' *Supervisory Management* 21/4: 11–17

Dandridge, T. 1983. '"Symbols": Functions and Use.' In L. Pondy et al, eds., Organizational Symbolism, 69–79. Greenwich and London: JAI Press

Daniel, W. 1976. Wage Determination in Industry. London: PEP

de Jong, J.R. 1972. 'Job Evaluation: History and Trends.' In *Some Approaches to National Job Evaluation,* 7–18. London: Foundation for Business Responsibilities

Dertien, M. 1981. 'The Accuracy of Job Evaluation Plans,' *Personnel Journal* 60/7: 566–70

Dessler, G., and J. Duffy. 1984. *Personnel Management,* 2d Cdn ed. Scarborough, ON: Prentice-Hall

Devons, E. 1961. 'Statistics as a Basis for Policy.' In *Essays in Economics,* 122–37. London: Allen and Unwin

Dick, A.D. 1974. 'Job Evaluation's Role in Employee Relations,' *Personnel Journal* 53/3: 176–9

Dickinson, Z.C. 1937. *Compensating Industrial Effort.* London: MacDonald and Evans

Douglas, T.W. 1966. 'The Job Evaluator and the Organization,' *Personnel Journal* 45/8: 475–7

Doverspike, D., A.M. Carlisi, G.V. Barrett, and R.A. Alexander. 1983. 'Generalizability Analysis of a Point Method Job Plan,' *Journal of Applied Psychology* 34: 225–8

Doyen, C.A. 1967. 'Diplomacy Needed in Job Evaluation,' *Administrative Management* 28/3: 63–4

Drucker, P. 1955. *The Practice of Management*. London: Heinemann

Dundes, A. 1984. *Sacred Narrative: Readings in the Theory of Myth*. Berkeley: University of California Press

du Pont, E.E. 1960. 'Snares and Delusions in Office Job Evaluation,' *The Management Review* 49/5: 15–22

Elizur, D. 1980. *Job Evaluation*. London: Gower

Ellul, J. 1964. *The Technological Society*. New York: Knopf

Evered, R. 1983. 'The Language of Organizations: The Case of the Navy.' In L. Pondy et al, eds., *Organizational Symbolism*, 125–43. Greenwich and London: JAI Press

Federal Board for Vocational Education. 1919. *Job Specifications*, Bulletin no. 45, Employment Series no. 3. Washington, DC

Flanders, A. 1975. *Management and Unions*. London: Faber and Faber

Foster, K. 1968. 'Job Worth and the Computer,' *Personnel Journal* 47/9: 619–26

Fox, W. 1962. 'Purpose and Validity in Job Evaluation,' *Personnel Journal* 41/9: 432–7

Frank, M.S. 1982. 'A State-of-the-Art Review and Analysis,' *Public Personnel Management Journal* 11/3: 239–47

Galenson, W. 1961. 'Why the American Labor Movement Is Not Socialist,' *The American Review*, 1/2: 1–19

Galenson, W., and R. Smith. 1978. 'The United States.' In J. Dunlop and W. Galenson, eds., *Labor in the Twentieth Century*, 11–84. New York: Academic Press

Gellerman, S.W. 1960. *The Uses of Psychology in Management*. London: Collier-Macmillan

Gephart, R. 1978. 'Status Degradation and Organizational Succession: An Ethnomethodological Approach,' *Administrative Science Quarterly* 23: 553–81

Ghobadian, A., and M. White. 1986. *Job Evaluation and Equal Pay*, Paper no. 58. London: Department of Employment Research

Gill, C., R. Morris, and J. Eaton. 1977. 'Managerial Control and Collective Bargaining: Some "Political" Aspects of Job Evaluation in a Multi-Site Enterprise,' *Personnel Review* 6/4: 51–7

Goffman, I. 1952. 'On Calling the Mark-Out – Some Aspects of Adaptation to Failure,' *Psychiatry* 15: 451–63

Gomberg, W. 1948. *A Labor Union Manual on Job Evaluation*, 2d ed. Chicago: Labor Education Division, Roosevelt College

– 1956. 'A Collective Bargaining Approach to Job Evaluation.' In J. Shister, ed., *Readings in Labor Economics and Industrial Relations*, 263–73. Chicago: J.B. Lippincott

Gomez-Mejia, L., R. Page, and W. Tornow. 1982. 'A Comparison of the Practical Utility of Traditional, Statistical, and Hybrid Job Evaluation Approaches,' *Academy of Management Journal* 25/4: 790–809

Gowler, D., and K. Legge. 1983. 'The Meaning of Management and the Management of Meaning: A View from Social Anthropology.' In M. Earl, ed., *Perspectives on Management: A Multidisciplinary Analysis*. Oxford: Oxford University Press

Grayson, D. 1982. *Job Evaluation and Changing Technology*, Occasional paper 23. London: Department of Employment, Work Research Unit

Harris, H.J. 1982. *The Right to Manage: Industrial Policies of American Business in the 1940s*. Madison: University of Wisconsin Press

Hay Group, n.d. *Job Evaluation Using the Hay Method*. Brochure

Hofstede, G. 1988. 'Book review of Mary Douglas's *How Institutions Think*,' *Organization Studies* 9/1: 122–4

Homans, G. 1961. *Social Behaviour: Its Elementary Forms*. New York: Harcourt, Brace

Hopwood, A.G. 1984. 'Accounting and the Pursuit of Efficiency.' In A. Hopwood and C. Tompkins, eds., *Issues in Public Sector Accounting*. London: Philip Allen

Hyman, A., and I. Brough. 1975. *Social Values and Industrial Relations: A Study of Fairness and Inequality*. Oxford: Basil Blackwood

Incomes Data Services. 1979. *Guide to Job Evaluation*. London, March *Industrial Relations Review and Report*. 1983. 'Staff Job Evaluation,' Series of four reports, 310, 311, 314, 315. London

– 1987. 'Equal Value in Local Authority Job Evaluation,' Report no. 388. London

International Association of Machinists. 1954. *What's Wrong with Job Evaluation: A Trade Union Manual*. Washington, DC: Research Department

International Labour Office. 1960. *Job Evaluation*. Geneva

Jacobson, R. 1977. 'Efforts to Resolve Problems in Federal Compensation.' In H. Suskin, ed., *Job Evaluation and Pay Administration in the Public Sector*, 449–80. Chicago: International Personnel Association

Janes, H.D. 1979. 'Union Views on Job Evaluation: 1971 versus 1978' *Personnel Journal* 58/2: 80–5

Jaques, E. 1958. 'An Objective Approach to Pay Differentials,' *New Scientist* 4: 313–15

– 1967. *Equitable Payment*, 2d ed. Harmondsworth: Penguin

Johnson, R., and P. Cooke. 1982. 'Subjectivity and Bias in Job Evaluations,' *Industrial Management and Data Systems*, Jul.-Aug.: 19–21

Kelday, G.J. 1922. 'Job Analysis – Occupational Rating,' National Personnel Association, 2 November

Kimball, A.T. 1964. 'Logics of Non-logical Position Evaluation,' *Personnel Journal* 43/6: 314–17

Kindig, F.E. 1963. 'Merit Rating and Job Evaluation: An Interrelationship,' *Personnel Journal* 42/8: 395–402

Klatt, L., R. Murdick, and F. Schuster. 1978. *Human Resources Management*. Homewood, IL: Richard D. Irwin

Klein, L. 1976. *A Social Scientist in Industry*. Epping, Essex: Gower

Koprowski, G. 1960. 'Job Evaluation: Tuxedo for an Amoeba,' *Personnel Journal* 38/8: 298–301

Kress, A.L. 1969. 'Job Evaluation for White Collar Workers in Private Sector Employment in the United States,' *International Labour Review* 100/4: 341–57

Lanham, E. 1955. *Job Evaluation*. New York: McGraw-Hill
 – 1963. *Administration of Wages and Salaries*. New York: Harper and Row

Lawler, E.E. 1981. *Pay and Organization Development*. Reading, MA: Addison-Wesley

Levi-Strauss, C. 1965. 'The Structural Study of Myth.' in T. Sebeok, ed., *Myth: A Symposium*, 81–106. Bloomington: Indiana University Press

Livy, B. 1975. *Job Evaluation – A Critical Review*. London: Allen and Unwin

Lockwood, D. 1958. *The Blackcoated Worker*. London: Allen and Unwin

Lupton, T. 1957. 'A Sociologist Looks at Work Study,' *Work Study and Industrial Engineering* 1/2
 – ed. 1972. *Payment Systems*. Harmondsworth: Penguin

Lupton, T., and A. Bowey. 1974. *Wages and Salaries*. Harmondsworth: Penguin

Lupton, T., and D. Gowler. 1969. *Selecting a Wage Payment System*, Federal Research Series. London: Kogan Page
 – 1972. 'Wage Payment Systems,' *Personnel Management*, Nov.: 25–8

Lutz, C.F. 1969. 'Quantitative Job Evaluation in Local Government in the United States,' *International Labor Review* 99/6: 607–19

Lytle, C.W. 1942. *Wage Incentive Methods*. New York: Ronald Press
 – 1954. *Job Evaluation Methods*, 2d ed. New York: Ronald Press

McArthur, L.Z. 1985. 'Social Judgement Biases in Comparable Worth Analysis,' *Comparable Worth: New Directions for Research*. Washington, DC

McCarthy, W.E.J. 1966. *The Role of Shop Stewards in British Industrial Relations*. London: HMSO

McConomy, S., and W. Ganschinietz. 1983. 'Trends in Job Evaluation

Practices of State Personnel Systems, 1981 Survey Findings,' *Public Personnel Management Journal* 12: 1–12

McCormick, E.J. 1976. 'Job and Task Analysis.' In *Handbook of Industrial and Organizational Psychology*, 651–96. Chicago: Rand McNally

McNally, J., and S. Shimmin. 1984. 'Job Evaluation and Equal Pay for Work of Equal Value,' *Personnel Review* 13/1: 27–31

Mahoney, T. 1990. 'Job Evaluation: Endangered Species or Anachronism?' Symposium presentation at Academy of Management, San Francisco, 13 August

Metcalfe, L., and S. Richards. 1984. 'The Impact of the Efficiency Strategy: Political Clout or Cultural Change?' *Public Administration* 62/4: 439–54

Merrie, A.H. 1968. *Notes for Managers, Number 13 – Job Evaluation*. London: The Industrial Society

Meyer, J.W., and B. Rowan. 1977. 'Institutionalized Organizations: Formal Structure as Myth and Ceremony,' *American Journal of Sociology* 83: 340–63

Milkovich, G., and R. Broderick. 1982. 'Pay Discrimination: Legal Issues and Implications for Research,' *Industrial Relations* 21: 309–17

Mills, C. Wright. 1940. 'Situated Actions and Vocabularies of Motive,' *American Sociological Review* 5 (February): 904–13

– 1963. *Power, Politics and People: The Collected Essays of C. Wright Mills*, ed. I Horowitz. New York: Oxford University Press

Miner, J.B. 1969. *Personnel and Industrial Relations: A Managerial Approach*. New York: Macmillan

Moberly, R.L., and E.S. Buffa. 1947. *Job Evaluation*, Wisconsin Commerce Reports, vol. 1. Madison: University of Wisconsin, School of Commerce, Bureau of Business Research and Service

Moch, M. 1980. 'Chewing Ass Out: The Enactment of Power Relationships through Language and Ritual.' Paper presented at the annual meeting of the Academy of Management, Detroit

Moore, F.G. 1950. 'Statistical Problems in Job Evaluation.' In M.J. Dooher and V. Marquis, eds., *The AMA Handbook of Wage and Salary Administration*, 324–35. New York: AMA

Morgan, G. 1986. *Images of Organization*. Beverly Hills: Sage

Morgan, G., P. Frost, and L. Pondy. 1983. 'Organizational Symbolism.' In L. Pondy et al., eds., *Organizational Symbolism*, 3–55. Greenwich and London: JAI Press

Morgan, G., and L. Smircish. 1980. 'The Case for Qualitative Research,' *Academy of Management Review* 5: 491–500

National Board for Prices and Incomes. 1968. *Job Evaluation*, Report no. 83. London: HMSO

– 1969. *100 Reports Summarized*. London

Nicolopoulos, L.G. 1954. *Formal Job Evaluation and Some of Its Economic Implications*. Montreal: Industrial Relations Centre, McGill University/ Quality Press

Offe, K. 1976. *Industry and Equality*, trans. by James Wickham. London: Edward Arnold

Oliver, P.M. 1976. 'Modernizing a State Job Evaluation Plan,' *Public Personnel Management* May-June: 168–72

Organization for Economic Cooperation and Development. 1967. 'Forms of Wage and Salary Payment for High Productivity,' International Management Seminar, Versailles

Patchen, M. 1961. *The Choice of Wage Comparisons*. Englewood Cliffs, NJ: Prentice-Hall

Paterson, T. 1972. *Job Evaluation, Vol. 1: A New Method*. London: Business Books

Patton, J., C. Littlefield, and S. Self. 1964. *Job Evaluation: Text and Cases*, 3d ed. Homewood, IL: Richard Irwin

Patton, J., and R.S. Smith. 1949. *Job Evaluation*. Chicago: Richard Irwin

Patton, J.A. 1961. 'Job Evaluation in Practice: Some Survey Findings,' *AMA Management Report no. 54*, 74–7. New York

Pay Board. 1974. *Relativities*, Advisory report no. 2 Cmd 5535. London: HMSO

Pay Research Bureau, Canada. 1981. *Salary Administration*. Ottawa

Pettigrew, A. 1973. *The Politics of Organizational Decision Making*. London: Tavistock

Pfeffer, J. 1981a. 'Management as Symbolic Action: The Creation and Maintenance of Organizational Paradigms.' In L.L. Cumings and B.M. Staw, eds., *Research in Organizational Behaviour*, vol. 3: 194–229. Greenwich, CT: JAI Press

– 1981b. *Power in Organizations*. Boston: Pitman

Phelps Brown, E.H. 1962. *The Economics of Labour*. New Haven, CT: Yale University Press

Pondy, L., P. Frost, G. Morgan, and T. Dandridge, eds. 1983. *Organizational Symbolism*. Greenwich and London: JAI Press

Pressman, J., and A. Wildavsky. 1973. *Implementation: How Great Expectations in Washington Are Dashed in Oakland: or Why It's Amazing that Federal Programs Work at All, This Being a Saga of the Economic Development Administration as Told by Two Sympathetic Observers Who Seek to Build Morals on a Foundation of Ruined Hopes*. Berkeley: University of California Press

Princeton University, Industrial Relations Section. 1941. *Job Classification and Evaluation*. Princeton, NJ

Purcell, J. 1983. 'The Management of Industrial Relations in the Modern Corporation,' *British Journal of Industrial Relations* 21/1: 1–16

Quaid, M. 1993. 'Job Evaluation as Institutional Myth,' *Journal of Management Studies* 30/2: 45–66

Remick, H. 1978. 'Strategies for Presenting Sound, Bias-Free Job Evaluation Plans' Paper presented at the Industrial Relations Counselors' Colloquium, Atlanta, GA

– 1984. 'Major Issues in A Priori Applications.' In H. Remick, ed., *Comparable Worth and Wage Discrimination*, 99–117. Philadelphia: Temple University Press

Rezler, J. 1969. 'Effects of Automation on Some Areas of Compensation,' *Personnel Journal* 38/4: 282–5

Richardson, A. 1987. 'Accounting as a Legitimating Institution,' *Accounting, Organizations and Society* 12/4: 341–55

Risher, H. 1978. 'Job Evaluation: Mystical or Statistical?' *Personnel* 55/5: 23–36

Roeber, J. 1975. *Social Change at Work: The ICI Weekly Staff Agreement*. London: Duckworth

Rossman, H.D. 1961. 'Job Evaluation Study – 1960,' *Personnel Journal* 39/8: 314–18

Routh, G. 1965. *Occupation and Pay in Great Britain*. Cambridge: Cambridge University Press

Runciman, W.G. 1966. *Relative Deprivation and Social Justice*. London: RKP

Scholten, G. 1979. *Functiewaardering met mate [Analysing Job Evaluation]*. Alphen a/d Rijn: Samson

– 1981. *Passen en meten met functienwaardering (Job Evaluation: Cutting and Contriving)*. Alphen a/d Rijn: Samsom

Schutz, A. 1962. *Collected Papers*, vols. 1 and 2. The Hague: Nijhoff

Scott, R. 1987. *Organizations: Rational, Natural and Open Systems*. Englewood Cliffs, NJ: Prentice-Hall

Scott, W.D., R.C. Clothier, and W.R. Spriegel. 1961. *Personnel Management*. New York: McGraw-Hill

Shils, E.B. 1984. 'A Perspective on Job Measurement.' In M. Rock, ed., *Handbook of Wage and Salary Administration*, 2d ed, 8/3–8/13. New York: McGraw-Hill

Shister, J. 1956. 'Methods of Remuneration.' In J. Shister, ed., *Readings in Labor Economics and Industrial Relations*. 2d ed., 260–3. Chicago: J.B. Lippincott

Sibson, R.E. 1967. *Wages and Salaries: A Handbook for Line Managers.* New York: AMA

Sisson, K., and W. Brown. 1983. 'Industrial Relations in the Private Sector: Donovan Revisited. In G. Bain, ed., *Industrial Relations in Britain*, 137–54. Oxford; Basil Blackwell

Slichter, S., J. Healy, and E. Livernash. 1960. *The Impact of Collective Bargaining on Management.* Washington, DC: The Brookings Institution

Smircish, L. 1983. 'Organizations as Shared Meanings.' In L. Pondy et al., eds., *Organizational Symbolism*, 55–65. Greenwich and London: JAI Press

Spencer, S. 1990. 'Developing Job Evaluation,' *Personnel Management* January: 48–50

Steinberg, R. 1991. 'Job Evaluation and Managerial Control: The Politics of Technique and the Technique of Politics.' In J. Fudge and P. McDermott, eds, *Just Wages: A Feminist Assessment of Pay Equity*, 193–218. Toronto: University of Toronto Press

Steinberg, R., and L. Haignere. 1987. 'Equitable Compensation: Methodological Criteria for Comparable Worth.' In C. Bose and G. Spitze, eds., *Ingredients for Women's Employment Policy*. Albany: State University of New York Press

Stelling, J.G., and R. Bucher. 1973. 'Vocabularies of Realism,' *Social Science Medicine* 7: 661–75

Stettner, N. 1969. *Productivity Bargaining and Industrial Change.* Oxford: Pergamon

Stimmler, P.T. 1966. 'The Job Evaluation Myth,' *Personnel Journal* 45/9: 594–6

Stone, C.H., and D. Yoder. 1970. *Job Analysis.* Long Beach: California State College

Thakur, M., and D. Gill. 1976. *Job Evaluation in Practice*, Report no. 21. London: Institute of Personnel Management

Thomason, G. 1968. *Personnel Manager's Guide to Job Evaluation.* London: Institute of Personnel Management

– 1980. *Job Evaluation Objectives and Methods.* London: Institute of Personnel Management

– 1981. *A Textbook of Personnel Management.* London: Institute of Personnel Management

Thomsen, D.J. 1978. 'Eliminating Pay Discrimination Caused by Job Evaluation,' *Personnel* 55/5: 11–22

Torrington, D., and L. Hall. 1987. *Personnel Management: A New Approach.* London: Prentice-Hall

Treiman, D. 1979. *Job Evaluation: An Analytic Review*, Interim report to the

Equal Opportunity Commission. Washington, DC: National Academy of Sciences

Trice, H., J. Belasco, and J. Alutto. 1969. 'The Role of Ceremonials in Organizational Behaviour,' *International Labour Relations Review* 23: 40–51

Trice, H., and J. Beyer. 1984. 'Studying Organizational Cultures through Rites and Ceremonials,' *Academy of Management Review* 9/4: 653–69

Turner, B. 1971. *Exploring the Industrial Subculture*. London: Macmillan

U.S. Department of Labor. 1950. *Glossary of Currently Used Wage Terms*, Bulletin 983. Washington, DC: Bureau of Labor Statistics

Van Horn, C. 1972. 'The Hay Guide Chart-Profile Method,' In M. Rock, ed., *Handbook of Wage and Salary Administration*, 12/4–12/17. New York: McGraw-Hill

Ward, D. 1973. 'Job Evaluation in Local Government,' *Personnel Management* 5/7: 34–9

Webb, G.H. 1973. 'National Job Evaluation in the Current Climate,' *Personnel Management* 5/10: 29–31

Weber, M. 1946. *From Max Weber Essays in Sociology*, ed., by H. Gerth and C. Wright Mills. New York: Oxford University Press

Weiner, N., and M. Gunderson. 1990. *Pay Equity: Issues, Options and Experiences*. Toronto: Butterworths

White, M. 1981a. *The Hidden Meaning of Pay Conflict*. London: Macmillan

–1981b. *Payment Systems in Britain*. Aldershot: Gower

Wilking, S.V. 1961. 'Seven Traps in Job Evaluation,' *The Management Review* 50/2: 38–41

Wilkins, A. 1983. 'Organizational Stories as Symbols.' In L. Pondy et al, eds., *Organizational Symbolism*, 81-92. Greenwich and London: JAI Press

Woods, K. 1976. 'Job Evaluation: More than Just a Management Technique,' *Personnel Management* November: 27–9, 39

Wooton, B. 1962. *The Social Foundations of Wage Policy*, 2d ed. London: Allen and Unwin

Index

accountability, guide chart, 110–11
Acker, J., 3, 8, 71–2, 75–6, 83
Ahlstrand, B., 65
Ahlstrand, B., and M. Quaid, 44
Akalin, M., 37, 46
analytical job evaluation schemes, 22
Armstrong, M., 249
Armstrong, M., and H. Murlis, 212–13
Arvey, R.D., 50, 53, 58, 71
Austin, W.C., 25, 37

Bacharach, S.B., and E.J. Lawler, 175
Baker, H., and J. True, 35, 47, 51, 56, 211, 219
Baldamus, W., 67
Barkin, S., 32–3, 35–6, 56, 209, 219
Bartley, D.L., 53, 122
Batstone, E.V.B., 37, 61, 63–5, 68, 251
Beatty, R.W., and J.R. Beatty, 58
Belcher, D.W., 37, 136
Bellak, A.O., 136, 212
Benge, E., 29
Bennis, W.G., K.D. Benne, and R. Chin, 240

Berger, P., and T. Luckmann, 6, 8, 15, 223–7, 243, 249, 254
Beyer, J., and H. Trice, 235
Blum, A., and P. McHugh, 227
Bolman, L.G., and T.E. Deal, 231, 235, 250
Bradley, K., 64, 115
Brandt, K., 40, 122
Braverman, H., 8
British Institute of Management, 51, 53, 68, 115
Brown, W., 56, 62, 211
Brown, W.A., 8, 41, 48, 63, 66, 73, 69, 219
Burns, M., 68, 72
Burton, C., 8, 71–3

Canadian Human Rights Act, 44
classification job evaluation schemes, 22, 28, 46
Cliff, T., 61–2
Cobb, A.T., and N. Margulies, 150
Collins, R., 8, 19, 39, 48, 61–2, 64, 66, 213
correlation, 150–2, 258–9
Craver, G., 37, 46
Crouch, C., 48, 66

Cuneo, C., 70
Curston, L.C., 52–3

Dandridge, T., 231
Daniel, W., 26, 68, 221
de Jong, J.R., 52
Dertien, M., 41, 50, 53
Dessler, G., and J. Duffy, 133
Devons, E., 242–3
Dick, A.D., 51, 53, 115
Dickinson, Z.C., 26
Donovan Commission, 65
Douglas, T.W., 50
Doverspike, D., A.M. Carlisi,
    G.V. Barrett, and R.A. Alexander,
    53
Doyen, C.A., 103–4
Drucker, P., 38
Dundes, A., 231
du Pont, E.E., 137

Elizur, D., 58
evaluation committees, in
    'Atlantis,' 133–49
Evered, R., 253–4

feminist school, 48–9, 70–8
Flanders, A., 65
Foster, K., 50
Fox, W., 50, 53
Frank, M.S., 21, 210

Galenson, W., 30–1
Galenson, W., and R. Smith, 39,
    40
Gellerman, S.W., 7
Gephart, R., 236
Ghobadian, A., and M. White, 42
Gill, C., R. Morris, and J. Eaton,
    68–9

Gomberg, W., 61, 67–8, 209
Gomez–Mejia, L., R. Page, and
    W. Tornow, 50, 53
Gowler, D., and K. Legge, 242–3
Grayson, D., 50

Harris, H.J., 38, 46
Hay Group, 84–5, 103
Hay plan, 9, 22, 84–5, 94, 96, 104–
    12; and pay equity legislation,
    102; decision to use by 'Atlantis,'
    99–103; guide charts, 106–11;
    philosophy, 101–2; position
    evaluation manual, 104, 149
hierarchy, 50–1, 206–18
Hofstede, G., 225
Homans, G., 67
Hopwood, A.G., 226
Hyman, A., and I. Brough, 8

Incomes Data Services, 9, 84, 115,
    156
industrial relations: job evaluation
    claims, 59–61; collective bargain-
    ing, 61–3; conflict reduction,
    67–9; pay grades, 61–2; problems
    with industrial relations claims,
    69–70; reform of, 65–7; shop
    stewards, 63–5
Institute for Workers Control,
    66
institutional isomorphism, 15, 224,
    227–8, 249–54
International Labour Office, 33–4,
    53, 203

Jacobson, R., 25
Janes, H.D., 69
Jaques, E., 67, 208
job descriptions, 28; in 'Atlantis,'

117, 121–32, 203–6; how to write, 121–2

job evaluation: and bureaucracy, 7, 19, 46–7, 228–30, 242–3; criticism of, 54–9, 69–70, 76–9, 202–22; definition/conventional, 20–3, definition/social constructionist, 15, 223–4, 230–49; feminist view, 48–9, 70–8; institutional isomorphism, 249–54; and politics, 213–18; purpose/conventional, 115; purpose/hidden, 4–8; industrial relations claims, 59–70; and myth, 4–6, 15, 224, 246; personnel management claims, 49–59; and symbolism, 4

job evaluation, history of: and automation, 38–9; Canadian experience, 42–5; early public sector, 23–7; early private sector, 27–9; equal pay legislation effect, 40–2, 43–5; Korean war wage controls, 39–40; large-scale development, 29–30; reason for early development, 25–7; recent history, 36–40; and technological change, 33; and trade unions, 30–3, 35–6, 38–9; and wage controls, 33–5

job evaluation schemes: hybrid, 22; non-analytical, 21–2; points rating, 22, 28–9, 46; ranking, 22

Johnson, R., and P. Cooke, 50

Kelday, G.J., 28
Kimball, A.T., 50
Kindig, F.E., 53
Klatt, L., R. Murdick, and F. Schuster, 212–13, 219
Klein, L., 9

know-how, guide chart, 106–7
Koprowski, G., 47
Kress, A.L., 50, 52

Lanham, E., 28–9, 32–3, 35
Lawler, E.E., 58, 175
Lévi-Strauss, C., 15, 254
Livy, B., 14, 27, 49, 58, 213
Lockwood, D., 210
Lott, M.R., 28–9
Lupton, T., 8, 55, 212, 215
Lupton, T., and A. Bowey, 53, 212, 221
Lupton, T., and D. Gowler, 195, 221
Lutz, C.F., 27, 39, 46, 50, 243, 248
Lytle, C.W., 29, 30, 32, 38, 56

McArthur, L.Z., 71
McCarthy, W.E.J., 67
McConomy, S., and W. Ganschinietz, 46
McCormick, E.J., 20, 230
McNally, J., and S. Shimmin, 50, 208, 217–18
Mahoney, T., 44
Merrie, A.H., 53, 173
Metcalfe, L., and S. Richards, 196
Meyer, J.W., and B. Rowan, 8, 15, 78–9, 224, 226–8, 230, 249–50
Milkovich, G., and R. Broderick, 58
Mills, C. Wright, 241
Miner, J.B., 27, 30–1, 53
Moberly, R.L., and E.S. Buffa, 36, 52
Moch, M., 236
Moore, F.G., 51, 57–9
Morgan, G., 243
Morgan, G., P. Frost, and L. Pondy, 231
Morgan, G., and L. Smircish, 10

National Board for Prices and
Incomes, 19, 21–2, 36, 46–7, 48,
62, 65–6, 68, 195
Nicolopoulos, L.G., 52

Offe, K., 8, 209–10
Oliver, P.M., 50
Organization for Economic Cooper-
ation and Development, 68

Patchen, M., 67
pay rates, 51–3
Peterson, T., 52, 208
Patton, J., C. Littlefield, and S. Self,
19, 24, 45
Patton, J., and R.S. Smith., 29, 35–6,
53
Patton, J.A., 36, 41, 46
pay equity, 1, 6, 15, 40–6, 48–9;
feminist perspective on, 70–8
pay equity legislation: in Canada,
42–5, 72–3; feminist perspective
on, 70–8; in United States, 40–2,
72–3
Pay Research Bureau, Canada, 46
personnel management: job
evaluation claims, 49–53; job
evaluation by-products, 53–4;
problems with job evaluation
claims, 54–9, 202–3
Pettigrew, A., 175
Pfeffer, J., 114, 175, 218, 233–4, 236,
241–2
Phelps Brown, E.H., 212
Pondy, L., P. Frost, G. Morgan, and
T. Dandridge, 230
Pressman, J., and A. Wildavsky, 87
problem solving, guide chart,
108–9
Purcell. J., 48, 61, 63–4, 66

Quaid, M., 224

Remick, H., 72, 75
research methods, 9–11, 85–8
Rezler, J., 38
Richardson, A., 225–6
Risher, H., 50
Rock, M.L., 187
Roeber, J., 122
Rossman, H.D., 57
Routh, G., 196
Runciman, W.G., 67

Scholten, G., 64
Schutz, A., 224
scientific management, 8, 29, 78,
27–8, 78
Scott, R., 224–5, 228–9
Scott, W.D., R.C. Clothier, and
W.R. Spriegel, 36
Shils, E.B., 23–4, 34, 40, 46
Shister, J., 36
Sibson, R.E., 219
Sisson, K., and W. Brown, 61–3
Slichter, S., J. Healy, and
E. Livernash, 27, 31–5, 38, 46,
50–1, 55, 63, 66, 68
Smircish, L., 234
social construction of reality, 6, 8,
15, 223–7, 243, 249, 254
sore-thumbing, in 'Atlantis,'
149–50
Spencer, S., 54
Steinberg, R., 71
Steinberg, R., and L. Haignere, 71
Stelling, J. G., and R. Bucher, 185
Stettner, N., 51
Stimmler, P.T., 39
Stone, C.H., and D. Yoder,
36–7

Thakur, M., and D. Gill, 19, 115
Thomason, G., 14, 20, 47, 49–50, 52, 114–15, 134
Thomsen, D.J., 40–1
Torrington, D., and L. Hall, 9, 41, 52, 122, 152
Treiman, D., 20, 23–4, 25, 37, 46, 49–50, 58, 64, 71, 234
Trice, H., J. Belasco, and J. Alutto, 243
Trice, H., and J. Beyer, 114
Turner, B., 235, 239

Ward, D., 50
Webb, G.H., 50
Weber, M., 239
Weiner, N., and M. Gunderson, 43
White, M., 9, 61, 63, 67, 69, 87
Wilking, S.V., 51
Wilkins, A., 254
working conditions: guide chart, 256–7
Wooton, B., 208